International and Development Education

The *International and Development Education Series* focuses on the complementary areas of comparative, international, and development education. Books emphasize a number of topics ranging from key international education issues, trends, and reforms to examinations of national education systems, social theories, and development education initiatives. Local, national, regional, and global volumes (single authored and edited collections) constitute the breadth of the series and offer potential contributors a great deal of latitude based on interests and cutting edge research. The series is supported by a strong network of international scholars and development professionals who serve on the International and Development Education Advisory Board and participate in the selection and review process for manuscript development.

SERIES EDITORS
John N. Hawkins
Professor Emeritus, University of California, Los Angeles
Senior Consultant, IFE 2020 East West Center

D1807417

W. James Jacob
Assistant Professor, University of Pittsburgh
Director, Institute for International Studies in Education

PRODUCTION EDITOR
Heejin Park
Project Associate, Institute for International Studies in Education

INTERNATIONAL EDITORIAL ADVISORY BOARD
Clementina Acedo, *UNESCO's International Bureau of Education, Switzerland*
Philip G. Altbach, *Boston University, USA*
Carlos E. Blanco, *Universidad Central de Venezuela*
Sheng Yao Cheng, *National Chung Cheng University, Taiwan*
Ruth Hayhoe, *University of Toronto, Canada*
Wanhua Ma, *Peking University, China*
Ka-Ho Mok, *University of Hong Kong, China*
Christine Musselin, *Sciences Po, France*
Yusuf K. Nsubuga, *Ministry of Education and Sports, Uganda*
Namgi Park, *Gwangju National University of Education, Republic of Korea*
Val D. Rust, *University of California, Los Angeles, USA*
Suparno, *State University of Malang, Indonesia*
John C. Weidman, *University of Pittsburgh, USA*
Husam Zaman, *Taibah University, Saudi Arabia*

Institute for International Studies in Education
School of Education, University of Pittsburgh
5714 Wesley W. Posvar Hall, Pittsburgh, PA 15260 USA

Center for International and Development Education
Graduate School of Education & Information Studies, University of California, Los Angeles
Box 951521, Moore Hall, Los Angeles, CA 90095 USA

Titles:

Higher Education in Asia/Pacific: Quality and the Public Good
Edited by Terance W. Bigalke and Deane E. Neubauer

International Students and Global Mobility in Higher Education

National Trends and New Directions

Edited by
Rajika Bhandari
and
Peggy Blumenthal

palgrave
macmillan

Contents

Tables and Figures

Tables

Figures

Series Editors' Introduction

It is not difficult to find in the very large literature on mobility and migration in higher education soaring language about how the world has forever or is in the process of being changed by globalization and internationalization and how these social phenomena have particularly impacted the world's universities and colleges. It is noted that the movement of students, scholars, skilled talent, ideas, institutional structures, the structure of knowledge, and almost everything else associated with mobility and migration, are a key part of these phenomena, ushering in a new age of higher education particularly in the Asian Pacific Region. Much of the literature is focused, as one might expect, on the movement of students and scholars through the world, however less attention has been placed on institutional change as a result of these and other movements. And the bulk of the literature on mobility and migration places it squarely in the context of the broader mega trends of globalization and its predecessor, internationalization. It is useful to keep in mind the distinctions among these terms, all of which describe social phenomenon that have been with us for some time, some would say a very long time. Students and scholars have roamed the world seeking new knowledge and experiences since the advent of higher learning, and despite the relative newness of the term "globalization" it too has a long history, and higher education institutions have been experiencing internationalization since the first foreign student or scholar walked through their doors. Yet we recognize that the contemporary use of these concepts is what is being discussed in this new study, that is, mobility defined and characterized by scope, pace, networking, and technology.

It is in this context that we are very pleased to add to our Palgrave MacMillan Series on comparative, international, and development education a new look at the issue of student mobility: *International Students and Global Mobility in Higher Education: National Trends and New Directions* edited by Rajika Bhandari and Peggy Blumenthal. Here we find a set of chapters that range through Asia, Europe, North America, Latin America, and Africa. This provides an important comparative dimension that allows the reader to see the wide range and scope of student mobility and the forces and factors that influence it. The editors have chosen the very best authors to assess this phenomenon and they are understandably enthusiastic and cautious about their topic. We do not yet know where this current trend of mobility and migration is heading, whether it is on an upward trend, has leveled off or will soon decline. What we do know from this volume and the chapter authors is that student mobility is in a state of rapid change and complexity. This volume helps set a research agenda for the future as well as inform us of the present.

John N. Hawkins
University of California, Los Angeles

W. James Jacob
University of Pittsburgh

Acknowledgments

Planning our book and bringing it to fruition involved the cooperation and contributions of many individuals and organizations in the United States and all over the world. The research reflected in the book would not have been possible without the generous support of the U.S. Department of State's Bureau of Educational and Cultural Affairs (ECA) for *Project Atlas*, and without the support of the Ford Foundation whose pilot grant enabled us to conceptualize and develop the unique project. *Project Atlas* international partner organizations have also provided invaluable support to the project by contributing their time and effort to the important endeavor of researching and measuring global student mobility. The views of many of our partners are reflected in this book.

At the Institute of International Education, we would like to acknowledge the thought leadership of the institute's president, Dr. Allan Goodman, and the assistance of Mary Paschall, Patricia Chow, Jae-Min Hwang, Loreny Socas, and many others. Their help provided us with the time and reflection required for a book of this nature.

We thank our series editors, John N. Hawkins and W. James Jacob, for selecting our book for inclusion in the Palgrave Macmillan *International and Development Education Book Series* and for providing in-depth feedback and guidance during the entire process. We also appreciate the editorial assistance provided by Samantha Hasey at Palgrave Macmillan.

Finally, we take this opportunity to thank and acknowledge two special individuals, Sudha Bhandari Anand and Douglas Murray, for their constant support and encouragement of all our endeavors.

RAJIKA BHANDARI AND PEGGY BLUMENTHAL
New York City
October 2010

Abbreviations and Acronyms

AAU	Association of African Universities
ADS	Australian Development Scholarships
AECI	Agency for International Cooperation
AEI	Australian Education International
AIDS	Acquired Immune Deficiency Syndrome
AIU	Association of Indian Universities
ANIE	African Network for Internationalization of Education
ANUIES	Association of Universities and Higher Education Institutions
APEC	Asia-Pacific Economic Cooperation
ASEAN	Association of Southeast Asian Nations
ASSOCHAM	Associated Chambers of Commerce and Industry in India
AUIDF	Australian Universities International Directors Forum
AUN	ASEAN University Network
AUQA	Australian Universities Quality Agency
BMBF	Federal Ministry of Education and Research of Germany
BRIC	Brazil, Russia, India and China
C$	Canadian dollars
CALs	Country assessment levels
CAPES	Coordenação de Aperfeiçoamento de Pessoal de Nível Superior
CIC	Citizenship and Immigration Canada
CINDA	Centro Interuniversitario de Desarrollo
CONACYT	Consejo Nacional de Ciencia y Tecnología
CONAHEC	Consortium for North American Higher Education Cooperation
CONICET	Consejo Nacional de Investigaciones Científicas y Técnicas
CREATE	Campus for Research Excellence and Technological Enterprise

CRICOS	Commonwealth Register of Institutions and Courses for Overseas Students
CSC	China Scholarship Council
CSCSE	Chinese Service Center for Scholarly Exchange
CUSPEA	China-U.S. Physics Examination and Application
DAAD	German Academic Exchange Service
DEEWR	Department of Education, Employment and Workplace Relations of Australia
DFG	German Research Foundation
DIAC	Department of Immigration and Citizenship
DRC	Democratic Republic of the Congo
EACEA	Education, Audiovisual and Culture Executive Agency
e-CoE	electronic Confirmation of Enrolment
ECTS	European Credit Transfer and Accumulation System
EdCIL	Educational Consultants India Limited
EHEA	European Higher Education Area
EIC	Education International Cooperation Group
ELICOS	English Language Intensive Courses for Overseas Students
ERASMUS	European Region Action Scheme for the Mobility of University Students
ESOS	*Education Services for Overseas Students Act*
EU	European Union
EUROSTAT	European Commission Statistics Database
GATE	German Higher Education
GATS	General Agreement on Trade in Services
GDP	Gross Domestic Product
GLP	Global Leadership Program
Go8	Group of 8
GRE	Graduate Record Examination
HEC	Pakistani Higher Education Commission
HEI	Higher education Institution
HESA	Higher Education Statistics Agency
HKIEd	Hong Kong Institute for Education
ICCR	Indian Council for Cultural Relations
ICETEX	Instituto Colombiano de Crédito y Estudios Técnicos en el Exterior
ICT	Information, Communication, and Technology
IDP	IDP Education Pty. Ltd.
IELTS	International English Language Test System
IIE	Institute of International Education
IITs	Indian Institutes of Technology

INSEAD	Institut Européen d'Administration des Affaires
ISEP	International Student Exchange Program
KAIST	Korea Advanced Institute for Science and Technology
KHDA	Knowledge and Human Development Authority Dubai
KLEC	Kuala Lumpur Education City
KV	Knowledge Village
LSE	London School of Economics and Political Science
MERCOSUR	Mercado Común del Sur
MHEST	Ministry of Education, Science and Technology
MIT	Massachusetts Institute of Technology
NAASCOM	National Association of Software and Services Company
NAFSA	Association for International Educators
NAFTA	North American Free Trade Agreement
NEPAD	New Plan for Africa's Development
NESI	Network of Emerging Scholars for Internationalisation
NGO	Non-government Organization
NSF	National Science Foundation
OECD	Organisation for Economic Co-operation and Development
OIM	Organization of Ibero-American States for Education, Science and Culture
OPT	Optional Practical Training
OSC	Overseas Student Charge
PIMA	Programa Interamericana Estudiantil
PIME	Academic Mobility Exchange Program
PMI2	Prime Minister's Initiative 2
PRISMS	Provider Registration and International Students Management System
PROMESAN	Program for North American Mobility in Higher Education
QEC	Qatar Education City
QF	Qatar Foundation
S&E	Science and Engineering
S&T	Science and Technology
SADC	Southern African Development Community
SARS	Severe acute respiratory syndrome
SCO	Shanghai Cooperation Organization
SE	School Education
SEGIB	Secretaría General Iberoamericana

STEM	Science, technology, engineering and mathematics
TEQSA	Tertiary Education Quality and Standards Agency
TOEFL	Test of English as a Foreign Language
UCGC	University College of the Gold Coast
UDUAL	Union of Latin American Universities
UGC	University Grants Commission
UKIERI	U.K.-India Education and Research Initiative
UMAP	University Mobility in the Asia Pacific
UNISA	University of South Africa
UQAIB	University Quality Assurance International Board
US GAO	U.S. Government Accountability Office
USSR	Union of Soviet Socialist Republics
VET	Vocational Education and Training

Chapter 1

Global Student Mobility and the Twenty-First Century Silk Road: National Trends and New Directions[1]

Rajika Bhandari and Peggy Blumenthal

With 3.3 million students currently studying outside their own country, global student mobility, or the migration of students across borders for a higher education, is a burgeoning phenomenon that affects countries and their academic systems. This number represents a 65 percent increase since 2000, and the greatest surge in international student enrollments in recent decades. The magnitude of this migration is so significant that in the United States alone higher education is the fifth largest service export sector, with in-bound international students contributing US$17.7 billion to the economy each year (Bhandari and Chow 2009). Similarly, a recent report by the industry body Associated Chambers of Commerce and Industry in India (ASSOCHAM) found that about 450,000 Indian students migrate overseas and spend US$13 billion each year on acquiring a higher education abroad, often because of the lack of capacity in domestic institutions. But although the rapid growth of mobility is relatively recent, the desire to acquire a higher education beyond national borders is itself not new: students and scholars have always sought learning at the best higher education institutions around the world as a way to broaden their educational and cultural horizons. What have changed, however, are the drivers of student mobility and the new modalities through which this migration occurs.

More recently, not only has the number of internationally mobile students grown, but the overall context of global mobility—in terms of both who is going where, and the mix of host and sending countries—has also changed significantly. While Anglophone and Western European countries such as the United States, United Kingdom, Australia, France, and Germany have historically attracted the largest number of international students, other countries have boosted their internationalization strategies in recent years to attract more students, build university linkages, and develop joint research programs. Most countries now view international academic mobility and educational exchanges as critical components for sharing knowledge, building intellectual capital, and remaining competitive in a globalizing world. It is also a way to foster mutual understanding and cooperation, especially in a climate of increased security and political concerns.

The rising number of mobile students is perhaps partly an outcome of the worldwide growth in higher education. Globally, domestic higher education enrollment in 2007 increased to 152.5 million students, up from 68 million in 1991, with countries in Asia and the Pacific seeing the largest growth (UNESCO 2009). Some rapidly growing Asian countries such as Malaysia and China have recently almost doubled their higher education enrollments. At the same time, these burgeoning higher education populations have put enormous pressure on the higher education systems of many developing countries, especially at the postgraduate level, leading large numbers of their students to seek higher education outside of their home country. India is one such example where the growth of the college-age population has outpaced the capacity of the country's existing higher education institutions. There remains, thus, an enormous unmet and growing demand for international education and a huge capacity worldwide to absorb more international students. In addition, increasing numbers of students have come to realize that study abroad will enhance their career options as they enter a marketplace that requires knowledge and skills beyond those available at home. Finally, there are growing numbers of programs through which students can combine study abroad with study in their home country, often leading to dual degrees or international qualifications by foreign providers.

In this current book we set out to capture these and other dynamics of the rapidly shifting field of higher education migration and mobility, a landscape that looks very different today than in the previous century when only a handful of countries sent or received significant numbers of students and when the acquisition of a foreign degree was limited to the elite. Now the pursuit of knowledge knows no boundaries, physical or virtual, and it is this exciting growth that we seek to analyze.

This opening chapter provides a broad overview of the field, covering key trends as well as new developments in global student mobility. The first section of the chapter examines the current status of data on student mobility as the accuracy and availability of data drives what we do and do not know about this phenomenon. Next, the chapter presents key national and regional trends in mobility, highlighting the competition for international students and the role of emerging and nontraditional destinations. We then discuss new developments in the field of mobility such as branch campuses and the growing popularity of virtual learning. This is followed by an analysis of what the future holds for mobility. The chapter concludes with an overview of the book.

Who Is an International Student? Defining and Measuring Global Mobility

How do we define an international student and how do we measure the movements of students around the world? The field of global student migration is vast and complex, and our ability to document and understand student mobility from a global perspective has not kept pace with the growth in numbers and variety of international study experiences. Reliable and consistent data is needed to respond effectively to global developments in higher education. Yet, there is surprisingly limited data available on which to base decision-making or frame policy discussion. Few countries outside of Australia, Germany, the United Kingdom, and the United States have developed data collection systems that produce high-quality and consistent statistics on which to base policy decisions. As a result, higher education officials in countries trying to develop policies in the context of global academic mobility need better information, as do campus-level officials and those in the press and public who are trying to understand critically important issues. These include, for example, how global academic migration affects brain drain; how it affects the current and future capacity of countries to accommodate a growing demand for higher education; and the implications of mobility for the labor market, the economy, and for the global search for academic talent.

Attempts to Measure Mobility

Which are the largest sending and host countries? Where do the students come from and where do they go? In an attempt to answer these critical questions, some countries have established systems for collecting information on international students. In the United States, for example, the Institute of International Education (IIE) has been collecting this type of data since the 1920s and publishing the material since 1954 as the *Open Doors* Report on International Educational Exchange, with support from the U.S. Department of State since 1972.[2] An annual census of U.S. international educational exchange, *Open Doors* presents mobility statistics based on data collected from all regionally accredited U.S. higher education institutions. Similar data for Australia is gathered by Australian Education International (AEI), for the United Kingdom by the Higher Education Statistics Agency, and for Germany by the German Academic Exchange Service (DAAD). Countries such as China (through the China Scholarship Council [CSC]) and Mexico (through the Association of Universities and Higher Education Institutions [ANUIES]) have more recently developed mechanisms to collect this type of data.

But because most current sources of information and knowledge about international students are derived from national data collection organizations such as the ones mentioned above, the resulting data vary widely from country to country in timeliness, data definitions, and scope. Country-specific data by itself is limited in that it tells us little about the implications of each country's mobility statistics within a global context. The variation in national degree and qualification structures across countries also makes comparative analysis difficult. What is needed is a global and consistent source of baseline data as well as a forum within which national efforts may be compared and benchmarked.

Although UNESCO and the Organisation for Economic Co-operation and Development (OECD) have instituted large-scale data collection efforts to collect mobility data for all countries, they face a number of well-recognized limitations. For one, there is typically a significant time-lag between data collection and data release. Second, because the data are primarily collected through Ministries of Education, they do not always capture enrollments at private institutions. The result is an underestimate of international students, since private institutions represent the fastest growing education sector in many countries. Third, according to the definitions used by UNESCO and OECD, only students enrolled for the duration of a year or more are counted in the data. Since internationally mobile students from the United States, Japan, and the European Union (EU) often study abroad for less than a full academic year, it can be safely assumed that the actual number of students who are globally mobile significantly exceeds the 2.8 million counted by UNESCO.

Project Atlas: A Shared Framework for Student Mobility Data

One effort to build upon the work of UNESCO and OECD and address some of its limitations is *Project Atlas*, a unique initiative that brings together a community of researchers from around the world to share more harmonized and current data on student mobility.[3] Initiated in 2001 with support from the Ford Foundation and currently supported by the U.S. Department of State and participating members in other countries, *Project Atlas* and its associated web portal, the *Atlas of Student Mobility,* currently provide a comprehensive global picture of international student mobility for 19 leading and emerging host countries, and enrollment by students from 76 places of origin. These data are gathered through data-sharing agreements with researchers based at national academic mobility agencies around the world. Table 1.1 lists the current 19 project partners, comprising 15 countries and 4 research affiliates, representing developed and developing countries.

Underlying the project is an unprecedented effort to engage these leading non-governmental and governmental agencies involved in international educational exchange to examine the broader implications of their work within a global context rather than through a narrow national lens. *Project Atlas* also helps IIE and the other member organizations to consider how international education patterns relate to other national developments

Table 1.1   Project Atlas Partner Organizations, 2010

Project Atlas Partners
• Association of Indian Universities (AIU)
• Australia Education International (AEI)
• British Council
• Canadian Bureau for International Education (CBIE)
• Campus France
• Center for International Higher Education (CIHE), Boston College
• Center for International Mobility (CIMO), Finland
• China Scholarship Council (CSC)
• Education Ireland
• German Academic Exchange Service (DAAD)
• Institute of International Education (IIE), United States
• International Education Association of South Africa (IEASA)
• International Association of Universities (IAU)
• National Association of Universities and Institutions of Higher Education (ANUIES)
• Netherlands Organisation for International Cooperation in Higher Education (NUFFIC)
• Organisation for Economic Co-operation and Development (OECD)
• Swedish Institute
• UNESCO Institute of Statistics
• Universidad.de, Spain

Source: Project Atlas, http://atlas.iienetwork.org.

such as home country investment in human capital, population growth, and the level of technological capacity, and how they are affected by international and transnational economic, diplomatic, and political factors. An improved understanding of these dynamics might also help potential international students make a better-informed choice regarding their study destinations.

Drawing on the experience of IIE's *Open Doors* project (which has collected and disseminated academic migration data for over 60 years), *Project Atlas* provides a shared framework within which to collect, synthesize, and disseminate data on the migration trends of the millions of students who pursue education outside of their home countries each year. The aim was to address the need for global migration data that measures student flows not just to the United States but also to several other leading and emerging destinations for transnational higher education. *Project Atlas* tells us, for instance, how China has moved from being the leading sending country for international students to now being one of the top ten host countries, and how South Africa is growing as a regional host for students from throughout Africa and beyond.

With the goal of highlighting national policies that facilitate global mobility, *Atlas* partner organizations use the project website to share the strategies and initiatives their countries and governments have undertaken to increase international educational exchange. To capture more fully the increasingly important role that newer "host" countries are now playing in global mobility, an ongoing priority for *Project Atlas* is to identify and involve more partners from Asia, Latin America, the Middle East, and Africa.

The Evolution of Project Atlas

The foundations for *Project Atlas* were laid down in May 2001 at a meeting in France that was attended by representatives from selected national bodies and non-government organizations (NGO) involved in international educational exchanges and mobility and who had expressed an interest in developing an effective approach to a common data set for global mobility. Staff from OECD and UNESCO also participated. The discussion would consider each group's needs, how best to take the project forward, and the possible funding implications. By creating a shared image of international mobility, the hope was to highlight the truly globe-spanning aspects of higher education, make apparent the emerging world higher education economy, and establish a conversation space for those concerned with global education mobility issues.

It was agreed that the first requirement was to establish mechanisms that would better and consistently describe international student mobility through the compilation of data available to national agencies and related organizations, aggregating the data and then disseminating findings internationally. With assistance from the British Council and IDP Education Australia, IIE took a first step in this direction by publishing the *Atlas of Student Mobility*, a seminal book bringing together international mobility data from 21 major host countries, using year 2000 data. The *Atlas of Student Mobility* graphically presented the data in various ways, including analyses by sending countries and comparisons with other relevant data sets (Davis 2003). This groundbreaking book was widely disseminated both in print and on the web among NGOs, universities, and scholars; its primary purpose was to enable the reader to view the emerging global higher education space as a whole—as more than just the sum of its national host country parts.

Current Project Activities

The project's regularly updated website makes the data available to a wider audience and provides an online forum for project partners; the group also meets at least once a year to engage in ongoing dialogue and cooperation. These collaborative meetings not only assist partners in developing joint data-collection standards and practices, but also strengthen collaboration and shrink the "competitive" prism through which international student mobility discussions are often viewed. Between 2006 and 2010, IIE has co-hosted international student mobility conferences and *Atlas*-related meetings with our *Atlas* partner organizations in China, Mexico, Scotland, India, the Netherlands, the United States, Kenya, and Spain. In addition to sharing mobility data, these meetings provide *Atlas* partners an opportunity to jointly develop research activities on topics such as cross-border education, student-level attitudinal surveys, and longitudinal trends in mobility for certain key host countries. A more recent goal of the project has been to engage in capacity-building activities for less-experienced emerging destinations to design and implement a system to collect mobility data. Along these lines, IIE collaborated with the African Network for Internationalization of Education (ANIE) in September 2009 to hold a two-day capacity-building workshop in Kenya on global student migration and best practices in collecting data on higher education migration.

National and Regional Trends in Global Mobility

The movement of students and scholars across borders is growing rapidly, driven by many factors and involving a wide range of vehicles and modalities. Many factors, real or perceived, can affect a student's choice of study destination, including the cost and quality of higher education programs; the value of the degree or professional credential for future careers; the availability of certain areas of specialization; access to the education system and a country (including, but not limited to, obtaining visas for entry); and important historical, linguistic, and geographic links between the home and destination countries (Bhandari and Laughlin 2009).

For the suppliers of international education—namely host countries and institutions—there are a variety of objectives and approaches to engaging in academic exchange, and those that are most effective in internationalizing are characterized by flexibility and a willingness to adapt to new realities in the complex world of higher education. Common to the best of them are certain elements such as commitment to academic excellence, to fair and open access for candidates, and to student diversity. Most also face similar challenges, such as how to cope with rapidly expanding opportunities and interest in study abroad with limited or shrinking resources. Given these dynamics in the field of higher education mobility, the following are some key trends that have emerged recently:

- Six countries host 64 percent of the world's tertiary-level mobile students: the United States (21 percent), the United Kingdom (13 percent), France (9 percent), Germany (8 percent), Australia (7 percent), and China (6 percent) (Figure 1.1) (*Project Atlas* 2010; UNESCO 2009). Anglophone countries such as Australia and the United Kingdom have seen large percentage increases in their international student populations, while the United States has seen a modest percentage decline. However, the United States continues to host the largest number and proportion of international students pursuing higher education outside

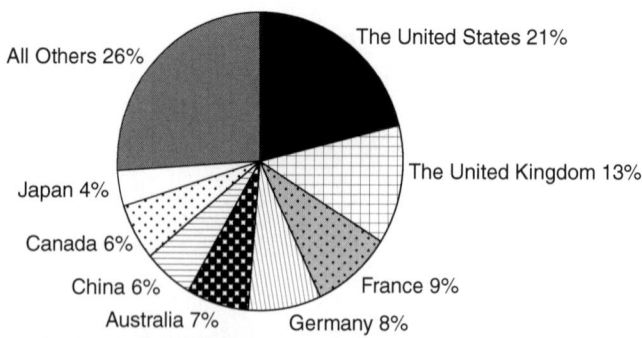

Figure 1.1   Top Host Destinations for International Students, 2007/2008.
Source: Project Atlas; UNESCO (2009).

of their home country (671,616 students in 2008/2009), followed by the United Kingdom at 415,585 students in 2009.

Looking at the rate of growth, the rate for the United States is understandably lower than those of other countries that are starting out from a much smaller base: the United States has hosted over half a million students for the past eight years while Australia, for example, hosted 223,508 students in 2008, resulting in a steeper rate of increase. The shift in the U.S. share is due to multiple factors such as the increased capacity of the higher education subsector in many nontraditional destinations, especially in Asia, to host domestic as well as international students; strong national-level internationalization policies and strategies in competing destinations; and the rise of nontraditional forms of educational delivery such as virtual learning and offshore education.

- The overall pie of global mobility is expanding with more countries emerging as important destinations for international students. Newer host countries such as China are seeing rapid increases in the numbers of international students. Several other countries in the Asia Pacific region—Thailand, Malaysia, Singapore, and New Zealand, to name a few—have stepped up their efforts to internationalize and to attract more international students (table 1.2). Although this has resulted in a somewhat smaller market share for top host countries, it is nonetheless a positive development as it has brought more countries into the field of international education and has changed the dynamic between sending and receiving countries from a unidirectional "brain drain" type of mobility to one of mutual exchange.
- The largest groups of internationally mobile students come from East Asia and the Pacific (29 percent). Students from China represent the largest share of internationally mobile students (421,000 or

Table 1.2 International Student Benchmarks among Emerging Hosts

Country	Total International Students	Target	Total Higher Education Enrollment
China	195,999	500,000 by 2020	25,346,000
Japan	123,829	300,000 by 2020	4,033,000
Jordan	21,509	100,000 by 2020	232,000
Malaysia	24,404	100,000 by 2010	749,000
Singapore	80,000	150,000 by 2015	184,000

Sources: Project Atlas; Singapore Education; UNESCO (2006, 2007).

15 percent), followed by students from India (153,300), South Korea (105,300), Germany (77,500), and Japan (54,500).

- Sub-Saharan Africa has the highest outbound mobility share of its total higher education population (5.8 percent), almost three times greater than the world average. North America has the lowest outbound ratio with only 0.5 percent of the region's tertiary students pursuing their education abroad.

Global "Competition" for International Students: Traditional Hosts and New Players

Developed countries in Europe, North America, and Oceania have dominated the global mobility picture of the late twentieth and early twenty-first centuries. The United States, the United Kingdom, France, and Germany, in particular, have long attracted large numbers of international students. For the most part, the movement of students has been from developing to developed countries (Altbach 2007; Altbach and Knight 2007; Knight 2006a; UNESCO 2006, 2009). And although this overall trend continues today, the situation is nonetheless changing for these key countries, with interesting variations emerging in which several unexpected players are now engaged in what might best be described as a "global competition" for international students (Wildavsky 2010). With strong financial incentives, geopolitical motives, and the need for immigrant labor in high-tech areas, the competition has become vigorous. As a result, international students are not only choosing nontraditional destinations but are also pursuing nontraditional forms of learning.

These changes have been propelled by a combination of factors that include aggressive recruiting by other countries to host more foreign students; the expanding capacity of countries such as China to not only provide more higher education opportunities for their own students but also host an increasing number of international students; the availability and global spread of alternative modes of educational delivery; and domestic economic, demographic, and workforce conditions that might affect students' decisions regarding an overseas education.

Government-supported efforts by key host countries, including nationally coordinated campaigns by the United Kingdom, Australia, Germany, France, New Zealand, and others, feature sophisticated marketing strategies. Launched in 1998, the United Kingdom's £5 million "Prime Minister's Initiative" was one of the earliest and was updated in 2000 as the "Education U.K." brand, a coordinated approach to marketing British institutions abroad that is available for use by any U.K. campus. Other recent U.K. initiatives include the Science and Engineering Graduate Scheme (2004), the U.K.-China Higher Education Program (2005), and the U.K.-India Education and Research Initiative (2006). Several traditional host countries, along with newer players in Asia and Europe, have over the past few years allocated tens of millions of dollars to launch large-scale initiatives. These efforts are proving very persuasive, especially to self-funded students from some of the large sending countries in Asia.

Countries that were primarily "sending" countries have now also developed their own internationalization strategies to attract foreign students and encourage international educational exchange. This new era of internationalization is most evident in Asia. Singapore has been making strides in this area with the establishment of Education Singapore, a new agency charged with promoting and marketing Singapore abroad and with attracting 150,000 foreign students by 2015. Malaysia seeks to attract 100,000 international students by 2010 (up from 45,000 in 2005); China seeks to host 500,000 by 2020; and Japan has reportedly set the ambitious goal of hosting 300,000 foreign students by 2020 (up from the current 132,720). But, the question remains: to what extent are recruitment strategies based on solid and complete information about the true nature of global mobility trends? Initiatives such as *Project Atlas* will play a vital role in filling this critical information gap.

Many countries are also formalizing the link between higher education and the skilled job market by implementing policies that encourage international graduates to enter the workforce of the host country, especially in scientific and technical fields. Scotland announced a "Post-Study Worker Scheme" aimed at attracting 8,000 foreign professionals per year up until 2009 by allowing international students who graduate from a Scottish university to remain for two years of postgraduation employment. Supplementing efforts by individual host countries in Europe, the EU has also launched initiatives to recruit science and technology researchers from around the world in an attempt to compete with America's well-funded research universities and labs that reputedly attract the world's best and brightest science and technology (S&T) talent.

The emergence and growing popularity of alternative higher education destinations, coupled with increasing return rates for a few key "source" countries such as China, India, and South Korea, leads to the inevitable question: can the perennial favorite hosts of the developed world—such as the United States, the United Kingdom, Australia, and Germany—maintain their competitive edge by attracting the best and the brightest from around the world? The United States, which remains to date the top choice of international students and scholars, is affected most by current trends in global student mobility and skilled migration. U.S. reliance on foreign-born talent grew in both absolute numbers and as a share of the science and engineering workforce and has continued to escalate during the 1990s and the first decade of the twentieth century (National Science Board 2010). Since 2006, foreign-born students have earned over 50 percent of US doctoral degrees in mathematics, computer sciences, physics, engineering, and economics, with most students coming from China, India, and South Korea. In engineering alone, foreign students earned 68 percent of all doctorates in 2007. The presence of foreign-born faculty at U.S. research institutions also continues to increase, with most constituting almost half of all STEM-related (science, technology, engineering, and mathematics) departments.

The key challenge for countries such as the United States that have come to rely on international talent is to strike the right balance between increasing domestic science and technology capacity and attracting the best minds from across the world. To view these strategies as mutually exclusive is to impose boundaries upon the science and innovation enterprise that, by its very nature, has become global and borderless. Keeping the doors open to international students and scholars, many of whom go on to become immigrants, also has multiplier effects: a study of engineering and technology companies started in the United States between 1995 and 2005 found that over a quarter of them were founded by immigrants (primarily Indians, followed by those from the United Kingdom, China, Taiwan, and Japan), employing 450,000 workers nationwide and accounting for US$52 billion in total sales (Wadhwa et al. 2007).

Developing countries have traditionally been the "suppliers" of international students but now face interesting challenges as they are poised to also become popular study destinations. They are likely to face the dilemma of how to increase the capacity of their higher education systems to provide adequate opportunities for their expanding college-age population while also accommodating incoming international students and engaging in the type of international educational exchange that is necessary in today's globally competitive world. Last but not the least, a related challenge for developing countries hoping to attract back their nationals will be to ensure adequate employment opportunities and an appropriate standard of living.

Redefining Mobility: New Paradigms and Developments

A range of new institutions and alternative approaches to international study has emerged to meet the growing need for a cost-effective education and, as a result, many students are choosing to stay home while also acquiring an "international" education (Blumenthal et al. 1996; Blumenthal 2002). These new modes of education include, among others, distance learning, joint and dual degrees, branch campuses, and "sandwich" programs involving short-term study abroad. According to Gray (2006), these types of nontraditional academic arrangements have succeeded because they offer alternative modes of organization and operation in the form of new program offerings (e.g., short courses, night classes), new pedagogical approaches, asynchronous and collaborative learning, and distributed physical infrastructure (including but not limited to remote campuses and distance education via the Internet).

Cross-border Education: Moving Education Overseas

Perhaps the most significant development in alternative forms of international education has been the advent of cross-border or transnational education—umbrella terms that include brick-and-mortar branch campuses as well as joint- and dual-degree programs. Broadly speaking, this approach involves "the movement of education across national jurisdictional or geographic borders" (Knight 2006b)—that is, "internationalization abroad" as compared with the more traditional form of "internationalization at home." As in the case of more traditional forms of global student mobility, the movement and spread of cross-border education has primarily been from the developed North to the developing South. Branch campuses dominate this type of overseas educational delivery, with U.S. institutions accounting for more than half of all overseas higher education, followed by Australia, the United Kingdom, and Ireland (Becker 2009; Verbik and Merkley 2006). Key host countries for overseas campuses include Singapore and China in Asia, and Dubai (Knowledge Village) and Qatar (Education City) in the Middle East.

Although branch campuses have the advantage of providing access to millions of students who cannot afford to travel to study abroad but who desire access to international education, such institutions are not easy to operate and face unique challenges. First, they need to be sensitive and responsive to the needs and requirements of the host country while also reflecting the mission and learning culture of the home institution—goals that might occasionally be incompatible and might lead to the foreign institution being viewed as engaging in "academic imperialism" (Becker 2009, 6). Second, they can never fully replicate the kind of intense learning experience that comes from plunging into a foreign environment and mastering the linguistic, cultural, and academic challenges of studying abroad. Despite their growing popularity,

11 international branch campuses have already closed their doors, five of them recently, including Australia's University of New South Wales' Singapore campus in 2007 and the U.S.-based George Mason University's United Arab Emirates (U.A.E.) branch in 2009. Reasons for the closures of these and other campuses have included low student enrollment, insufficient revenues, political instability in the host country, and strained relationships with local partners. For many of the same reasons, Japan's branch campus "bubble" of the 1980s attracted over 100 U.S. partners, of which only one (Temple University) still remains (Chambers and Cummings 1990).

In recent years, new forms of international collaborative partnerships, such as joint and double degree programs, consortial arrangements, twinning and other forms of close curricular integration, have been rapidly gaining attention at colleges and universities around the world as a way to offer particularly deep and meaningful international experiences to college and university students. Although the United States has relatively few international joint- and double-degree programs—especially when compared to European countries, where such degrees have long been a vital part of internationalization strategies in higher education—U.S. interest in such degrees has increased substantially. A survey of U.S. and European institutions conducted in 2008 by IIE and the Freie Universität Berlin found that universities on both sides of the Atlantic are working to establish more international joint- and dual-degree programs, with 87 percent of respondents saying that they wanted to develop more joint and dual degrees, especially with countries such as China and India.

Virtual Learning: Knowledge Is Just a Click Away

Finally, we cannot ignore the growth of "virtual mobility," the use of the Internet to deliver courses anywhere in the world to anyone who has access to a computer and a modem (Blumenthal 2002). This type of Internet-based learning may also undercut the need for students to cross physical borders to obtain an international credential. Among the many challenges of Internet-based education are monitoring of quality and equity of access. One creative response to both challenges has been the "open courseware" offered by the Massachusetts Institute of Technology (MIT), which posted hundreds of its courses online and made them available without cost to anyone in the world. Other universities around the globe are also developing creative ways of delivering education remotely and reaching students and professionals who may never have considered studying abroad. The Internet can also be an invaluable tool for alumni of study abroad programs to stay in touch with their host campuses even after they return home and to benefit from the continuing educational opportunities available online.

Cross-border education and the expansion of virtual learning have significant implications for domestic and international higher education. It is conceivable, for example, that as prospective international students choose branch campuses located in their own countries over the institution's home campus, traditional student mobility, as we know it, might decline (Knight 2006b). Conversely, it is also possible that these diverse forms of internationalization will continue to grow rapidly, serving different types of students with varying educational needs. Thus, we see an important role for different forms of internationalization and hope that they can reinforce each other in the coming decades.

The Future of Mobility

Changing economies and political situations at home, as well as the evolving landscape of higher education around the world, have created new opportunities for internationally mobile students. Indeed, according to some estimates, the desire for higher education—and the subsequent demand for international education—is expanding so rapidly that in 20 years there will not be enough classroom seats in the whole world to meet the needs of students who want to pursue higher education. Creative and collaborative solutions will be needed to provide higher education and training to those who seek it. Distance learning, joint-degree programs, and new approaches we cannot yet imagine will all be needed to address the educational needs of the hundreds of millions of undergraduates around the world. Governments will, of course, be the primary responders to this need, but the private and nonprofit sectors are also likely to play key roles. In this section of the chapter we examine the future implications of mobility within the framework of the circulation of "brains" and knowledge. While staying clear of projecting a rate of growth in the future, we also take a look at whether student mobility numbers might continue to grow.

From "Brain Drain" to "Brain Circulation"

As mobility continues to grow, it is imperative for those involved in international education to revisit the "brain drain" debate. Early assessments of skilled migration emphasized the negative aspect of such mobility, arguing that because mobility was primarily from the developing to the developed world, it resulted in a drain of the former's human resources. Later interpretations of skilled migration rejected the inequitable aspect of mobility and suggested that the drain should be regarded as a "brain gain" situation whereby sending countries actually stand to benefit, primarily financially, from skilled migration.

We too employ the brain drain metaphor, while also offering a new and more nuanced interpretation of it that takes into account current mobility trends. The terms "brain circulation" or "brain exchange" more accurately describe the increasingly multidirectional nature of international flows and the growing awareness that such mobility patterns or exchanges are mutually beneficial for sending and receiving countries, albeit in varying ways. It is important to mention, however, that the one major exception to this shift is Africa, as it continues to lose a disproportionate amount of its human resources to skilled migration. Coupled with the widespread destruction of human capital caused by the AIDS epidemic and repeated political upheavals, outward migration of talented individuals has taken a heavy toll on the continent's social, economic, and educational sectors (Teferra and Knight 2008). As mentioned previously, Africa has the highest outbound mobility ratio of any world region in that more African students are enrolled in higher education overseas than at home.

Although there is limited empirical evidence to support this assertion, anecdotal evidence suggests that international mobility or skilled migration no longer follows a strictly linear pattern where people move between just two countries, typically from South to North. In an increasingly connected world, a student from Asia, for example, might choose to obtain an undergraduate degree in her home country, a master's degree in the United States, and a doctoral degree in the United Kingdom, returning home subsequently to work for a European multinational firm. The mobility of international scientists and researchers, too, has become increasingly complex as the field of science and engineering itself has evolved into a borderless enterprise. Not surprisingly, this type of multi-country mobility is difficult to measure. For instance, even though Finn's (2010) research on the "stay rates" of international postdoctoral researchers and scholars in the United States sheds light on who remains in the United States and who leaves, it is not able to tell us whether those who leave are heading to another country or back to their home country, or even whether those staying on in the United States are commuting between the United States and their home country regularly to work in joint ventures.

The strengthening of overseas higher education partnerships, facilitated by advances in telecommunications and the Internet, has also contributed to the shift from a drain to a balance in the sharing of knowledge and information. For instance, faculty and researchers at universities across many parts of the world have significantly increased their collaboration, and research activities now regularly span multiple countries while capitalizing on worldwide knowledge and talent (Adams et al. 2004; Obst and Kuder 2009; Wildavsky 2010).

Another growing trend is that many students educated abroad are returning to their home countries to take up competitive positions in the private, public, and academic sectors. Research by Wadhwa (2009) has shown that large numbers of Indian and Chinese students in the United States plan to return home. To take advantage of the global knowledge and skills required in a knowledge economy and to meet the demand for skilled labor, Asian places of origin such as China, Singapore, South Korea, and Taiwan have launched extensive efforts and initiatives to recruit scientists and engineers to return home. Returning skilled workers are seen as improving a country's productivity and global competitiveness because of the direct transfer of knowledge and skills and the indirect benefits that accrue through returnees' access to overseas professional and trade networks that can have a positive impact on domestic growth and development (Thorn and Holm-Nielsen 2006).

One of the newest players in the Asian region is Pakistan. Launched in 2002, the Pakistani Higher Education Commission (HEC) is an umbrella organization vested with creating academic linkages between Pakistani higher education institutions and foreign universities through an initial investment of US$5 million (Atta-ur-Rahman 2007). Among its key strategies to promote bidirectional exchange is the Foreign Faculty Hiring Program, which recruits highly qualified faculty members from abroad for both short- and long-term appointments. Efforts to attract back highly skilled Pakistani migrants are complemented by the goal to provide more Pakistani students with the opportunity to obtain an international education and to reinvigorate their country's higher education subsector with their newly acquired knowledge.

Will Numbers Continue to Grow?

At the turn of the millennium, several studies documented the rise in international student mobility and suggested that the numbers would inevitably increase. In a prominent report published in 2002, IDP Education Australia projected a dramatic expansion in the demand for international education, doubling over the next ten years and then perhaps doubling again, with as many as 7.2 million students studying outside their home country by the year 2025 (Böhm et al. 2002). Eight years after these initial projections, it appears that these high estimates did not fully account for the rapid expansion of the higher education subsector in countries such as China that have since gone beyond functioning primarily as sending countries to also become attractive host destinations, especially for students from within the region. For example, in just one year, international enrollment in Chinese universities has risen from 162,695 students in 2006 to 195,503 in 2007–2008, a 20 percent increase (*Project Atlas* 2008). In a more recent forecasting study conducted in 2007, the IDP, revising its calculations of student mobility growth, estimated a total of 3.7 million mobile students by 2025 (Banks and Olsen 2008).

In contrast, the estimates released by UNESCO and OECD have remained fairly stable over time. In 2000 UNESCO estimated that almost 2 million higher education students were being educated in countries other than their homes; current estimates indicate that approximately 2.8 million students (most from the developing world) are mobile, a large proportion of whom—43.8 percent—are in major Anglophone host countries, defined as Australia, Canada, the United Kingdom, and the United States. Students from traditional destination countries in Europe and North America are also pursuing international education in increasing numbers. Data from *Open Doors* show that the number of American students studying abroad (primarily on short-term programs) has more than quadrupled since the mid-1980s (Bhandari and Chow 2009). Countries within the EU have experienced even greater expansion of their internationally mobile student populations due to EU-funded programs such as Erasmus, Socrates, and Leonardo, as well as the structural reforms initiated through the Bologna Process. The EU estimates that since the beginning of the Erasmus program more than two decades ago, more than 2 million European students have participated in the program at over 3,000 higher education institutions in 31 participating countries.

Forecasting is in general an imperfect science, and even more so for a dynamic phenomenon like higher education mobility that is affected by multiple factors and developments around the globe that are beyond any one nation's control. However, in addition to analyzing the rapid growth taking place in Asia, it is worth exploring current developments in some key host nations and the implications that these will have for mobility. Beginning first with the United States, the top host country, the picture appears to be mixed. Although numbers increased by a significant 8 percent to an all-time high of 671,616, other surveys suggest an impending decline in international graduate students in the United States, especially from India, which has thus far been the top sending country (Council of Graduate Schools 2009; IIE 2009). At the same time, international undergraduate enrollments in the United States are rising sharply, particularly from China (Bhandari and Chow 2009). It remains to be seen whether the increases in international undergraduate enrollments will offset the declines at the graduate level.

From the perspective of higher education capacity, the United States has a large untapped capacity to absorb significant future growth in international student enrollment as compared with other key host countries (figure 1.2). The 671,616 international students in the United States comprise less than 4 percent of total U.S. higher education enrollment, with only 150 institutions hosting 54 percent of all international students in the United States.[4] This suggests that there is much room for a larger number and variety of accredited U.S. institutions to host future international students, especially at the undergraduate and non-degree level.

Turning next to two other popular hosts, the United Kingdom and Australia, the forecast is more uncertain. Despite strong efforts in both countries to attract large numbers of international students, the recently implemented strict visa restrictions for international students may lead, in the near future, to a significant decline or flattening of the international student population in the United Kingdom. According to various news reports, this decline is most likely to occur from India and Pakistan, countries that send large numbers of students each year. Because of the tightening of the visa process, the United Kingdom is likely to witness a drop in enrollments similar to what the United States saw in the years immediately after September 11. As for Australia, a recent spate of racial attacks and violence against Indian students and the wider Indian community has affected relations between the two countries, with many Indian students now wondering whether Australia is a safe and welcoming destination. In

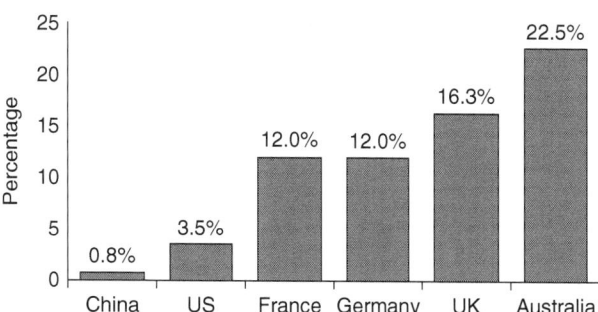

Figure 1.2 Top Countries' International Enrollment as a Percentage of Total Higher Education Enrollment, 2007/2008.
Source: Project Atlas.

addition, the Australian government recently tightened its visa regulations that are likely to affect thousands of prospective international students.

Overview of the Book

The last book similar in global scope to this one—*Academic Mobility in a Changing World: Regional and Global Trends*—was published back in 1996 by Blumenthal and colleagues. A lot has changed in higher education in general and in student mobility in particular since then. Using a country- and regional-level approach, the current book captures many of the developments that have taken place over the past 15 years. In addition to sharing specific strategies that their countries have adopted to facilitate mobility, the authors also examine what key developments mean for their country as both host and sender. This national and regional focus also allows us to examine the implications of these trends at the institutional and national levels, and how each country's governmental and non-governmental sector continues to adapt its marketing and recruitment efforts to attract international students.

Our book attempts to cover most world regions and key countries. Many of the authors and their organizations are current *Project Atlas* partners and are experts on understanding and interpreting mobility trends for their countries or regions. With the increasing demand for higher education in the developing world, chapters by Xinyu Yang and Pawan Agarwal are devoted to addressing the capacity of rapidly growing economies such as China and India, and whether their educational systems can continue to absorb more international students while also adequately meeting the demand from their own students. Through his case study of the developing countries of Africa, Roshen Kishun highlights the continuing brain drain problem caused by high outbound mobility. He also provides an in-depth look at the current paucity of mobility data for Africa and the need for more complete and current data collection at the national level.

In their chapter on Europe, Christian Bode and Martin Davidson, chief executives of two of the world's largest educational exchange organizations—the German Academic Exchange Service and the British Council—provide complementary and contrasting perspectives on mobility-related developments in two of the top host destinations and in the wider European context. Allan Goodman and Robert Gutierrez in their chapter on the United States analyze in detail both in- and outbound trends for the United States, the world's top host for international students.

Melissa Banks and colleagues provide an overview of the rapid growth of international education in Australia, and the increasingly market-based approach to attracting international students. In their chapter on Latin America, Hans de Wit and Isabel Jaramillo attempt to provide a regional perspective on mobility, while also highlighting the diversity and complexity inherent in Latin American countries. A final country-level chapter by John McHale focuses on the various strategies and incentives in place to attract international students to Canadian universities and the costs and benefits of this type of recruitment.

The concluding chapters of the book assess the implications of a changing landscape of global student mobility. Veronica Lasanowski documents how English has become the lingua franca for most countries and the implications this has for international student flows. Finally, Jane Knight, an expert in the area of higher education internationalization, examines the growth of a new form of cross-border education—"education hubs"—and how such developments force international educators to think about student mobility in new ways, while also posing unique challenges and opportunities for measuring mobility trends.

NOTES

1. A similar chapter by the primary author appeared in *Higher Education on the Move: New Developments in Global Mobility*. New York: Institute of International Education, 2009.
2. See http://opendoors.iienetwork.org.
3. http://atlas.iienetwork.org.
4. A larger proportion of international students are enrolled at the graduate level in the United States.

BIBLIOGRAPHY

Adams, James D., Grant C. Black, J. Rogers Clemmons, and Paula E. Stephan. 2004. *Scientific Teams and Institutional Collaborations: Evidence from U.S. Universities, 1981–1999*. NBER Working Paper No. 10640. New York and Palo Alto, CA: National Bureau of Economic Research.

Altbach, Philip G. 2007. *Tradition and Transition: The International Imperative in Higher Education*. Boston, MA: Center for International Higher Education, Boston College.

Altbach, Philip G., and Jane Knight. 2007. "Higher Education's Landscape of Internationalization: Motivations and Realities." In *Tradition and*

Transition: The International Imperative in Higher Education, ed. Philip G. Altbach. Boston: Center for International Higher Education, Boston College.

Anderson, Stuart. 2004. *The Multiplier Effect.* Arlington, VA: National Foundation of American Policy. Available online at: http://www.nfap.com.

Atta-ur-Rahman. 2007. "Higher Education in Pakistan: A Silent Revolution." *IIENetworker* Spring: 36–39.

Atlas of Global Student Mobility. 2010. *Atlas of Student Mobility.* New York: (IIE). Available online at: http://atlas.iienetwork.org.

Banks, Melissa, and Alan Olsen. 2008. "Defining and Measuring Global Student Mobility: An Australian Perspective." Paper presented at the NAFSA Annual Conference 2008 Special Research Seminar, Washington, DC, May 29, 2008.

Becker, Rosa. 2009. *International Branch Campuses: Markets and Strategies.* London: The Observatory on Borderless Higher Education.

Blumenthal, Peggy. 2002. "Virtual and Physical Mobility: A View from the U.S." In *The Virtual Challenge to International Cooperation in Higher Education. ACA Papers on International Cooperation,* ed. Bernd Wächter. Bonn, Germany: Lemmens.

Bhandari, Rajika, ed. 2010. *International India: A Turning Point in Indo-U.S. Higher Education Exchange.* New York: IIE.Bhandari, Rajika, and Patricia Chow. 2009. Open Doors 2009: Report on International Educational Exchange. New York: IIE.

Bhandari, Rajika, and Shepherd Laughlin, eds. 2009. *Higher Education on the Move: New Developments in Global Mobility.* New York: IIE.

Blumenthal, Peggy. 2002. "Virtual and Physical Mobility: A View from the U.S." In *The Virtual Challenge to International Cooperation in Higher Education. ACA Papers on International Cooperation,* ed. Bernd Wächter. Bonn, Germany: Lemmens.

Blumenthal, Peggy, Alan Smith, Ulrich Teichler, and Craufurd Goodwin., eds. 1996. *Academic Mobility in a Changing World: Regional and Global Trends.* London: Jessica Kingsley Publishers.

Böhm, Anthony, Dorothy Davis, Denis Meares, and David Pearce. 2002. *Global Student Mobility 2025: Forecast of the Demand for International Higher Education.* Sydney: IDP Education Australia.

Chambers, Gail S., and William K. Cummings. 1990. Profiting from Education: Japan-United States International Educational Ventures in the 1980s. New York: IIE.

Council of Graduate Schools. 2009. Findings from the 2009 CGS International Graduate Admissions Survey. Phase III: Final Offers of Admission and Enrollment. Washington, DC: Council of Graduate Schools.

Davis, Todd M. 2003. *Atlas of Student Mobility.* New York: IIE.

Finn, Michael G. 2010. *Stay Rates of Foreign Doctorate Recipients from U.S. Universities, 2007.* Oak Ridge, TN: Oak Ridge Institute for Science and Education.

Gray, David. 2006. *Global Engagement in a Virtual World.* Paper presented at the Assuring a Globally Engaged Science and Engineering Workforce Workshop of National Science Foundation, Washington, DC, September 20–22, 2006.

Institute of International Education (IIE). 2009. *Fall 2009: Joint Survey on International Student Enrollments in the U.S.* Open Doors. New York: IIE. Available online at: http://opendoors.iienetwork.org.

Knight, Jane. 2006a. Internationalization of Higher Education: New Directions, New Challenges. 2005 IAU Global Survey Report. Paris: International Association of Universities.

Knight. Jane. 2006b. "Crossborder Education: An Analytical Framework for Program and Provider Mobility." In *Higher Education: Handbook of Theory and Research, 21,* ed. John C. Smart. Dordrecht, The Netherlands: Springer.

National Science Board. 2010. *Science and Engineering Indicators—2010.* Arlington, VA: National Science Foundation.

Obst, Daniel, and Matthias Kuder, eds. 2009. Joint and Double Degree Programs: An Emerging Model for Transatlantic Exchange. New York: IIE.

Teferra, Damtew, and Jane Knight. 2008. *Higher Education in Africa: The International Dimension.* Accra: Association of African Universities.

Thorn, Kristian, and Lauritz B. Holm-Nielsen. 2006. *International Mobility of Researchers and Scientists: Policy Options for Turning a Drain into a Gain.* Research Paper No. 2006/83, United Nations University-World Institute for Development Economics Research. Available online at: http://www.wider. unu.edu.

UNESCO. 2006. Global Education Digest 2006: Comparing Education Statistics across the World. Montreal: UNESCO Institute for Statistics.

UNESCO. 2007. Global Education Digest 2007: Comparing Education Statistics across the World. Montreal: UNESCO Institute for Statistics.

UNESCO. 2008. Global Education Digest 2008: Comparing Education Statistics across the World. Montreal: UNESCO Institute for Statistics.

UNESCO. 2009. Global Education Digest 2009: Comparing Education Statistics across the World. Montreal: UNESCO Institute for Statistics.

Verbik, Line, and Cari Merkley. 2006. *The International Branch Campus: Models and Trends.* London: The Observatory on Borderless Higher Education.

Wadhwa, Vivek. 2009. Losing the World's Best and Brightest: America's New Immigrant Entrepreneurs, Part V. Kansas City, MO: The Ewing Marion Kauffman Foundation.

Wadhwa, Vivek, AnnaLee Saxenian, Ben Rissing, and Gary Gereffi. 2007. *America's New Immigrant Entrepreneurs, Part I.* Duke Science, Technology & Innovation Paper No. 23. Available online at: http://ssrn.com.

Wildavsky, Ben. 2010. The Great Brain Race: How Global Universities Are Reshaping the World. Princeton, NJ: Princeton University Press.

Chapter 2

Mobility Strategies and Trends: The Case of China

Yang Xinyu

Since the adoption of China's Open Door Policy 30 years ago, higher education mobility and educational exchange has grown tremendously from a few student participants to many forms of exchange, including student/faculty exchange, research collaboration, joint- and dual-degree programs, jointly operated schools and programs, and joint academic conferences. On December 26, 1978, the arrival of 52 Chinese visiting scholars at the John F. Kennedy International Airport in New York marked the first Chinese government-sponsored study abroad program since the Cultural Revolution. This was the first group of scholars supported by the Chinese government to study in the United States after 1941. Since then, more and more higher education institutions all around the world have opened their doors to Chinese students, and China now sends the largest number of students abroad for international education. In spite of the recent global economic slow down, in 2008, the number of Chinese students and scholars who went overseas to pursue study or conduct research was 179,800, a 20 percent increase over the previous year (Ministry of Education 2008). Among them, 18,200 were on government sponsorships or supported by their home institutions; the rest got scholarships from host universities/professors, were supported by their families, or received assistance from other sources. It is also reported that nearly 70,000 study fellows returned to China after completion of their study/research overseas in 2008. This is a 60 percent increase as compared with the number of returnees in 2007.

With the development of higher education in China and increasing recognition of the quality of Chinese higher education by the international community, China has also gradually become one of the most popular destination countries for international education. As a popular international education destination in the region, China attracted 223,499 international students from 189 countries and regions in 2008, a 14 percent increase over the previous year. These students attended 592 higher education institutions across 31 provinces in China. Korea, the United States, and Japan are the top three countries of origin of international students in China. During the same period, scholarships provided by the Chinese government to international students increased by 33 percent totaling 13,516.

Chinese Students Overseas: Study Abroad Trends

Ever since the late Deng Xiaoping initiated the government-sponsored study abroad program in 1978, over 100,000 fellows have studied overseas under Chinese government scholarship programs and approximately 1.3 million Chinese students sponsored by other resources have pursued study in over 100 countries and regions. Over the same period of time, 390,000 Chinese returnees brought back not only knowledge but also new ideas and innovation that have contributed significantly to China's rapid development.

Significant strides have been made in China's higher education system in the past 30 years. In 2008 the total student population in higher education institutions was 27 million, resulting in a 23 percent gross enrollment rate. However, the rapid growth of the student population in the past decade has also created challenges in the areas of quality control of programs, government investment, and hiring and retaining faculty members. Although there are more than 1,900 higher education institutions in China, the system as a whole is not able to meet the public's demand for high-quality higher education. Thus there will continue to be a high demand for overseas study opportunities: according to the information released by the Ministry of Education, in 2007/2008 alone there were 195,503 Chinese students studying overseas and this number is likely to increase in the future.

Chinese Government Policy in Support of Study Abroad

Study abroad activities in China are greatly supported by Chinese government policy. In the early eighties, only government-sponsored study fellows had the opportunity to study abroad. The focus at that time was to send as many highly qualified candidates abroad as possible because after the Cultural Revolution China desperately needed a large number of well-trained, talented graduates for its development. At that time no one without government sponsorship would have dreamed of pursuing overseas studies as an individual or for personal reasons. Only students who had close relatives living overseas to support them financially were allowed to study abroad independent of government sponsorship. The policy changed in 1986 to allow self-financed students and scholars to study abroad. This new policy encouraged them to return to China on completion of their study abroad. Chinese citizens could apply for approval to pursue self-financed study abroad from their home institution but had to pay back to the home institution an amount equivalent to the government expenditure per student. At this time, the cost of higher education in China was covered entirely by the government.

The establishment of China Scholarship Council (CSC) was a milestone in study abroad policy development. As a result of the rearrangement of central government departments, CSC was set up by the Ministry of Education and charged with administering government scholarship programs. The selection of scholarship recipients underwent a major change from assigned allocations to open competition.

The Chinese government also set up a number of favorable policies to encourage students to return to China after their studies. By the late 1980s, the government was facing public pressure because many government-sponsored study fellows, for various reasons, were not returning to China immediately after the completion of their studies. This was not an isolated issue. It was more complicated than the choice not to return; it was an issue of policy, environment, and living and working conditions. The situation became even worse after the June 4, 1989 Tiananmen Square event. Some countries extended special immigration policies to Chinese students, and some even provided them political protection. It was a difficult time for the Chinese government, and for Chinese institutions who worried about losing their staff and students.

It was Deng Xiaoping, once again, who offered comments on how to deal with this issue. When he traveled to Shenzhen, China's first special economic zone, he stated that the Chinese government should think about making special policies to encourage overseas study fellows to return. He suggested that the government and home institutions should provide good working and living conditions and necessary funds to help them settle down, regardless of their political attitudes. He then passed on the message to overseas Chinese students, telling them that it was better to return if they wished to contribute to the social and economic development of China.

Following these developments, the Chinese government issued a number of official documents clearly indicating preferential policies on salary, health care, welfare, working conditions, employment of spouses, and other areas. The Ministry of Education also set up projects especially for overseas Chinese study fellows, including the "Research Fund of Returned Study Fellows," the "Cheung Kong Scholars Project," and the "Chunhui Project." The Natural Science Foundation of China also set up special programs to attract overseas Chinese students, the most important of which is the "National Research Fund for Outstanding Young Scientists." Winners of this project can get funds sufficient to conduct research either in natural science or applied basic research. Another example is the "One Hundred Talents Project" of the Chinese Academy of Sciences, which aimed to attract back 100 talented overseas Chinese students annually to be leading scientists in their research institutes. Provincial and local governments also made efforts to welcome study fellows to start businesses or bring investments to their regions. Local governments have established over twenty Science Parks for Returned Study Fellows throughout China to serve as incubators for returnees to start businesses. It is estimated that these programs have funded over 40,000 returned study fellows and 12,000 overseas Chinese study fellows to temporarily work in Chinese higher education institutions.

In recent years, "The Mid to Long-Term Strategy of Scientific Research," a national strategy project for the development of science and technology, and the launch of Project 211 and Project 985 provided great opportunities to those who remained overseas to return and join in the exciting process of social and economic development.

In view of the growing tendency of talented researchers to compete on a global scale, the Chinese government, like many others, is making more efforts to attract top scientists from all around the world to be leaders of major national projects.

Chinese Government Scholarship Programs

China is among the few countries that provide large numbers of scholarships to support international education for its own citizens as well as international students. When the late Chinese leader Deng Xiaoping initiated support for young Chinese students to study abroad in 1978, the Chinese government set up a special budget to provide 3,000 scholarships each year for study abroad. The number of outgoing scholarships has expanded dramatically in recent years to 12,000 annually. The scholarships for international students to study in China have also increased, and currently the government provides over 10,000 scholarships each year. By 2010, the Chinese government will offer 20,000 scholarships to international students in China annually.

In the late 1970s and early 1980s, Chinese government scholarship holders for study abroad were mainly university faculty or researchers from the Chinese Academy of Sciences and Chinese Academy of Social Sciences. They were selected by their home institutions and approved by the Ministry of Education, which administered all government scholarship programs. The first ever group of scholars sent by the government after 1978 went to the United States under a verbal agreement between the two governments. After that, the governments of the United Kingdom, Germany, France, Japan, Canada, and Australia reached similar agreements with Chinese government on student exchange. Since there were very few contacts between Chinese universities and universities in other countries, governments had to work carefully to place Chinese students in foreign universities. There were no Test of English as a Foreign Language (TOEFL), Graduate Record Examination (GRE), or International English Language Test System (IELTS) examinations in China in those days. Foreign universities found that it was difficult to judge the quality of Chinese students who wished to pursue graduate study because they had no idea of Chinese students' academic background and language level. To solve this problem, the American-Chinese Nobel Laureate Dr. Tsung-Dao Lee initiated a program named "China-U.S. Physics Examination and Application" (CUSPEA), with the support of the Chinese government. For this program, a number of U.S. universities set up a special test in English at the same standard as they set to take international students. Chinese students who passed the test were accepted by U.S. universities for PhD study. From 1989 to 1999 over 900 Chinese students attended PhD programs in more than 50 U.S. universities under CUSPEA. As a result of the program U.S. universities came to recognize the quality of Chinese students.

Today, government scholarship holders make up only a very small proportion of all study abroad students, compared to the large number of students who are self-sponsored or sponsored by the host university. But because of the opportunities originally provided by government scholarships, a channel was established, and the fortunate scholars and students who studied abroad in the early 1980s brought back the message that study abroad was possible and that Chinese students had a good chance of being admitted to foreign universities.

After the CSC was established, many tailor-made scholarship programs were designed in line with the development of Chinese higher education institutions and China's social and economic growth. For example, the "University Young Faculty Training Program" was designed to support development of young faculty members at Chinese universities through study abroad. The "Special Professional Development Program for Western China" was designed to support the national goal of development in western China by funding study abroad fellows from universities and research institutes in that region.

On January 8, 2007, the Chinese government launched a new postgraduate study abroad scholarship program that provides 6,000 scholarships every year to university students for graduate study overseas. Another 6,000 scholarships are for postdoctoral research or academic visit for university faculty or people in a field of work different from their own discipline to gain some overseas study or research experience. The main objective of the program is to contribute to the development of Chinese universities and to support the national project of building world-class universities. A select number of Chinese universities are invited to participate in this program. The participating universities have the obligation to select the best students and send them to the best programs under the best possible supervision. Ideally, the program envisions that when students return on completion of their study overseas, they could become university faculty members. The ideal model is that through sending students abroad, the Chinese universities can strengthen academic links with their international partners, and cooperation between Chinese and foreign universities will thus be more efficient.

The postgraduate study abroad scholarship program sets clear priorities for certain fields of study that are seen as being critical to the nation's development strategy. These seven fields include: agriculture, information technology and telecommunication, life science and public health, material science, energy and environment, engineering, and the applied social sciences. Participating Chinese universities are encouraged to work closely with their partner institutions around the world in selecting candidates and to integrate students into existing and new research collaborations. With the help of CSC scholarships, Nankai University established a program in which each year the top 100 among students who finish their first degree are selected to pursue doctoral degrees in prestigious foreign universities and are appointed as faculty at Nankai University upon their return to China. Students are required to sign a letter of commitment that signals their intent to work at the sponsoring Chinese university upon their return. During their study overseas, Nankai University stays in close contact with these students, informing them of the progress and development of their home institution.

As yet another effort to encourage their faculty members to engage in international collaboration, many Chinese universities set overseas study or research experience as requirements for faculty promotion. The CSC works closely with Chinese universities to jointly fund postdoctoral research or academic visits overseas to support the development of young faculty. Eligible faculty are selected through an open competition and are typically those who have made some progress in their career and need some international research experience to enhance their knowledge.

As part of bilateral cultural or educational exchange agreements that the Chinese government has signed with other governments, scholarships are also provided for undergraduate students who major in foreign languages to visit countries where that language is spoken.

The Chinese government has also made efforts to assist students who self-finance their overseas study. China is the most significant place of origin for students seeking transnational education, and many self-sponsored Chinese students can be found in countries worldwide. To honor academic achievements, the Chinese government set up the "Award to Outstanding Self-financed Chinese Study Abroad Students" in 2003; 300 PhD students receive the award each year based on their study and research performance.

Impact of Study Abroad

The scholarship programs described above have been widely accepted by Chinese universities and institutions in other countries and have contributed significantly to the development of higher education in China. Even though great progress was made in China's higher education in the past decades, the need for talented manpower for rapid social and economic development has exposed Chinese universities to challenges they had never encountered before. Apart from inefficient financing, unbalanced development, increasing unemployment amongst school leavers, and a lack of quality control, the shortage of high-quality faculty members is the most crucial challenge. Statistics show that in 2007 among the 1.16 million faculty members in 1,908 Chinese higher education institutions, 42 percent held master's degrees and only 11.7 percent held doctoral degrees (China Education Yearbook 2008). Since most of the university faculty gained their graduate degrees from Chinese universities, the quality of China's graduate education affects directly the quality of university faculty.

China established its graduate education system only in 1978. Rapid development over a period of three decades has enabled Chinese universities and research institutes to train students at both the master's and doctoral levels in almost all fields. From 1998 to 2007 the number of graduate students in Chinese higher education institutions increased from

198,885 to approximately 1.2 million (Ministry of Education 1997, 2008). Although the total enrollment of graduate students is quite high, it still cannot meet the needs of a rapidly developing nation. The scale as well as the quality of graduate education, research projects, and supervisors are the main challenges of graduate education in China.

International cooperation is a key strategy for improving the overall quality of China's graduate education. The return of Chinese graduate students who have studied overseas has demonstrated valuable outcomes such as a broadened vision, improvement in the quality of research and dissertations, the establishment of research collaborations, and the ability of students to communicate and engage with the international community. Many of these Chinese study fellows are now serving in Chinese higher education institutions and are mentors to the next generation of Chinese graduate students. The academic links they built with their international partners are beneficial for their research and for training young students. As part of a project to analyze the results of government-sponsored study abroad programs (carried out by Peking University with support from the Chinese Ministry of Education), a 2002 survey conducted in 100 Chinese universities on the impact of study abroad programs showed that 58 percent of PhD supervisors were returned study fellows. In Peking University, 80 percent of the PhD supervisors and 79 percent of the fellows of Chinese Academy of Sciences and Chinese Academy of Engineering had overseas study experiences.

A question remains: with such a large number of self-sponsored Chinese students studying abroad every year, should the Chinese government not be setting policies to attract these students back to China rather than providing scholarships for graduate education overseas? The Chinese Service Center for Scholarly Exchange (CSCSE) is authorized by the Ministry of Education of China to accredit degrees acquired by self-sponsored Chinese students from universities outside China. Of the 48,541 foreign degrees accredited by CSCSE from 2002 to 2006, 8.13 percent were doctoral degrees, 70.5 percent master's degrees, and 18.31 percent bachelor's degree. This shows that only few of these returned self-financed students gained a PhD, which is the basic academic requirement for a university teacher. In terms of field of study, the discipline of agriculture was not so popular (0.47 percent) among these students, but it's one of the very important fields for China's future development.

Demand for High-Quality Higher Education

Although China has the largest higher education system in the world with 1,700 higher education institutions and 27 million students, there is still great demand for high-quality higher education. Among the 1,700 higher education institutions, only 770 award bachelor's degrees, and 697 and 347 award master's and doctoral degrees respectively. Increased recruitment by higher education institutions since 1999 has meant that more high school graduates have the opportunity to receive a higher education: between 1999 and 2007, the university student population expanded from 6.8 million to 25 million (a 73 percent increase). The implementation of the specially funded Projects 211 and 985, whose goal is to build 112 world-class universities, has enabled the fast development of a number of participating Chinese universities. But the quick expansion of higher education in a very short period of time has also caused a demand and supply problem when it comes to quality higher education. The main reason is that there are now more good students but only a limited number of high-quality higher education institutions that can serve their needs. As a result, many capable students are likely to continue seeking international education opportunities if they cannot gain admission to top universities in China.

Recent social and economic development has also had a positive impact on the demand for quality higher education in China. Over the past 30 years, the living standard of ordinary Chinese has improved dramatically. In addition, the one-child policy results in most families wanting the best—which includes a high-quality education—for their only child. Many families are willing to invest their life's savings to pay for their children's education. Because of all these factors, China has become one of the biggest countries of origin for international education. It is estimated that the total number of Chinese students overseas has reached 700,000. Even though study abroad is affordable to only a few Chinese families, because of its large population even a small proportion in China is equivalent to hundreds of thousands of students.

Most Chinese students who study abroad come from the more advanced and economically developed regions of Beijing, Shanghai, Shenzhen, Hangzhou, and Guangzhou. The relatively higher value of the Chinese currency makes international education affordable for an increasing number of Chinese families; the annual expense for study in the United Kingdom was likely 25 percent less in late 2008 than the previous year. This is one of the reasons that even with the global financial crisis, the number of Chinese students going to study abroad increased by 20 percent in 2008.

Contributions of Study Abroad Returnees

The return of Chinese students who studied abroad has contributed significantly to the country's development and progress. On December 24, 2008,

China's Ministry of Education held a conference: Achievements of Thirty Years' Study Abroad Programs. Returned study fellows from different fields were invited to express their views on the benefit they gained from study abroad experiences. Liu Baicheng, one of the 52 Chinese study fellows who studied in U.S. universities in 1978 under an informal agreement between Chinese and U.S. governments, spoke of his success and accomplishments upon returning to China after two years of study at the University of Wisconsin and the Massachusetts Institute of Technology. He was elected a fellow of the Chinese Academy of Sciences for his academic achievements.

In addition to adding to the realm of academics, returned study fellows also contribute to applied work and research in fields such as economics, finance, business, law, social work, and education and take up important positions in the government, research institutes, state-owned enterprises, national banks, joint venture companies, and research and development companies. According to data from the Ministry of Education (2008), 80 percent of the fellows of the Chinese Academy of Sciences and the Chinese Academy of Engineering, 78 percent of university presidents under the Ministry of Education jurisdiction, and 72 percent of directors of national key laboratories had studied abroad.

Attracted by the government's favorable policies, many returned study fellows have started their own companies. There are more than 100 science parks designed for returned study fellows; over 6,000 enterprises owned by returned study fellows have been incubated in these science parks. These returnees have had the opportunity to participate in international exchange and cooperation and to promote mutual understanding between China and other countries. Their successful stories have encouraged more young students to follow their footsteps.

To sum up, study abroad will continue to be a popular choice among Chinese students in the future. Even though only a small proportion of Chinese families can afford the cost of international education, there will still be quite a large number of Chinese students seeking study abroad opportunities every year. The government scholarship programs, on their part, will continue to target high-priority fields and candidates at advanced levels of education.

International Students in China: Trends in In-bound Mobility

Providing education opportunities to international students is one of the important elements of the opening up and internationalizing of the

Chinese higher education. In 1950, after the founding of the People's Republic of China in 1949, Chinese universities started receiving international students from Eastern European countries. The past 30 years have seen significant development in the number of international students coming to China. According to UNESCO, in the 2005–2006 academic year, China was ranked 13th in the world as a host destination for international degree students. China gradually became a major destination for international education, especially in Asia. With the continued development of its higher education subsector, China is in a position to attract more international students. The low cost of study in China and reasonable admission requirements are other factors that attract international students, especially those from less developed countries.

Although Chinese higher education continues to face challenges, the country's rapid growth has been recognized worldwide. The implementation of Project 211 from 1995 onward saw great achievements in Chinese higher education within a very short period of time. The project guaranteed funding from central and provincial governments for the development of a select number of universities. As a result, the quality of teaching and research as well as the facilities and the overall environment were greatly improved. All of these developments have made Chinese higher education more attractive to international students and scholars. A number of institutions are now recognized as world-class for certain disciplines such as material science at the Tsinghua University and chemistry at the Peking University. The importance of educational exchange between China and other countries is also evident in the fact that foreign alumni from Chinese universities are in key positions in politics and other fields in their own countries: over 20 foreign ambassadors to China, and more than 30 ministers in their governments all have experiences of studying in China.

The Growth of International Students in China

During 2002–2007 (China's Tenth Five-year Plan), the average annual increase of international students was 20 percent in China. The Severe Acute Respiratory Syndrome (SARS) epidemic in 2003 made some international students withdraw from Chinese universities, and the number of international students decreased that year. In 2007, the total enrollment of international students in China was 195,503, a 56 percent increase from the year 2002. Traditionally, international students travel to China just for language learning or for taking some non-degree courses. But in

2002–2007, the increase in the number of students in degree programs was higher than that of non-degree programs. Among all the degree students, more are enrolled in undergraduate programs (82.5 percent) than in postgraduate programs (15.9 percent).

International students in China come from 189 countries and regions, but most of them come from Asia and neighboring countries. The number of students from a certain country studying in China also reflects that country's geographic location and its relationship with China. In terms of key sending countries in 2008, South Korea was the top country of origin, followed by the United States and Japan. These three countries all have close economic relations with China and two are located in the Asia Pacific Region. The students from these top three countries of origin make up 46 percent of the international students in China, and the number of Korean students (66,806) accounts for 30 percent. According to *Open Doors*, China is now one of the most popular destination countries for U.S. students (Bhandari and Chow 2009). In terms of host institutions, the Beijing Language and Culture University receives the most international students, with 10,622 in 2008.

International students in China tend to cluster in more developed regions such as Beijing, Shanghai, and the coastal cities in east and southeast China. The living standards, working conditions, and environment in these cities are likely to be attractive to international students. There are also job opportunities in these cities for international students when they graduate from Chinese universities. Most of the China branch offices of major international companies are located in these cities and the companies are likely to benefit greatly if their potential employees are from the company's home country, are familiar with Chinese culture, and speak the Chinese language.

Government's Efforts to Attract International Students to China

As part of its open-door policy, the Chinese government encourages Chinese universities to attract more international students to study on their campuses. In recent years, the Ministry of Education has signed 34 agreements with foreign governments on mutual recognition of academic degrees. These countries include the United Kingdom, Germany, France, Australia, New Zealand, and Spain, among others. The signing of these agreements demonstrates the confidence of the international community in the quality of higher education in China. The good performance of Chinese postgraduate students in foreign universities has also added to the credibility of Chinese higher education.

Chinese government scholarships for international students provide opportunities to students all around the world to study in Chinese institutions. In 2008, 13,516 scholarships were provided to international students from 171 countries, a 25 percent increase over the previous year. These scholarships increased to 20,000 in 2010. In an effort to assist students in developing countries, President Hu Jintao announced at the China-Africa Summit in November 2006 that scholarships to students from African countries would be doubled from 2,000 to 4,000 per year.

International students receiving government scholarships are placed at 134 Chinese higher education institutions and are typically enrolled in a full range of subject areas. The most popular subjects in 2008 were: Chinese languages (25 percent of all international students), engineering (20 percent), economics (9 percent), medical science (9 percent), and management (8 percent).

There are also Chinese government scholarships that target strategic interests. These scholarship programs include the following: China/ UNESCO-The Great Wall Fellowship; Study In Asia Scholarship; China/Association of Southeast Asian Nations (ASEAN) University Network (AUN) Scholarship; Chinese Government Scholarship Program (European Union Window); China/Shanghai Cooperation Organization (SCO) Scholarship Scheme; China/Pacific Island Forum Scholarship Scheme; Chinese Government Scholarship—University Postgraduate Study Program; and the Chinese Culture Research Fellowship.

Other scholarships for international students in China are provided by the local government (for example, in Beijing, Shanghai, and Yunnan), and by private sector companies such as Huawei Technologies Co. Ltd., the China Development Bank, and the China National Petroleum Corporation.

Some foreign governments have also set up scholarship programs for their students to study in China. For instance, the governments of Pakistan, Thailand, Tanzania, Saudi Arabia, and Vietnam all provide scholarships to their students/scholars to study in China.

Institution-Level Efforts to Attract International Students

Almost all universities in China place a high priority on attracting international students and have taken specific steps in this direction. Because China has not traditionally been considered a top destination for international education, the promotion of Chinese higher education is essential to make Chinese universities and their programs known to international students. To this end, Chinese institutions participate in China Education Fairs in many countries and showcase what they can offer to international students. The first such fair organized by the China Scholarship Council in Australia in 2003 attracted a large audience that was surprised to learn about China's active participation in international education.

Great efforts have also been made at the institutional level to improve the quality of teaching and research facilities, and accommodations and services for international students. Since students in Chinese universities are required to live on campus, most universities have accommodations specially prepared for international students. English-taught programs are provided to attract international students at the master's and doctoral levels who may be not be comfortable using Chinese as a medium of instruction. Chinese language programs are also provided throughout the academic year to meet the needs of international students.

Student exchange programs between universities in China and in other countries are also very important to promote Chinese higher education. For instance, the Tsinghua University-Aachen University of Technology student exchange program in engineering sends 30 master's students every year to the other campus after the first year of study at their home university. After study in the host university in the second year, successful students are awarded a master's degree from each of the two universities. In the first year of the program, 30 students from Tsinghua University participated, but only six German students took up the opportunity to study in Tsinghua University. The number of German students coming to Tsinghua has slowly increased. In 2009, 190 applications were received. The positive experience of the German students who participated in the program has made the program very popular among students at the Aachen University of Technology.

Challenges in Recruiting International Students

Although the number of international students in China has grown rapidly in the past few years, Chinese universities are facing their fair share of challenges in their drive toward internationalization, especially as a result of the global economic crisis.

Even though there were 223,500 international students in China in 2008, these students account for less than 1 percent of the total enrollment in Chinese universities. If one takes this as an indicator of world-class universities, the number of international students enrolled in Chinese universities is far less than in prestigious universities in more developed countries. Thus, Chinese universities have a long way to go to become internationally recognized.

The immediate impact of the global economic crisis on international students in China is that due to the depreciation of certain currencies, some students could no longer afford the study cost in China. Some students withdrew, while others asked for an extension of their admission. Some foreign governments suspended their Study in China programs because of the financial situation they were facing in their own countries. At the same time, some overseas universities lowered their cost of study in their countries to attract international students. As a result, the competition in the international education market is even keener.

Conclusion

The internationalization of higher education benefits greatly from the global mobility of students and scholars. The future social and economic development of a country requires that graduates from higher education institutions have the capability to play and compete on a global stage. International education experiences are also beneficial to an individual's career and personal development.

As a country with a large student population and rapid economic development, China will continue to be one of the most important countries for student mobility. A 2009 survey conducted by the Education International Cooperation Group (EIC), an international education service provider, forecasts the following trends for Chinese student mobility, especially with the global economic crisis placing great pressure on the job market worldwide, including the Chinese job market. Many Chinese students will choose to study abroad to avoid facing this pressure. The increased value of the Chinese currency has made international education more affordable for more Chinese families. At the same time, key destination countries such as the United States, Canada, the United Kingdom, and Australia have introduced more favorable policies on immigration, employment, and financial assistance to attract more international students. While the choice of destination country/region for Chinese students will vary, it is likely that the United States will continue to be their first choice, but Europe, Asia, Russia, Australia, and New Zealand may also feature in their list of preferences. The subjects Chinese students choose to study abroad will be more job-oriented and will meet their professional and personal development needs.

On the other side of the equation, despite China being a comparatively new destination country for international education with a very short history, Chinese institutions are striving to attract more international students by providing high-quality programs and services. The recent success of the 2008 Olympic Games, the Shanghai Expo in 2010, the rich culture, lucrative job opportunities, a safe environment, the hospitality of Chinese people, improved living standards, and a booming economy are all factors that are attracting young students from other countries to explore China.

BIBLIOGRAPHY

Chen, Xuefei. 2003. Wo guo gai ge kai fang yi lai gong pai liu xue xiao yi yan jiu [Costs and Returns: A Study on the Efficiency of Government-Sponsored Overseas Education Since 1978]. Beijing: Education Science Press.

Fang, Maotian, 2007, Beijing: Remarks on the Conference of Post-graduate Study Abroad Programs.

International Cooperation Department. 2009. *The Statistics and Analyses of International Students in China in 2007.* Beijing: International Cooperation Department, Development Research Center of the State Council (DRC).

Liu, Yandong. 2008. Welcoming Remarks at the Annual Meeting of State Degree Committee, December 27, 2008.

Ministry of Education. 1998. "Number of Regular School Entrants by Level and Type." Beijing: Ministry of Education. Available online at: http://www.moe.edu.cn.

Ministry of Education. 2007. Beijing: Ministry of Education. Available online at: http://www.moe.edu.cn.

National Research Group on Education Reform and Development Over 30 Years. 2008. *The Rising of a Country Through Education:1978–2008.* Beijing: Educational Science Publishing House.

Pan, Chenguang. 2008. "Opportunities and Challenges of Talents Cultivation in China in an Environment of Globalization." *Research on Study Abroad* 60 (4): 47–54.

Wang, Zhengfu. 2009. "Promote Sustainable Development of International Education in China Facing Global Economic Crisis." *Study on International Education in China* 1: 11–14.

Yang, Xinyu. 2008. "National Policy Goals: PRC Government Activities Supporting U.S.-China Exchange." In *U.S.-China Educational Exchange: Perspectives on a Growing Partnership, The Series of Global Education Research Reports.* New York: Institute of International Education and AIFS Foundation.

Yuan, Wei. 2009. "Study Abroad Programs Upgrade the Quality of Talents Cultivation." *World Education Information* 260 (4): 34–36.

Zhan, Tao. 2005. *Global SDU 2010*. Shandong: Shandong University. Available online at: http://youthtw.wh.sdu.edu.cn.

Western Returned Scholars Association. 2009. *Study Abroad and the Impact on China's Social Development*. Zhuhai: Zhuhai Press.

Chapter 3

India's Growing Influence in International Student Mobility

Pawan Agarwal

India is a key player in international student mobility, in particular as a source country. The country's large and growing number of young people, rapidly growing economy, and middle class boom make it a favorite source country amongst the nations eying to recruit internationally mobile students. Currently, India contributes about 7.5 percent of this pool, second only to China, the leading source country. Apart from this, India also hosts a growing number of international students. Currently this number is noticeably small, but the country has potential and aspiration to host much larger numbers. Thus, India's importance in international student mobility is destined to grow.

This chapter maps the patterns and trends of student mobility in respect to India. The chapter begins with an overview of the Indian higher education system and its key trends. This is followed by an examination of outward and inward mobility looking at the future trends in the context of growing complexity of student flows in a highly interconnected world.

Overview of Indian Higher Education and Trends

Indian higher education is complex, extremely fragmented, and riddled with many contradictions. It is both large and small. In terms of absolute enrollment (around 12.8 million students), it is the third largest system of higher education in the world (next to China and the United States), but in terms of gross enrollment ratio, it is small—just around 11 percent. Female participation rates are even lower. The bulk of this enrollment is in affiliated colleges that have uniform and often outdated curriculum. These colleges are affiliated to the universities that award degrees. The number of universities and colleges together is more than 20,000, and yet the number of institutions that are eligible to grant degrees is merely 400 (Agarwal 2009). Because the number of institutions is large, the average enrollment in each institution is small, just about 600. This makes many institutions nonviable. Most of the country's students (88.9 percent) are pursuing undergraduate study, with merely 9.4 percent enrolled in postgraduate studies and just 0.7 percent in doctoral programs. Enrollment is skewed in favor of arts and humanities (45 percent), followed by science (20.5 percent), commerce (18 percent); only 17 percent students pursue professional studies dominated by engineering and medicine. Thus, a large part of higher education lacks vocational focus and churns out unemployable graduates (Agarwal, 2009).

The vocational education and training (VET) subsector catering to lower-level skills is small and separated from higher education. Lack of pathways between the two creates a situation where vocational education is regarded as a noncompetitive option with little possibility for upward mobility. With low prestige and low quality, it suffers from poor demand. Demand for high-end vocational skills, broadly termed as professional education, is met by the burgeoning private sector. In certain streams such as engineering, medicine, management, nursing, and teacher education, more than four-fifth enrollment is in private institutions. Accreditation is not effective and regulatory oversight is burdensome. As a result, quality institutions are few.

In recent years, the government has been funding higher education more liberally, yet public funds continue to be scarce and spread unevenly. This results in a majority of institutions facing financial hardships, forcing them to raise tuition fees and start self-financing programs to substitute or supplement public funds. As a consequence, higher education has become expensive. With only a small fraction of students eligible for education loans, access has turned out to be more difficult.

With a growing college-age population of young people, better school education, and rising prosperity, demand for higher education is destined to grow over the next decades. India is forecast to be the most populous country by 2030 and the population of its young people is likely to grow even faster. Despite the global slowdown, India has one of the fastest growing economies in the world resulting in a middle class boom in the country.

Consequently, there is both an increasing demand and a growing capacity to pay for higher education. This demand driven by rising aspirations is "income elastic," hence growth in demand outstrips the growth in income.

With higher education receiving high priority in government spending, public higher education has expanded. At the same time, the private sector has also grown considerably. The growth in domestic capacity is, however, unable to meet rapidly rising demand. Thus, a large and growing number of students go abroad for studies.

Outward Mobility

Prior to India's independence from British rule in 1947, only a small group of the country's elite went abroad for studies. Many Indians who led the struggle for the country's independence studied abroad, in particular in the United Kingdom. This trend continues to date. The national government formed in May 2009 has at least 14 ministers who graduated from Ivy League universities and Oxbridge (*The Economic Times* 2009). Post independence, many graduates from premier institutions such as the Indian Institutes of Technology went abroad for postgraduate studies and research and stayed. Several of them went into entrepreneurship and were financially successful, serving as leaders in the Indian diaspora and as role models who inspired a whole generation of Indians to study abroad.

Thus, not surprisingly, the number of Indians who study abroad has been increasing over the years. However, now this is no more confined to the rich or intellectual elite: studying abroad is now a possibility even for ordinary students from middle-income families. There has been a twenty-four-fold increase in the number of Indian students abroad from 11,192 in 1965 to 268,000 in 2008. Though these are less than the corresponding figures for China, where the numbers sharply grew from about a few thousands in the 1960s to 417,350 in 2008, it is more than twice the global tenfold growth from 290,000 in 1963 to 2.9 million. Currently, Indians constitute about 7.5 percent of the world's globally mobile students, representing the second largest share (after Chinese students).

About a decade ago, the main destination for Indians seeking foreign degrees was the United States, with some going to the United Kingdom. Though the United States continues to lead as the most favored destination, it is less predominant now. In 2000, three-fourths of Indian students studying abroad went to the United States; this reduced to about half in 2008. Now Indians study in a more diverse set of countries, with countries such as Australia and the United States serving as important

Table 3.1 Size of Indian Diaspora and Trends in Indian Students' Outward Mobility to Key Destinations, 2000 and 2008

Country	Indian Diaspora	Number of Indian Students in the Host Country		Increase (%)
		2000	2008	
The United States	2,662,112	47,411	94,563	200
Australia	235,000	6,195	96,555	1,558
The United Kingdom	1,600,000	4,649	35,245	758
China	Negligible	...	7,234	Very large
Canada	960,000	1,431	7,200	503
Singapore	320,000	...	6,700	Very large
Germany	35,000	1,412	5,200	378
Malaysia	2,400,000	714	2,600	364
New Zealand	105,000	355	2,500	704
Sweden	11,000	92	1,500	1,630
France	75,000	239	640	268
Japan	20,589	...	544	Large
Switzerland	13500	84	400	476
Other countries	...	1,000	5,000	...
Total	23,000,000	63,000	267,889	425

Sources: OECD Database, UNESCO Institute of Statistics Database, EUROSTAT Database, country-based sources: The United States (IIE 2008); Australia (AEI); *Atlas of International Student Mobility*; Indian Diaspora data from Ministry of Overseas Indian Affairs (updated where updated data from source country available).

destinations because of their large Indian diaspora that tends to attract a large number of Indian students. Table 3.1 gives countrywide trends in outward mobility growth and the current stock of Indian diaspora in destination countries. There appears to be a positive correlation between the number of Indian students and size of Indian diaspora in host countries. The subsequent section of the chapter maps country-wise pattern and trends.

Country-Wise Analysis

The United States

There is a long history of Indians going to the United States for higher studies. In 1923–1924, there were 231 Indian students in the United States, this number increased to 1,006 by 1947 at the time of India's independence and comprised the third largest group after Canadian and Chinese students. The numbers kept growing and reached a peak of 11,327 in 1969/1970. During these years, India was amongst the top three countries of origin of international students in the United States and eventually topped the list in 1972/1973. This predominance was, however, lost thereafter. The number dropped to 8,760 in 1979/1980, when India slipped to number-nine position. From 1980/1981 onward, there was a revival and India came in at fourth place (after China, Japan, and Taiwan) in 1988/1989. Beginning in 1997/1998, the number of Indian students studying in the United States has increased dramatically; in 2000/2001, this grew by 30 percent, followed by two years of double-digit growth (22 percent and 12 percent). India took the leading place once again in 2001/2002, when it surpassed China and has since held the position. Figure 3.1 below shows long-term trends in the growth of Indian students in the United States and its comparison with other major sending countries (IIE 2005).

Following a period of sustained growth, total international student enrollment in the United States declined in 2002/2003 due to tightened security procedures in the wake of September 11. Notwithstanding a fall in overall numbers, India maintained its leading position and saw continued growth except for a marginal drop in 2005/2006. This was followed by a 9.6 percent increase in 2006/2007 and a 12.8 percent increase in 2007/2008, when there were 94,563 Indian students (15.2 percent of the total) in the United States (IIE 2008).

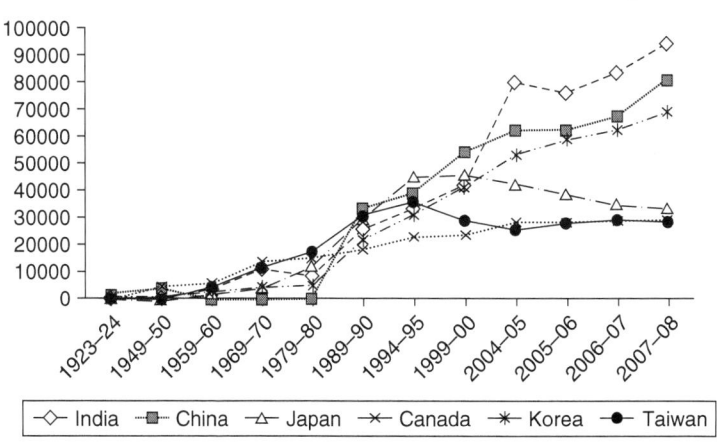

Figure 3.1   International Students in the United States: Trends 1923–2008.

The majority of Indian students are at the graduate level. In 2007/2008, 72 percent were graduate students, while only 14.4 percent were undergraduate students, with the remaining 13.6 percent enrolled in non-degree programs. Almost one quarter of all international graduate students in the United States come from India. The number at 68,069 is significantly higher than that for China (53,047). For degree programs, Indian students are enrolled mainly in science, technology, engineering, and mathematics (STEM), business and management, public health, and health administration. The number of Indian students enrolled in optional practical training has also increased in recent years (IIE 2008).

The majority of international students finance their U.S. studies through personal and family funds. This is true for applicants of all academic levels except graduate students who rely on U.S. university funds and personal and family funds in equal measure. According to calculations based on estimates from an *Open Doors* report, overall about one half of Indian students use personal and family funds for their U.S. study. Indian students contribute over US$1.2 billion (out of a total of US$15.5 billion) to the U.S. economy through living expenses for themselves and accompanying dependents, as well as through expenditures on tuition, books, fees, and other education-related expenses.

In addition to Indian students, Indian scholars also have a strong presence on U.S. campuses: 9,959 Indian scholars were teaching or doing research in the U.S. in 2007/2008. India surpassed South Korea as the second most popular place of origin for scholars, with 9 percent increase over the previous year. With a majority of the research scholars in STEM fields, biological and biomedical sciences, and health sciences, Indian scholars make a significant contribution to research and innovation in the United States. The large and growing population of Indian students and scholars in the United States provides financial resources and innovative capacity for U.S. higher education.

Recent developments, however, suggest that the current growth momentum would be difficult to sustain. The weakening of the Indian rupee has made U.S. education unaffordable. Hiring restrictions in the United States and clamping down on H1-B job visas for international students would make studying in the United States less attractive. A recent study by the University of California, Berkeley, shows that almost 84 percent Indian students think that it will be difficult for them to find a job in their field in the United States (Brown and Linden 2008). The students covered by the study also felt that their home country will grow faster in future and that, as a result, they plan to return to India after their studies. These findings are supported by reports of Indian students turning down admission offers in U.S. universities.

Australia

There has been rapid, recent growth in the number of international students in Australia. Immigrants were not welcome until 1973 and it was much later that Australia began to host international students. Thus, Australia's experience as a host country is relatively new. There were less than 30,000 international students in 1985; since then, this number has increased over ten times. Student admissions in Australia take place three times during the year: February, July, and November. Australian Education International (AEI) maintains countrywide data on monthly stock and arrivals for the four education subsectors: higher education, Vocational Education Training (VET), English Language Intensive Courses for Overseas Students (ELICOS), and school education (SE). There is significant enrollment in short-duration VET and ELICOS programs, thus monthly enrollment numbers vary widely. Total international student enrollment (across all levels of education) fell from a peak of 541,714 in December 2008 to 289,609 students in January 2009. Many students study in multiple subsectors. For instance, they first enroll in the ELICOS subsector and then transfer to VET or higher education subsectors, or they come for vocational studies (VET subsector) and then transfer to the higher education subsector. This mobility across education subsectors needs to be kept in mind while discussing Indian students in Australia.

Indians started going to Australia for study in the early 1990s. The number increased from 488 in 1993 to 2,400 in 1997; by 2002, there were 11,312 Indian students studying at all levels in Australia. The most dramatic growth has been from 2002 onward, when this number reached 38,662 in 2006, before growing by two-and-a-half times to 96,555 in December 2008. Australia surpassed the United Kingdom in 2005 and had more Indian students than even the United States in December 2008. From the eighth position in 2002 (4.5 percent share), the number of Indian students has now grown to second position (18.4 percent) (AEI 2009).

For Indian students, VET has been the fastest growing subsector: from 2,223 students in 2002, the number rose sharply to about 52,000 in 2008. Currently, India leads with the number of students enrolled at 51,990, which is almost double that from China. There are large enrollments in management and commerce; food, hospitality, and personal services; and society and culture courses. There has been a very rapid growth in ELICOS subsector as well, from a mere 80 in 2002 to over 16,000 in 2008. In April 2009, this number stood at 6,782, since many students shifted to higher education and VET subsectors. Growth of enrollment in the higher education subsector has also been significant, from 8,834 in

2002 to 27,455 in December 2008. This number dropped marginally to 22,033 in April 2009.

There are several factors responsible for the dramatic growth in the number of international students in Australia. A few years ago, Australia launched a AUS$3.5 million advertising campaign to attract students from emerging economies such as India. In addition, the Australian government established a AUS$20 million Australia-India Strategic Research Fund to promote collaboration in science and technology, with the government of India committing to match this fund. This represents the largest bilateral collaborative fund that the Australian government has established with any country in the world. Further, Australia launched a AUS$5 million endeavor scholarship program to facilitate inbound mobility.

For several years now, student recruitment for Australian institutions has been carried out through education agents that adopt aggressive practices. Though the Association of Australian Education Representatives, with 143 members located in over 400 offices across India, has a code of ethical practice that includes a schedule of maximum fees that can be charged to students, there have been complaints about agents adopting unfair practices and charging hefty fees. Education is Australia's third largest export industry (after coal and iron ore), with Indian students contributing about US$1.6 billion (out of US$11.8 billion) to the Australian economy. Some universities now generate a quarter to almost a half of their income from foreign student fees.

Although the number of Indian students in Australia has increased sharply over the past six years—a compounded annual growth rate of over 40 percent—recent developments might slow the growth. There have been physical assaults on Indian students in recent times, leading to the concern that Australia may no longer be as appealing to Indian students as before. While some view the assaults as the latest wave of resistance to immigration in a country that has a mere 35-year-old history of being a multiracial society, others view these attacks as a manifestation of the frustration of disaffected youth that have few prospects for work or education during the economic slowdown. Whatever be the reason, Indian student flows to Australia might not grow as rapidly in the coming years.

The United Kingdom

The United Kingdom has embarked upon a comprehensive strategy for international education. Under the 2006 prime minister's initiative, institutions are encouraged to internationalize in a broader sense, while still focused on generating additional revenue via inbound student mobility. This involves solidifying the long-term reputation and standing of U.K. higher education both at home and overseas through international partnerships. India is a key nation under this strategy. U.K.-India Education and Research Initiative (UKIERI), a £23-million initiative aimed at improving educational and research links with India, was launched in April 2006.

The United Kingdom has a long history of hosting international students both from within Europe and outside. Links established during India's days as a British colony and a large Indian diaspora (1.6 million) have helped the United Kingdom attract Indian students. To begin with, however, this number was small. In 1993, there were 1,388 Indian students in the United Kingdom, a number that increased to 2,131 in 1995 and 4,649 in 2000. However, when faced with financial constraints, U.K. universities began to recruit full-fee-paying international students. Thus after 2008, the number of Indian students increased rapidly and there has been more than a sixfold increase over the past five years. From its position as the seventh largest host country for Indian students in 2003 (4 percent share), the United Kingdom rose to the second position in 2008 (7.2 percent share).

In 2007/2008, there were 28,318 Indian students at U.K. universities, an increase of nearly 17.6 percent over the previous year. A recent study by the British Council that counted students by their nationality revised this number to 35,245 (British Council 2009). This revised approach indicates that the United Kingdom hosts 513,570 international students rather than the 389,330 previously thought (Lightfoot 2009). India (amongst the non-EU countries) sends the second highest number of students (after China).

The United Kingdom has courses of shorter duration: an undergraduate degree is of three-year duration, while a master's degree takes a year. Hence, study in the United Kingdom works out to be less expensive, giving it an advantage over other nations in attracting international students. The most popular subjects for study are management and business studies, engineering (led by electronic and electrical engineering), IT and multimedia studies, law, medicine, and science (led by the biosciences). Two-thirds of Indian students study one of the top three subjects, one-third study business and administration studies, a further fifth engineering and technology, and 14 percent computer science.

Since the recent assaults on Indians in Australia, many Indian students are now opting to study in the United Kingdom. With proactive governmental and institutional efforts, the number of Indian students in the United Kingdom, which is merely one-third of that in the United States and Australia, is bound to increase in the coming years. However, in the wake of reported misuse of student visas, the United Kingdom has recently tightened its student visa regime; this could prove to be a dampener.

Emerging Asian and Middle Eastern Destinations

In recent years, many developing countries have worked toward increasing the capacity of their higher education systems to accommodate more of their own students (who might otherwise have gone overseas), as well as opening their doors to a larger number of international students. Thus, they have made a transition to being an "emerging destination." Amongst the Asian nations that are emerging as important host nations are India's neighbors China, Singapore, and Malaysia. In 2005, these three countries had a combined share of approximately 12 percent of the global student market (about 250,000). In addition, the Middle East is home to two emerging educational hubs—Knowledge Village in Dubai (the United Arab Emirates) and Education City in Doha (Qatar)—both of which are establishing themselves as hosts for several foreign providers. These destinations are quite popular amongst Indian students now. Several Indian institutions, from the private sector in particular, have set up their campuses in these nations and target Indian students, including overseas Indians.

China, a traditional source nation, has now emerged as an important host nation with 7 percent share of the global student market. It hosted 195,503 international students in 2007/2008, with international enrollments having increased more than twofold since 2001. In order to promote itself as a key destination, China is offering liberal scholarships to international students. The number of scholarships increased from 4,400 in 1997 to more than 10,000 in 2010. A majority of students in China are from South Korea (25 percent) and Japan (20 percent); India currently has a very small share (3.7 percent), but this is growing fast. The main attraction for Indian students in China is the cost. Typically, a course in China costs about half that of a similar course at an Indian private institution. Indian students are also mainly enrolled in programs in medicine that have limited capacity at home. Therefore, it is not surprising that from just a few hundred students in 2000, China now hosts 7,234 Indian students, making it the fourth most important destination country for Indian students. Chinese education delegations regularly visit India now. Although language of instruction and recognition of qualifications are continuing challenges, several Chinese institutions now offer programs in English, and Chinese authorities' efforts to get recognition for their qualifications in India has resulted in a recent agreement between the two countries to recognize each other's qualifications for a period of five years.

In 1999, Singapore announced that it would attract "world-class" academic institutions to become the regional destination of choice for students, researchers, and industry. Over the past ten years, more than 16 leading foreign universities have set up their facilities in Singapore.

Currently, Singapore hosts more than 86,000 students from over 120 nationalities and aims to attract 150,000 by 2015. From less than a hundred students in 2000, the number of Indian students has now increased to over 6,700, with the majority of these students pursuing management, engineering, and science programs. The fees for foreign students are higher than those for local students, 1.5 times more in 2008. A large number of students receive government subsidies to cover their tuition fees and in return are bound by an obligation that requires them to work for Singapore-based companies for three years upon graduation. Those who are unable to meet this obligation pay full fees with no public subsidy. However, with increasing prosperity and tight and very competitive labor market at home, this requirement is not a serious deterrent for prospective students from India.

In addition to Singapore, neighboring Malaysia is emerging as a key host nation providing high-quality and affordable higher education opportunities. In 2009, Malaysia enrolled about 75,000 international students from over 110 countries and appears to be well on its way to meeting its target of enrolling 100,000 international students. A growing number of Indians now go to Malaysia for study, a fourfold increase from 714 students in 2000 to 2,600 in 2008. Manipal University, one of the biggest private institutions in India, attracts several hundred Indian students to its campus in Malaysia.

Other English and Non-English Speaking Destinations

Other popular English-speaking destinations for Indian students are Canada and New Zealand. Canada has 5 percent of the international student market (about 145,000). Although Chinese students in Canada far outnumber those from India, the number of Indian students increased significantly from 1,431 in 2000 to over 7,200 in 2008. Considering that students can stay on even after undergraduate studies, work for up to three years, and even apply for permanent residency if they wish to stay on, it is understandable why undergraduate studies in Canada is a popular option for international students. Thus, compared to the United States, Canada attracts a larger share of Indian students for undergraduate studies (35 percent compared to 17 percent in the United States). Canada has the third largest Indian diaspora (close to 1 million, second only to the United States and United Kingdom) and this is mainly from the northern Indian states of Punjab and Haryana. With family ties playing an important role, it not surprising that the majority of Indian students in Canada are from this region of India.

New Zealand is another important destination country, though it started attracting international students rather late. The numbers increased from

9,200 in 1998 to 92,000 in 2006 despite a drop in 2004. International students contribute about US$ 1.4 billion annually to the New Zealand economy. Over the years, New Zealand has emerged as a popular destination for Indian students: there has been a sevenfold increase from 355 in 2000 to about 2,500 in 2008. The fact that one out of four Indian students in New Zealand is able to get permanent residency makes New Zealand a popular choice amongst them. Between July 1997 and June 2005, out of 5,761 first-time Indian students, 1,515 (26.5 percent) had obtained permanent residency.

Other countries such as Sweden, Ireland, Cyprus, and Switzerland are now actively pursuing Indian students with Sweden, in particular, emerging as an important destination. From just 26 students in 2000, the number jumped to 892 in 2004. Now, about 1,500 Indian students study in Sweden, constituting the second largest group of students from outside the EU (the largest being from the United States) in Sweden. In 2008, about 900 Indian students were studying in Irish institutes. Cyprus, located in the eastern Mediterranean region, attracted 729 Indian students in 2007. Most of these students were in private institutions pursuing undergraduate degrees. Switzerland hosted 84 Indian students in 2000; this increased to 226 in 2003 and to about 400 in 2008. Other countries such as Austria, Norway, Finland, and South Africa also view India as an important source country and have begun to recruit Indian students in growing numbers.

Amongst other non-English speaking destinations, Germany, France, Japan, Russia, and the Netherlands are most prominent. In these countries, the largest numbers of students come from countries where the same language is spoken or from China. In order to access a larger pool of students, most of these countries have started offering programs in English. For example, France started attracting Indian students in 1998 by publicizing its English language courses. Within this group of countries, Germany has attracted the largest number of Indian students. Since 1997, the number of foreign students who come to Germany to study has increased steadily—from 100,033 to the 189,450 in 2008. This places Germany among the leading academic destinations in the world. Indian students in Germany increased from 800 in 1996/1997 to 1,412 in 2000 and tripled by 2005 to 4,339; in 2008 the share of Indian students in Germany was 3.1 percent of all international students in the country (BMBF 2008).

Germany has a policy to attract postgraduate and doctoral students in science and technology. Thus, a large number of Indian students pursue postgraduate and doctoral studies in Germany. In 2004/2005, one-third of Indian students in Germany came for undergraduate studies, another one-third for postgraduate studies, and one-fifth for doctoral studies. Indian students are mostly enrolled in programs in engineering, mathematics, and natural sciences. In 1997, Germany signed an agreement with the Indian Institutes of Technology to foster student mobility at the master's level. Over 700 Indian students have been to Germany under the program. The number of research scholars has also increased from 554 in 1999 to over a 1,000 in 2008. Thus, Germany has been successful in increasing the number of Indian postgraduate students and research scholars over the years and has provided liberal financial support to foster mobility at this level (Hahn and Schelewsky 2006).

Due to an aging population, higher education in Japan is contracting. Thus, Japan needs international students to keep universities open. They also seek young bright people to join their future workforce. As a result, the number of overseas students in Japan increased by more than 230 percent, from 51,000 to about 118,000 students, between 1998 and 2008. Earlier, international students in Japan were mostly from China. Now, Japan is attracting students from other countries including India. Currently the number of students from India is small. But this is likely to change with the offer of liberal scholarships and a massive drive to recruit bright Indian students with the Japanese government offering full scholarship for undergraduate studies (Chakraborty 2009).

Future Trends for India as a Sending Country

Although China continues to send the largest number of students abroad, more than twice that from India, recent trends suggest that the gap between China and India is closing. With a declining youth population and a dramatic increase in domestic higher education provision (a 2.5 million increase, which amounts to adding one new U.K. higher education system every year), the number of Chinese students accessing an overseas education is likely to decline over time. In comparison, outward mobility for India may not increase as rapidly as now, but due to the rising youth population and limited growth in domestic capacity, there would continue to be a large number of Indian students opting to study abroad for at least the next two decades. With an estimated 1.5 percent growth rate in outbound mobility for China and 6 percent for India, India would surpass China as the main source country of international students by 2025.

Demography, rising prosperity, and a large and growing diaspora will likely make India the leading source country of international students. Over the next 25 years, India's population is slated to rise by almost 350 million, twice as fast as that of the United States, Western Europe, and China combined. It would surpass that of China by 2028, peaking at about

1.46 billion. India's young population (15–24 years) will rise even faster. By 2025, while China's young population is projected to plummet to 172 million, India's young are likely to soar to 245 million. By 2025, India's young population would be about five times that of North America, over three times that of Europe, and 1.7 times that of the entire developed world (United Nations 2008).

India is currently witnessing a middle-class boom. According to the Delhi-based National Council for Applied Economic Research, the middle-class share that was merely 5 percent in 2005 would rise to 20 percent by 2015 and will be over 40 percent by 2025. This would mean that a 100 million young people would belong to middle-income households. Middle class is not merely an income category but reflects a set of attitudes. Drawing upon empirical and anecdotal evidence, Safran, Sahoo, and Lal (2009) argue that Indian middle classes have the advantages of skill, mobility, cultural rootedness, and the ethic of hard work. With a reasonably sizable share of their income left for discretionary spending, and with a global outlook and high aspirations, the Indian middle class is most likely to scout globally for the best higher education options.

Finally, India has the third largest diaspora in the world (after the British and the Chinese). Recent estimates suggest that there are 23 million overseas Indians in more than 70 countries, including the United States (2.66 million), Canada (0.96 million), the United Kingdom (1.6 million), European countries, Australia, Middle East, and Asian countries. Cultural affinity and family linkages help facilitate student mobility in both directions. Huang and Khanna (2003) note that while the Indian diaspora may not be able to match the Chinese diaspora as far as "hard" capital goes, Indians abroad have substantially more intellectual capital to contribute, an advantage that could prove even more valuable. The large and growing Indian diaspora would thus be critical to maintaining the momentum of student flows in the years to come.

Several developments in the key destination countries would impact student flows in both positive and negative ways. Demographic, economic, political, and cultural factors would impact future inward mobility in destination countries. Europe and Japan are facing a rapid decline in birth rates, resulting in an inverse population pyramid with a shrinking proportion of 18-to-24-year-olds and a growing segment of the aging population. It is predicted that only immigration could reverse this trend.

Participation in higher education grew in almost all these countries over the last decade, with most spectacular increases in Central and Eastern Europe after the end of the post-1989 planned access policy. However, there are clear indications that the demographic impact would result in a decline in total student numbers before 2020, despite a growing demand for education in general and the rising number of older students. The potential implications of these changes are enormous: unless foreign students are imported in large numbers, higher education institutions in Europe and Japan will inevitably be reduced in numbers and size.

Although the imperative of demographic shifts is likely to motivate advanced nations to welcome foreign students, cultural issues might create tensions in certain destinations, in particular in those countries where the numbers increase very rapidly. Recent racial attacks on Indian students in Australia, where the number of Indian students grew almost fivefold in just the past four years, is a case in point. In several advanced countries, foreign students already constitute 15–20 percent of the total student population. In such cases, a further increase of foreign student enrollment may not be sustainable, particularly in times of an economic slowdown.

Advanced countries have often used the practice of attracting and retaining bright foreign students, particularly from the developing world. These highly qualified immigrants bring significant benefits in the form of tuition fees as well as academic and innovative capacity to the host academic institutions and the host country. Over the years, the United States has advanced its higher education and research system—and, therefore, its national technology and innovation systems—by importing talent from countries such as India and China. The United States may now face competition from countries in Continental Europe as they gear up to attract bright graduate students from India.

Although the overall trend in advanced nations has been toward immigration policies that help retain highly qualified people, recent developments suggest that potential immigrants may find it increasingly difficult to find suitable jobs in advanced nations faced with a serious economic slowdown. As a result, many Indian students would find a stint of education abroad meaningless. With the possibility of living at one-fifth of the cost and options for entrepreneurial activities, many Indians now like to stay home. In recent years, a growing number of Indian students are declining admission offers from reputed institutions abroad.

Further, as the options for study abroad increase, students would become more price-sensitive. The United Kingdom, Australia, and several other host countries that charge hefty fees from international students may price themselves out of competition. They would have to compete with other European countries and emerging Asian nations.

Thus, several factors would impact outward mobility from India. While overall there is likely to be continuing growth especially for emerging nations and new destinations, there will also be a slowdown in outward mobility to the United States, the United Kingdom, and Australia that have seen spectacular growth in recent years. The coming years will see more aggressive marketing by all host nations targeting the rapidly growing Indian market. While many advanced nations will take advantage of the limited capacity of the postgraduate education and research sector in India, some such as Australia would target India's weakness in the vocational education and training sector.

Policy Implications

Outward mobility is driven more by individual choice than public policy. Nevertheless, the growing number of Indians studying abroad and its implications for India as a source country have been a matter of public debate for many decades. Is the country losing precious foreign exchange due to outward mobility? Would an increase in domestic capacity help in reducing outward mobility? Often the debate is represented in simplistic terms.

There is concern that the country is losing revenue and valuable foreign exchange due to a large exodus of students. Based on student numbers and cost of education in various host countries, it could be estimated that India currently imports higher education worth over US$7 billion. The figure is comparable to the total public expenditure on higher education. Thus, the concern appears to be genuine; however, it is unclear whether these students or their families would have spent the money on higher education if they had stayed back. Further, the figure itself appears to be a gross overestimation. As per the Reserve Bank of India, in 2005 total outward remittances that included education and travel added up to US$9.6 million. In 2008/2009, the figure rose sharply to US$808 million, half of which was expenditure on education and travel. Even if a large outflow is through informal channels, such as *hawala*, the above estimate is grossly inflated.

Interestingly, growing inward remittances are linked to increased outward mobility. India gets one-tenth of global remittances, making it the world's largest single recipient. Total remittances from overseas Indians have grown steadily over the past 15 years, and dramatically in the past ten, skyrocketing from US$2.1 billion in 1990/1991 to US$24.1 billion in 2005/2006 and accounting for about 3.2 percent of the country's gross domestic product (GDP). One of the factors responsible for the growth in reported remittances is the shifting emigration pattern to high-skilled technology jobs (Chisti 2007). This has been crucial for balancing the trade and capital flows. Social networks created by Indian immigrants have also fostered trade and capital flows. A sizable immigrant population in many advanced countries is also influencing the foreign policy of advanced countries toward India. Many of these immigrants are students who study in advanced countries and stay on (Freeman 2006).

There is also concern about brain drain caused by an exodus of a large number of bright students. Concerns have been primarily centered on graduates of the elite Indian Institutes of Technology (IITs) who leave India and stay in the destination country. It is estimated that about 24 percent of IIT graduates were abroad in 2004. The upside of this flow is now being realized. It is becoming increasingly clear that the so-called brain drain from India to advanced countries is now a more complex, two-way process of "brain circulation" (Public Policy Institute of California 2002). This is further substantiated by empirical evidence that suggests that Indian engineers educated in the United States are transforming developmental opportunities in India by building professional and business connections between technological hubs in the two countries. These engineers and entrepreneurs are transferring technical and institutional know-how to accelerate development of high-technology industries. Initially, they tap low-cost skill in India, and over time they contribute to highly localized processes of entrepreneurial experimentation and upgrading (Saxenian 2006).

Outward mobility of students may, in fact, be an opportunity. Bhagwati (2004) argues that for India, with its large population and huge capacity to generate skilled professionals at home and (through education) abroad, out-migration of professionals is an opportunity and not a threat. Migration, particularly to developed countries, often takes place after a stint of study abroad. Given the limited capacity of the organized sector in India to absorb growing numbers of graduates, opportunities for work overseas through either temporary or permanent migration ease the pressure on the domestic labor market. Freeman (2005) observes that India, with its large pool of scientists and engineers both within the country and overseas, could threaten the North's monopoly in hi-tech sectors by producing innovative products and services.

It is evident from the above not only that the notion of brain drain is being substituted by new developments in the form of brain gain and brain circulation but also that there is reverse brain drain now. Foreigners or foreign citizens of Indian origin are coming to India in large numbers for short-term work experience. Indian Americans settled abroad for years are coming back to their homeland for good because many Indian companies provide the same work environment and opportunities for growth as any U.S. firm anywhere. Such returnees include fresh graduates as well as high-level professionals with PhDs (NAASCOM 2005). Thus, concerns about revenue loss and brain drain are misplaced.

It is often argued that building India's domestic higher education capacity would enable the country to retain students. This may not be true. An econometric study by Professor Mark Rosenzweig indicates that student migration is strongly affected by the promise of wage opportunities, and not by constraints in the domestic educational capacity of the source countries. Students from today's low-wage, source countries appear to seek schooling in high-wage countries as a means of augmenting their chances of obtaining a high-wage job in the United States and other nations. Rosenzweig's research finds that an increase in the number of colleges and educational capacity in source countries actually increases the flow of foreign students to the United States (Rosenzweig 2006). This argument is substantiated by the Indian experience where despite growth in domestic capacity in recent years, outward mobility has increased.

Considering the above, it is now realized that for countries such as India, outward mobility may, in fact, be beneficial. It is, therefore, not surprising that the focus of public policy has shifted from preventing brain drain to managing migration better by promoting the integration of the migrants in host societies. A well-managed migration, where student flows play an important role, could positively contribute to increased employment and rapid global economic growth. Migrant workers could become the nucleus of a worldwide network that can be harnessed for the home country's development. Such networks might enable knowledge transfer and promote new businesses in the home country. With the recent physical attacks on Indian students in Australia, plans to register students abroad and to take action against agents and middleman who exploit students by giving them false information are all steps in the right direction.

Inward Mobility

Although ancient Indian universities such as Nalanda (circa first to fourth century AD) hosted students and scholars from across the world, modern Indian universities are focused on meeting domestic demand and are inward looking. At the time of independence, India had a relatively well-developed system of higher education compared to other developing nations. Thus, India hosted students from several developing countries with a genuinely altruistic motive to provide and contribute to the development of these countries and offer students with an international curriculum and promote better understating between nations, regions, religions, and so on. Enrolling foreign students was considered an important part of public diplomacy (Agarwal 2008b).

Most international students in India have traditionally come from neighboring countries in South Asia that have a large Indian diaspora.

The Association of Indian Universities (AIU), the nodal agency for collecting student mobility data, has faced difficulties in collecting and collating data on international students because of the porous borders with neighbors such as Nepal, Bhutan, and Bangladesh. Thus, though data is available for developments since 1988/1989, there are large gaps in the data. For instance, according to AIU there were 615 U.S. students in India in 2006/2007, but this number stood at 2,627 as per the *Open Doors Report*. In recent years, 400 to 600 Chinese students studied engineering, IT, and computer science in India, but these are not reflected in AIU data.

Long-term trends of inward mobility show that the number of students stood at 11,844 in 1988/1989 and steadily increased during the first half of the 1990s and reached a peak of over 13,707 in 1993/1994, and thereafter it declined steadily. A marked drop occurred in 1996/1997 and, by the end of the millennium, the number of international students in India had halved. While many developed countries, especially the United Kingdom and Australia, were aggressively marketing their education abroad, India stood inactive. However, the numbers began to grow from 2001/2002 onward, after India adopted a more positive approach. Currently India hosts 18,594 international students (AIU 2009).

India hosts students from about 195 countries; 28 of them send more than 100 students. Iran sends the highest number, followed by the U.A.E., Nepal, Ethiopia, Saudi Arabia, and Kenya. Over 90 percent of the students come from the developing countries of Asia and Africa: two-thirds from Asia and one-fourth from Africa. Nearly half of the students come from low-income countries and one-fourth from upper-middle income countries (AIU 2007).

In terms of regional distribution, South and Central Asia leads with more than 30 percent. About 20 percent of the students are from North Africa and the Middle East. Trends over the past 18 years (table 3.2) indicate that while in the earlier years, countries in North Africa and the Sub-Saharan Africa (Kenya, Sudan, Ethiopia, Nigeria, and Somalia) sent the largest numbers, by the late 1990s, numbers from these countries (except Ethiopia) had fallen drastically. In Southeast Asia, the number of students from Malaysia, Thailand, and Vietnam, which were sending a significant number earlier, has fallen (AIU 2000, 2007, 2009). Mauritius, which has a sizable Indian diaspora, still sends some students. In recent years, the largest numbers of students have come from the Middle East (Iran, the U.A.E., Saudi Arabia, Oman, and Yemen).

India's neighbors send a much larger number of students to advanced countries than to India (Agarwal 2008a). For instance, Nepal sent 8,936

Table 3.2 Top-12 Countries of International Students in India (1988/1989–2006/2007)

	1988/1989	1998/1999	2006/2007
1	Kenya (2,332)	Kenya (639)	Iran (2,180)
2	Sudan (1,692)	Nepal (574)	UAE (1,878)
3	Jordan (1,247)	Bangladesh (461)	Nepal (1,728)
4	Nepal (912)	Ethiopia (403)	Ethiopia (1,033)
5	Malaysia (824)	Sri Lanka (368)	Saudi Arabia (771)
6	Iran (553)	Sudan (245)	Kenya (621)
7	Ethiopia (455)	Thailand (197)	USA (615)*
8	Sri Lanka (430)	Uganda (196)	Oman (608)
9	Somalia (429)	Iran (108)	Yemen (598)
10	Nigeria (339)	Vietnam (88)	Bhutan (531)
11	Bangladesh (252)	Jordan (60)	Sri Lanka (466)
12	Thailand (187)	Afghanistan (59)	Korea (452)

Source: Association of Indian Universities (*2,627 as per IIE 2008).

students to the United States compared to merely 1,728 to India. Similarly, Pakistan, Sri Lanka, and Bangladesh sent 5,345, 2,591, and 2,305 students to the United States compared to merely 7, 466, and 361 students respectively to India.

Most students from advanced nations come to India for short-duration study abroad programs. Though the overall number of foreign students is still small, it has been growing in recent years. For instance, the number of U.S. students in India increased from 382 in 1993/1994 to 2,627 in 2006/2007. Although this increase is encouraging, in absolute terms the number is small, especially when compared with the number of Indian students who study in the United States (94,563 in 2007/2008). The small number is particularly striking in comparison to the number of United States students who studied in other "non-traditional" study abroad destinations such as China (11,064) or even Costa Rica (5,383) (*Open Doors* 2008).

The majority of international students in India are enrolled at the undergraduate level (77.6 percent), 12.5 percent are enrolled in postgraduate studies, and only 1.4 percent students are in research programs. International students are mainly concentrated in the western (especially Maharashtra) and southern parts of India. They prefer to study in and around metropolitan cities such as Delhi, Mumbai, Chennai, and Pune. The top-10 Indian universities account for 80 percent of the total. At the very top is Indira Gandhi National Open University enrolling 3,925 students in its programs offered through distance education mode.

The top-ten host institutions include four private universities (Symbiosis International University, 3,554; Manipal University, 1,325; Bharati Vidyapeeth, 473; and Jamia Hamdard, 349). Private institutions have been allowed 15 percent supernumerary seats to admit foreign students and enjoy greater leeway in deciding the fees for foreign students. As a result, private institutions are playing an increasingly important role in attracting international students.

Despite the upward trend, the growth of international students in India is stunningly low compared to that in China. While China hosted only a few hundred students in the early 1990s, it now hosts about 200,000 students, while in Indian this number increased from about 13,000 students in 1990/1991 to the current 18,594. There are several reasons for this. Academic structure, academic calendars, grading procedures, and methods of instruction in Indian higher education need to change and align with global norms to ensure higher international student enrollment. For example, international students from certain countries are used to being able to select their courses, while Indian students generally take sequenced courses, mostly within their discipline of study. Additionally, facilities on Indian campuses are often not suitable for foreign students, with dorms and cafeterias offering standards of living below those to which some international students are accustomed.

India has also not been proactive in attracting international students and its coordination, communication, and recruitment strategy is weak. Most institutions recruit foreign students themselves, though some universities coordinate recruitment for affiliated colleges. The coordination mechanism for promotion of Indian higher education abroad put in place by the University Grants Commission in 2004/2005 has failed to take off. EdCIL (formerly Educational Consultants India Limited) is the coordinating agency for the admission of foreign nationals and overseas Indians, but it recruits less than a thousand students each year. EdCIL is responsible for admission to 1,400 seats in 20 central government technical institutions (only about half are filled up each year) and 200–250 seats in 45 other institutions (mainly private), and it selects 100 overseas Indian students for a scholarship program for children of the Indian diaspora.

The Indian Council for Cultural Relations (ICCR), the public diplomacy arm of the government, facilitates exchange visits and offers scholarships under various schemes. Its special focus is on neighboring countries and the Indian diaspora. There are over 1,800 scholarship slots, with most being country-specific (500 for Afghanistan, 100 for Bangladesh, 60 for Sri Lanka, and 30 for Mauritius). Last year, with the exception of Afghanistan, only 60–65 percent slots were used.

Although India hosts a small number of international students overall, the consistent increase in the international student population since 1998/1999 is an indication of the country's desire and potential to emerge as an important host nation. In recent years, the government has taken several steps to attract international students, including the streamlining of the visa process and the granting of multi-entry visas for students of long-term courses. Universities have been advised to set up international student centers, special websites, familiarization sessions, and periodic monitoring of foreign students.

The government plans to set up five universities to cater to the needs of overseas Indians with half of the seats reserved for them. The first such university, to be located in Bangalore, is to be set up in partnership with the Manipal Group. Several private institutions are aggressively wooing foreign students. For instance, Vellore Institute of Technology hosts several hundred students from China. Several institutions have world-class infrastructure and facilities for foreign students. A few education hubs are coming up that will create such facilities for a group of institutions. Education cities in Chandigarh and Sonepat near Delhi and the Lavasa hill town near Mumbai are such initiatives that have the potential to attract large numbers of international students. Developed as a center of excellence for education and research in hospitality and management education, Lavasa has already commenced academic programs.

Attracting a larger number of international students is important for India. Although inbound student mobility might not be a significant source of revenue (except for a few institutions), it should be viewed as a means to promote mutual understanding and as an opportunity for India to maintain its influence in the region and within countries with a large Indian population. Other benefits could be benchmarking of standards for quality control purposes, stimulating course innovation, enriching cultural and intellectual life, and creating an environment conducive to increased international understanding.

The Indian higher education has a better reputation than that of China, the language of instruction is mostly English, and its capacity to absorb foreign students is comparable. Thus, there is no reason for India not to attract as many or even a larger number of international students than China. However, international student recruitment in India is driven by private providers and not the state as in China, thus it might take longer to reach its targets.

Three recent developments suggest increased inward mobility to India. One, in several key host countries, foreign students already constitute a large enrollment share (e.g., Australia, 21.1 percent; the United Kingdom, 15.8 percent; Sweden, 19 percent). Further growth in such countries might not be sustainable. Two, there has been a steep increase in tuition fees in the United Kingdom and Australia in recent years, and countries such as Germany and France have introduced tuition fees for foreign students. Over the past 25 years, average college tuition and fees have been raised by 440 percent in the United States—more than four times the rate of inflation and almost twice the rate of medical care (Cronin and Horton 2009). As a result, students from low-income families are likely to look for more affordable alternatives.

Finally, study abroad programs in nontraditional destinations are likely to become more popular for students from advanced countries. These countries that place a premium on creativity and innovation to stay competitive have begun to understand that experiences abroad are critical for creative output (Maddux and Galinsky 2009). This would increase demand for short-duration courses as well as longer-term programs. Thus, India has the potential to become an important host country of international students seeking different and enriching experiences.

Summary and Conclusion

Currently, India is the second most important source country of international students. Recent trends suggest that with its young population and large middle class, India will surpass China as the main source country by 2025. While the United States is likely to remain the top destination for Indian students, the rate of growth of Indian students in the United States is likely to be slower than that in other competing nations. While the recent sharp increase in Indian students going to Australia is likely to receive a setback, the number of Indian students in the United Kingdom might hold steady or continue to grow. Most other countries that started out with a much smaller base of Indian students and have only recently come to be viewed as "major players" or "emerging destinations" will see significant growth in numbers from India. Some European countries and Japan, where higher education enrollment would shrink due to demographic changes, would attract many Indian students. However, countries already having a significant foreign student share would find it difficult to accommodate more.

At present, India hosts a small number of international students. This number has grown in recent years, albeit slowly. Trends in inbound mobility and recent developments suggest that India has the potential to attract a much larger number. In India, education entrepreneurs and not the state will drive international student recruitment. Despite these efforts and rising numbers, it might take many years before India receives as many international students as does China.

BIBLIOGRAPHY

Agarwal, Pawan. 2008a. Privatization and Internationalization of Higher Education in the Countries of South Asia: An Empirical Analysis. South Asia Network of Economic Research Institutes. http://www.saneinetwork.

Agarwal, Pawan. 2008b. "India in the Context of International Student Circulation." In *The Dynamics of International Student Circulation in a Global Context*, ed. H. de Wit. Rotterdam and Taipei: Sense Publishers.

Agarwal, Pawan. 2009. Indian Higher Education: Envisioning the Future. New Delhi: Sage India.

Association of Indian Universities (AIU). 2000. AIU Status Report 2000/2: International Students in Indian Universities. New Delhi: AIU.

AIU. 2009. International Students in Indian Universities 2006–2007. New Delhi: AIU.

AIU. 2007. AIU Occasional Paper 2007: Student Mobility: International Students in Indian Universities. New Delhi: AIU.

Banks, Melissa, Alan Olsen, and David Pearce. 2007. *Global Student Mobility: An Australian Perspective Five Years On.* Sydney: IDP Education Australia Limited.

Bashir, Sajitha. 2007. Trends in International Trade in Higher Education: Implications and Options for Developing Countries. Washington, DC: World Bank.

Bhagwati, Jagdish. 2004. *In Defense of Globalization.* New Delhi: Oxford University Press.

British Council. 2009. *Britain Challenging the USA as the World's Top Study Destination, New Analysis Shows.* London: British Council. Available online at: http://www.britishcouncil.org.

Brown, Claire and Greg Linden. 2008. *Is There a Shortage of Engineering Talent in the U.S.?*

Center for Work, Technology, and Society, IRLE, University of California, Berkeley. Available online at: http://www.irle.berkeley.edu/worktech/papers/brown_linden_engineer_shortage08.pdf.

Chakraborty, Mou. 2009. "Study in Japan, Get Full Scholarship." *Hindustan Times HT Live*, May 11.

Chishti, Muzaffar A. 2007. *The Phenomenal Rise in Remittances to India: A Closer Look. Policy Brief.* Washington, DC: Migration Policy Institute.

Cronin, Joseph Marr, and Howard E. Horton. 2009. "Will Higher Education be the Next Bubble to Burst?" *Chronicle of Higher Education* 55 (37): A56.

The Economic Times. 2009. "PM's Dream Team's in a League Apart. Kolkata." *The Economic Times*, June 13.

Ministry of Education and Research of Germany (BMBF). 2008. Internationalization of Higher Education—Foreign Students in Germany—German Students Abroad. Bonn: BMBF. http://www.bmbf.de.

Freeman, Richard B. 2006. *People Flows in Globalization.* National Bureau of Economic Research (NBER) Working Paper No. 12315, Cambridge. MA: NBER.

Hahn, Karola, and Andre Schelewsky. 2006. *Academic Mobility and Scientific Cooperation between the European Union and India*. Bonn, Germany: German Academic Exchange Service (DAAD).

uang, Yasheng, and Tarun Khanna. 2003. *Can India Overtake China?* Available online at: http://www.foreignpolicy.com.

Institute of International Education. 2005. Open Doors: Report on International Educational Exchange (1948–2004). New York: IIE.

Institute of International Education. 2008. Open Doors: Report on International Educational Exchange (2008). New York: IIE.

Lightfoot, Liz. 2009. "More Overseas Students Found." *BBC News*. Available online at: http://news.bbc.co.uk.

Maddux, William W., and Adam D. Galinsky. 2009. "Cultural Borders and Mental Barriers: The Relationship Between Living Abroad and Creativity." *Journal of Personality and Social Psychology* 96 (5): 1047–1061.

National Association of Software and Services Company (NASSCOM). 2005. *The IT Industry in India: Strategic Review 2005*. New Delhi: NASSCOM.

Public Policy Institute of California (PPIC). 2002. *"Silicon Valley Immigrants Forging Local and Trans-National Networks."* Issue #58. San Francisco: PPIC.

Rosenzweig, Mark R. 2006. *Global Wage Differences and International Student Flows*. New York: New York University.

Safran, William, Ajaya K. Sahoo, and Brij V. Lal, eds. 2009. *Transnational Migrations: The Indian Diaspora*. New Delhi: Routledge Publications.

Saxenian, Annalee. 2006. *The New Argonauts: Regional Advantage in a Global Economy*. Cambridge, MA: Harvard University Press.

United Nations. 2008. *World Population Prospects, 2008 Revision*. New York: United Nations Population Division. http://esa.un.org/unpp.

Chapter 4

International Student Mobility: A European Perspective from Germany and the United Kingdom

Christian Bode and Martin Davidson

Introduction

The global financial and economic crisis, the emergence of new economic and political power centers, and the growing awareness of problems and risks such as climate change are transforming the way we see the world. The dominance of the West and its political, military, and cultural influence are gradually giving way to a multi-polar setting of a multicultural and decentralized world that at the same time needs more cooperation, coordination, and common solutions than ever before. Of course, this also has a direct and massive impact on the higher education subsector that not only provides research and technologies for new solutions and economic growth but, more importantly, also educates future world leaders on whom the fate of our global village will depend. There is no doubt that internationalization will play an increasing role in higher education and move from its former peripheral role into the center of institutional and national strategies.

Internationalization in this new sense will go far beyond recruiting international students although students' (in particular graduates') mobility will continue to play a major role. Mobility and competitive recruitment of staff will also grow and so will cooperation in thematic and institutional networks, both regional and global. This process includes a political coordination of higher education policy at different international levels, such as the Bologna Process that would have been unthinkable two decades ago. Insofar as developments in the European Union (EU) are concerned, the Bologna Process—and its interaction with national policies, as illustrated in the case of Germany and the United Kingdom—gives an example of an emerging new pattern of internationalization that may also be instructive for other parts of the world.

Europe

The EU—which started as the European Communities with purely economic agendas such as coal and steel, agriculture, and foreign trade—has grown into a driving force in other areas of policy as well, particularly in research and education. The launchpad for this new dimension was the Lisbon Agenda, which set the EU goal of becoming "the most dynamic and competitive knowledge-based economy in the world" by 2010. This goal is unlikely to be achieved but the distance to go has become shorter.

In the area of research and development, European political leaders have set themselves the goal of committing 3 percent of gross domestic product per year. Currently the European average share is still below 2 percent. In Germany, as in the United States, it stands at 2.6 percent, and in the United Kingdom at 1.8 percent (where the government has set a target of 2.5 percent for gross domestic product spend on research by 2014). Investment in the seventh European Union Framework program will grow to €60 billion and will involve various non-European partners. A European Research Council has been established and a European Institute of Technology will follow. All these programs are, by definition, international and will create thousands of new opportunities for doctoral and postdoctoral students. Many of these positions will be filled by non-European candidates.

The developments in European higher education are even more astounding. The Bologna Process was an unprecedented international harmonization of national reform policies in Europe—a process EU member states would have cursed until recently. At celebrations for the 900th anniversary of the University of Bologna in 1988 and at the European education ministers' conference 11 years later, participants elaborated two Bologna Declarations, which could not have been more different. The first, in Latin and signed by hundreds of rectors, presidents, and principals, confirmed the legacy of European universities' humanist tradition. The other, in English and signed by 30 European ministers of higher education, set political goals to develop a unified European higher education area (EHEA), the three central themes being "mobility, quality and international competitiveness." In the period between the two declarations the Iron Curtain fell, opening up a new dimension of globalization. In evidence of this, the Bologna Process has expanded, conference by conference, to 20 more countries from the Atlantic to the Pacific. Membership seems to be completed by now but at the same time a systematic dialogue with non-European partner countries has been opened, in particular on issues of quality assurance, accreditation, and the rules for recognition and revalidation. Not surprisingly, the Bologna ministers decided at their recent meeting in Leuven to carry on the process beyond 2010, the original target date for completion. They also formulated the future agenda, where mobility of students and staff is back in the center of the process.

The main instrument of the EU to enhance mobility of students and staff (including administrative personnel) is the Erasmus program that last year alone sent 183,000 students (including placements) and 27,000 university teachers for a period of up to one year to another European country and several associated nonmember states such as Iceland, Norway, and Turkey. The program has been extremely successful and the European Union plans to double these numbers over the next few years. One may question whether this new target will be achieved, since former growth rates have significantly slowed down. There is a growing concern that the introduction of the bachelor-master system into continental higher education might be counterproductive for integrated student mobility since courses are often shorter (three years for a bachelor course) and the delivery of instruction more school-like and less flexible.

The driver for the Erasmus program was primarily political—to achieve greater cohesion between EU member states through mutual connections and better understanding between future leaders. The spin-off effect of the program on university structures and strategies, however, has been enormous. The Erasmus program combines individual mobility with institutional responsibility. It requires commitment from participating universities and member states and has introduced new mechanisms for curriculum design and mutual recognition, such as European Credit Transfer and Accumulation System (ECTS) and Diploma Supplement. It now includes staff mobility and exchanges of administrative personnel.

This broadening of content has been accompanied by two significant extensions. One dimension is the extra-European expansion. In the course of the last 15 years, bilateral and multilateral agreements with non-European countries have established a set of exchange and cooperation programs (third-country programs) with most parts of the world and higher education has become an integral part of the EU Neighbourhood Policy with adjacent regions such as the Mediterranean or Central Asia.

Academic exchange and cooperation has developed into a nucleus of a gradually emerging foreign cultural policy of the EU. The second dimension is the growing role that the EU plays as a driver of higher education reform policy in its member states, setting targets and benchmarks for institutional development, quality assurance, management, and funding, partly using the Bologna Process as a vehicle for its own political goals. This confirms a trend that can also be observed at the national level: increasing internationalization means growing exposure to international comparisons and competitions and that leads back to a self-critical assessment of one's own strengths and weaknesses ending up with either resignation or vigorous institutional reforms. In short, internationalization has become an important and successful instrument of institutional development.

The following case studies from Germany and the United Kingdom illustrate differences in trends and developments in the two countries with a view to the internationalization of higher education as well as a common agenda of partnership.

Germany

Germany was one of the major destinations for students from all over the world seeking a modern and research-oriented higher education throughout the nineteenth century and the first quarter of the twentieth century. Japanese doctors, American engineers, and Russian students of law or natural sciences all came to obtain their degrees in Berlin, Göttingen, Munich, or Tübingen. Visiting Heidelberg in 1879, Mark Twain noted, "The summer semester was in full tide; consequently the most frequent figure in and about Heidelberg was the student. Most of the students were Germans, of course, but the representatives of foreign lands were very numerous. They hailed from every corner of the globe—for instruction is cheap in Heidelberg, and so is living, too."

This highlights a feature of Germany that still holds true: university tuition is generally free of charge or subject to very low fees (approx € 1,000 per year), and living costs are still reasonable. However, for obvious political and economic reasons, Germany's "market share" in internationally mobile students decreased sharply during the Nazi period, World War II, and the following reconstruction period. By the late 1990s, the number of internationally mobile students coming to Germany had recovered to a level of around 100,000. In the following decade, coinciding with the Bologna Process, Germany adopted an explicit policy of enhancing its international attractiveness, recruiting more students from abroad and increasing the international mobility of its own students and academic staff.

Today the number of international students enrolled at Germany universities is approximately 233,606 (including 55,000 foreign students who obtained their secondary education in Germany), which ranks Germany as the fourth biggest host country for international students worldwide. International students account for roughly 8 percent of the total student population, with much higher proportions in technical universities (15–20 percent) and music colleges (up to 40 percent). The yearly intake is stable at around 66,500 beginners, two-thirds of them for undergraduate education. Apart from the Chinese (25,500) and the Turks, who are mainly permanent residents (21,500), the biggest national groups are from Germany's Eastern European neighbors. This reflects not only geographical proximity but also strong traditional relations and the privileged position of the German language in this region. However, almost half of the international students come from developing countries, mainly from Africa and Asia.

This enormous increase in international students in Germany over the last 20 years was partly a result of the aforementioned geopolitical developments (the fall of the Iron Curtain, emerging economies, and new political orientations in Asia that increased globalization) and partly due to a deliberate political decision to promote Germany as a preferred destination for international students. This decision was inspired in part by a critical discussion about Germany's economic competitiveness, in particular its role as a champion in exports (which it still is), and in part by the successful new recruitment policies in the United States, the United Kingdom, and Australia that had a strong impact on the intensified higher education policy debate that was triggered off by the Bologna Process and the pushing of EU policy (Lisbon, Maastricht, etc.). In the mid-1990s the German Academic Exchange Service (DAAD) established a new consortium of higher education institutions for the worldwide promotion of German higher education (GATE) supported by public funds from the departments of both foreign affairs and higher education. This consortium is now actively represented in all major student fairs around the globe and organizes promotion tours; provides information through all kinds of media; offers seminars, training facilities, and consultancy; and sets standards for best practice in international education. The target is to maximize not the volume of international student intake but the quality of the candidates. The expected benefit is not cash (fees) but the establishment of an international campus at home (for the 70 percent domestic students who do not leave their university for study abroad), the recruitment of potential PhD candidates and young researchers, and, above all, the development of an international network of partners and friends all over the world that may pay off one day in different, mostly indirect ways including economic cooperation.

The DAAD, which was founded shortly after World War I by a group of students and which has grown into the world's biggest agency in the field with a budget of €360 million (US$453 million) and 60,000 grantees per year, didn't leave it at that. In its continuously updated action plan it identified two more political aims: a major increase in outbound mobility and the internationalization of the higher education institutions (HEIs) themselves.

As for outbound mobility (study abroad), Germany's record of 83,000 students enrolled in foreign universities and 26,300 participants in the European Region Action Scheme for the Mobility of University Students (Erasmus) program is not bad, actually it is better than in most other highly developed countries but not good enough for a country that is so intensively involved in world trade and European integration. Therefore, the DAAD has set the target that by 2015 every second higher education graduate should have had a substantial international experience, be it study abroad, an integrated internship, or an intensive language course of several months. This coincides with the mobility policy of the Bologna Process that has also set a more moderate benchmark of 20 percent. The DAAD supports this mobility through a great variety of fellowship programs at all academic levels (undergraduates, doctorates, postdoctorates, internships, language courses, summer schools, etc.) and through regular campaigns (e.g., "Go out," "Go East!"). The DAAD's traditional "philosophy" for study abroad is still the idea that a longer period of living and working in a different cultural, linguistic, and personal setting leads to more understanding, tolerance, and, last but not least, promotion of character and personality, not just simple skills for professional behavior abroad. Therefore, the core program of DAAD fellowship is still a one-year stay abroad although there is an obvious tendency among candidates toward shorter periods in order not to "lose" any time.

More recently DAAD and political authorities have come to the conclusion that fellowships and individual motivation alone do not meet the requirements of academic mobility at large but should be complemented by explicit professional support from the side of the HEIs themselves. As mentioned above, this had already been part of the success story of the Erasmus program. Therefore, the "internationalization of HEIs" has become the third pillar of the DAAD agenda and it encompasses a great variety of support programs that aim at professionalizing institutional structures for academic exchange and cooperation: language courses, marketing activities, information and advice, targeted selection and admission procedures, tutoring, career services for international students, fund raising, program design, quality control, alumni programs, international guest lecturers, and dedicated professional staff in the international office. More and more universities have begun to collate these elements in a coherent internationalization strategy.

As inter-university cooperation moves from simple bilateral exchange agreements to more sophisticated multilateral research and study networks, the more professionalism is needed. Universities join groups such as U 21, the Coimbra Group, and the Utrecht Network to improve their competitiveness as sending and receiving institutions and as successful applicants in international funding programs. These international funding programs, often focused on global problems such as climate change, energy supply, environment protection, and so forth, frequently serve as a starting point for thematic university networks that include a range of "embedded" mobility options for staff and students.

It is obvious that this kind of operation needs external funding. In the case of Germany, and the rest of Europe, this means predominantly public funding (since private investment does not account for a major share of educational costs). This highlights another trend in recent years: national governments have assumed an active if not dominant role in the promotion of international education marketing and cooperation, not only as a funding source but also as a driving force and steering power. Motivation may vary from program to program and differ in detail but the principal aims are obvious: economic competitiveness, political influence, and, to a lesser extent, development aid.

In Germany, the need for more international qualification, engagement, and investment is common sense among government departments and political parties. The German federal government has recently adopted an explicit "Internationalization Initiative." The foreign minister has referred to international cultural, education, and science policy as the "third pillar" of foreign policy, comparable in importance with political or economic issues, and the German Parliament in 2009 increased DAAD's budget by 20 percent (in comparison to 2008). Many of DAAD's member universities and also non-university research institutions have adopted a clear internationalization mission, sometimes with quantitative benchmarks, and funding agencies such as the German Research Foundation (DFG) are internationalizing their programs.

The main aims of these initiatives are the following:

- to raise Germany's attractiveness and efficiency in the international competition for talent, international cooperation, and reputation

- to increase Germany's contribution to solving important global problems
- to qualify Germany's own future leaders in politics, economics, and science at the best destinations, in the spirit of global citizenship
- to contribute to sustainable institution building in developing countries
- to encourage peaceful dialogue between different cultures.

Operational outcomes of these political considerations can be seen in the recent development of DAAD's programs. They have developed from simple fellowship programs to far more complex projects such as the promotion of the Millennium Development Goals through higher education and research or the founding of German universities abroad, such as the ones in Cairo, Amman, Istanbul, and Ho Chi Minh City. There are even more difficult and policy-oriented projects such as the academic contribution to European-Islamic dialogue, reconstruction of higher education in Afghanistan, or the establishment of a new partnership with Iraq.

It will be a major challenge to maintain these initiatives in the face of increasing pressure on public funding and the economic crisis. However, international cooperation and exchange are simply too important to be neglected or postponed. To paraphrase Derek Bok's famous quotation concerning education, one could say, "If you think international cooperation is expensive, try isolation!"

The United Kingdom

Higher education in the United Kingdom today is preparing itself to meet the global challenge of internationalization. Of course, internationalization of academia is not a twenty-first-century phenomenon but its dynamics and political dimension have changed dramatically in recent years.

Until recently, much of the internationalization of higher education in the United Kingdom, both in teaching and research, had developed at the level of university faculties and departments, often quite selectively focusing on specific areas of academia. These endeavors tended to be opportunistic and not part of a wider and coherent national agenda of internationalization in academia as a whole. In the past, many HEIs in the United Kingdom would often focus on inward international student recruitment as the main or even sole strand of their internationalization strategies. A fundamental driver for this was the introduction by the U.K. government of full-cost fees for international (i.e., non-EU) students in the early 1980s, while EU students' admission was permitted on the same terms as those set for U.K. students.

The introduction of full-cost tuition fees for overseas students brought about a much more businesslike and competitive culture in U.K. higher education. In its wake, the great majority of U.K. HEIs developed a stronger, more entrepreneurial approach, professionalized their marketing strategies, and prioritized the recruitment of international students. At the same time, U.K. HEIs actively sought out and participated in European mobility programs. If the latter brought diverse academic and cultural benefits, the recruitment of overseas students generated additional economic benefits both to individual institutions and to the U.K. economy as a whole. Fees from non-EU students in higher education alone currently total some £2.5 billion a year.

Today, the United Kingdom is the second most popular destination for students worldwide: the total number of non-U.K. students for 2007/2008 was 389,330, of whom 131,805 were non-U.K. EU students (Higher Education Statistics Agency [HESA]). The recruitment of overseas students will undoubtedly remain one strand of the international activities of U.K. HEIs in the near future. Above and beyond that, there are the beginnings of a shift in approach toward setting a clearly focused, joined-up agenda for the internationalization of the higher education subsector, catalyzed as a political priority of the U.K. government. Programs such as PMI2 (Prime Minister's Initiative 2) and UKIERI (U.K.-India Education Research Initiative) recognize these drivers and support the development of strategic alliances and partnerships between U.K. and overseas institutions.

This is clearly affirmed in the recent *Denham Review*[1] on the future of higher education, which made special reference to internationalization. This report states emphatically that a forward-looking agenda for U.K. higher education is needed to elevate the United Kingdom's position as a leading global player in using the research and learning strengths of the global higher education subsector to address the primary global challenges of the next 20 years. It is also argued that a genuinely international approach is necessary, not only to maintain non-U.K. student recruitment numbers but also to enhance the United Kingdom's overall research, innovation, and education capability. Such a strategy needs to have an impact on university campuses, faculties, and students through stronger worldwide connections.

This is a clear signal for the U.K. higher education subsector and all related stakeholders to move toward an inclusive, holistic approach to internationalization. Its aim is to incorporate student exchange, teaching partnerships, joint-research development, and policy dialogue as the way to develop both domestic and global capacity in higher education.

The Bologna Process and Outward Mobility of U.K. Students

The United Kingdom has been a participating country in the Bologna Process since higher education ministers from 29 European countries, including the United Kingdom, met in Bologna in June 1999 and signed a declaration establishing what was necessary to create a European higher education area by the end of the decade.

One of the key objectives of the Bologna Declaration is the "promotion of mobility by overcoming obstacles to the effective exercise of free movement" (European Ministers for Education, 1999). At the London Summit in 2007, mobility was designated as a key priority for the Bologna Process until 2009. EU mobility programs such as Erasmus provide support across Europe for students wishing to spend a period of study aboard. However, there has historically been a low level of outward student mobility from the United Kingdom compared to other countries. Only about 1 percent of U.K. students spend a period of time abroad as part of their studies. Many factors affect the mobility (or lack there of) of U.K. students such as

- lack of knowledge about mobility schemes
- lack of a tradition of mobility
- social factors
- language barriers
- lack of opportunity/support offered by the institution
- family/work commitments.

However, after a period of decline in the early part of this decade, outward mobility of U.K. students is now increasing; with the introduction in 2008 of work placements to the Erasmus program, the total number of U.K. students on the Erasmus program has now risen from 7,235 in 2006/2007 to 10,278 for 2007/2008, representing about a 40 percent increase (HESA). The year 2008 was the second year in a row that showed an increase in numbers after many years of decline and suggests that the challenges in overcoming the barriers U.K. students face in taking up these opportunities are gradually being addressed by the U.K. higher education subsector.

The British Council, as the United Kingdom's international cultural relations organization, has responded dynamically to these challenges. Education in the broader sense has always been at the core of our activities precisely because education at all levels is part of a wider cultural engagement. To support and facilitate the internationalization of higher education is now a priority for the British Council because of the rapidly changing and competitive international higher education environment. It demands very different approaches if the United Kingdom is to retain and build its position. The growing differentiation in the U.K. higher education subsector in terms of universities' missions, international strategies, capacities, and resources makes this undertaking even more challenging.

However, as current trends show, the forces of competition and cooperation often coincide. This is particularly evident in the case of transnational education that has transformed the global educational landscape since the late 1990s. This unprecedented growth in program mobility is driven by the commitment of overseas governments to develop knowledge economies. The consequence of this has been a rapidly changing and far more competitive environment for higher education for the United Kingdom and other established educational markets, in particular the United States, Canada, and Australia. Another important trend is the emergence of new models of partnership and collaboration. Although the establishment of overseas campuses, such as Nottingham University's Malaysia and China campuses, remain limited, there is an increasing focus on multifaceted international partnerships involving both research and teaching. Through these, universities look for mutually beneficial opportunities to increase their brand profile, research capabilities, and their teaching reach. On top of this the private sector is playing an increasingly important role in the delivery of teaching in countries across the world. Partnership with private providers is opening up significant opportunities for U.K. universities to develop new and innovative models of teaching and learning.

Although there is no indication that the global higher education market has peaked, established markets are changing dramatically, so that although the growth in student inflow in traditional English language destinations such as the United Kingdom, the United States, and Australia is slowing, education hubs are developing fast in other regions. Students look increasingly to Malaysia, Singapore, China, or the Middle East rather than the West for the provision of international undergraduate education, delivered by either state or, increasingly, private institutions. Many of these students will go on to seek postgraduate education in the United Kingdom, the United States, or other Western countries. Student mobility increasingly involves a journey across two or three countries. These developments challenge the notion of traditional student recruitment to one institution in one country. Rather they suggest a much more complex market in which international partnerships between universities may begin to drive student mobility between institutions and countries. In this context, the U.K. policy agenda focus on internationalization and international partnerships is seen as fundamental to the United Kingdom's position in an increasingly competitive and globalized market.

Globalization of the education market is a dynamic process that is constantly undergoing changes to which national agendas and institutional strategies will need to adapt. The latest HESA data indicates that in 2007–2008 just under 200,000 students outside of the country were studying for U.K. higher education awards. It is estimated that at least 65 percent of students have participated in some form of transnational education activity.

In 2006 the British Council commissioned research into the motivations of the U.K. sector in delivering transnational education. A study by Sheffield Hallam University found that the main motivation for U.K. universities is internationalization. It also found that as universities look more strategically at their international engagement, rationalization of transnational education provision is occurring in some institutions and being scaled up in others. There is also an increase in central transnational education roles and/or departments as institutions tighten up on quality controls and try to ensure a better "strategic fit."

This trend is consistent with wider changes within the U.K. higher education subsector. Universities are moving away from international strategies defined through student recruitment to something far broader encompassing teaching and research partnerships and ensuring that U.K. students also have exposure to an international dimension in their education. Transnational education is one part of this broader international remit.

Financial issues are also important for U.K. universities as the international arena becomes more volatile. Since 2003/2004, most U.K. universities have seen more modest growth in terms of international student inflow. Vastly increased domestic provision, including transnational education, in many of the United Kingdom's major source countries has had an impact—particularly in countries such as China. International students now expect, and have, more flexibility. The length of time spent in the United Kingdom by international students has decreased substantially with more and more students choosing to come for just one or two years of study. It shows that the implication for most U.K. providers is that *some* transnational education delivery is essential to ensure continued flow of international students to U.K. campuses.

Meeting the demands of the higher education subsector while bearing in mind that higher education itself is international, global pursuit will remain a priority because international education is critical to the United Kingdom's knowledge economy and its long-term wealth and prosperity. U.K. higher education is a dynamic and sustainable export industry worth more than £10 billion. By internationalizing its higher education provision and strengthening its position within the global education market, the United Kingdom attracts intellectual capital, making a vital contribution to its capacity for research, technological growth, and innovation. Both the U.K. government and the U.K. higher education subsector have ambitious agendas that strive to do this. If in the past the U.K. higher education subsector had a tendency to equate international strategy with inward student recruitment alone, all stakeholders, both at the governmental and institutional level, have fully realized that student recruitment is only one strand of a wider portfolio of internationalization. The United Kingdom has moved away from inward student recruitment and is now seeking a healthy balance in its international activities between recruitment, partnerships, research, and capacity building.

Conclusion

The internationalization of higher education is felt at international, national, and local levels. Higher education is no longer a domestic concern to which international engagement is an added benefit. This process is now unstoppable. The question is not whether a country wishes to internationalize its higher education system, but how can it do so for the greatest benefit and most efficiently. The university of the future will either be international or it will be no university at all.

Emerging consensus and practice are that a holistic approach to internationalization is the way to develop capacity not only in the domestic system but also in global higher education. It is clear that gaining an international perspective in education—whether from a short-term study abroad as part of a national degree, a degree in a foreign country, or an international qualification in one's own country—is an integral part of internationalization. If this is to develop in a sustainable manner, however, higher education systems need to advance in line with the changing requirements of the market.

Higher education institutions now need to see their role not in terms of supply but in terms of how they can meet these demands. National governments, educators, and institutions need to ask whether their courses are fit for the purpose. Do they really provide students with the skills and experiences they will need to prosper in a global economy? Governments have an important role in supporting an increased international mobility and so do cultural relations organizations, for education is an integral part of a wider cultural engagement.

The experience offered by studying abroad is not solely about education. For international students, a good educational experience builds a lifelong connection to the country in which they study. An educational tie becomes a cultural tie, which in turn becomes a personal tie and is one of the most powerful ways to augment traditional diplomatic relationships.

In this landscape the role of national education and culture organizations needs to change to keep pace with the changes in both the subsector and the wider world. Countries need to ask what the internationalization of higher education really means and ensure fair access to international experience for students from all backgrounds. What additional efforts need to be mobilized and at what level to maintain the process of internationalization? What quality-assessment practices might be introduced to ensure the sustainability and high quality of higher education provision by national institutions and in cooperation with international partners? From a position of self-interest it has to be about maintaining a world-class education system to underpin the development of the knowledge economy that globalization is demanding of more and more nations. So to some extent this is about ensuring the quality of a country's higher education system with a view to international achievements, and this is a competitive argument.

However, in a multi-polar world, where the education debate can no longer be dominated by the voices of the traditional recipient countries for international students, a merely competitive attitude that is not complemented by a willingness to cooperate on equal footing will be counterproductive and ultimately doomed to failure. Universities, the leading ones in particular, as driving forces of the international knowledge society have a special responsibility to combine their indispensable competition for best academic achievements with a knowledge-sharing cooperation, thus creating a win-win situation that is in their best interests and serves the world at large. Nonprofit professional organizations such as DAAD and the British Council have a key role in enabling that change.

NOTE

1. John Denham, secretary of state for innovation, universities, and skills from 2007 to June 2009.

BIBLIOGRAPHY

Drew, Sue, Ning Tang, Ben Willis, and Claire Wolstenholme. 2006. *Transnational Education—U.K. Higher Education Institutions' Response to Increasing Global Demand.* London: British Council. Available online at: http://www.britishcouncil.org.

Chapter 5

The International Dimension of U.S. Higher Education: Trends and New Perspectives

Allan E. Goodman and Robert Gutierrez

Introduction

Most people are not very mobile. And the vast majority of the roughly 40 million who are do so because they are forced to become refugees. Most people undertaking higher education also live and study only inside their own countries, and today of the 192 sovereign states who are members of the United Nations, in only twenty does the enrollment of international students exceed 1 percent. For the United States, that proportion is just under 4 percent and yet the United States is and has been the leading destination for international students and scholars for half a century.

At the turn of the twentieth century, the first pathways for students and scholars from other countries to enter the United States were created with the support of the U.S. government, and pioneering academic institutions and nonprofit organizations, including the Institute of International Education (IIE) that saw the benefit to progress in science, learning, diplomacy, and commerce.

Almost 100 years later, the dynamics of student and scholar mobility are still shifting. Along with new paths of academic mobility being carved out in international education come opportunities and challenges that the United States will need to address if global competitiveness and security remain equally important national goals. As international students and

scholars play a key role in the internationalization of U.S. higher education, so also do U.S. students who are increasingly pursuing their studies
abroad. Mobility is a two-way street.

This chapter will focus on exploring higher education mobility from the
U.S. perspective, with an analysis of the current picture of flows of students
based on trend data from *Open Doors*, IIE's longstanding annual publication on student and scholar mobility statistics, supported by the Bureau
of Educational and Cultural Affairs at the U.S. Department of State. We
will also examine the key drivers of mobility into and out of the United
States and highlight the impact of scholar mobility and exchange and its
relation to internationalization efforts on U.S. campuses. Finally, we will
address implications of mobility and its new forms, as these will no doubt
play a vital role in the way higher education is delivered across borders and
how they influence the mobility of students and scholars worldwide. Their
movement around the globe and the innovations in research and teaching
that result from their work are creating the twenty-first-century Silk Road,
multidirectional and more diffuse, but with no less profound an impact on
cultures, economies, and international relations.

Student and Scholar Mobility
Trends across U.S. Borders

In terms of absolute numbers, growth in the international student population in the United States has increased almost constantly (figure 5.1).
Although there were slight declines in the two years following September
11, the number rose by more than 80 percent over the past two decades
to more than 671,000 students in 2008/2009, outpacing the 40 percent
growth in overall total enrollment in the U.S. higher education subsector
(Bhandari and Chow 2009).[1] Compared to other leading host countries,
the United States remains the top destination for international students,[2]
hosting approximately 21 percent of all international students worldwide,
followed by the United Kingdom, France, Germany, Australia, China,
Canada, and Japan (Atlas of Student Mobility 2009).

Although international students contribute substantially to the diversity
of the student body at many U.S. institutions, on a national level they represented only 3.7 percent of total U.S. higher education enrollment in 2009.
However, this aggregate figure fails to convey their uneven distribution across
institutions—with roughly over half of all international students (54 percent)
in the country located within only 150 U.S. institutions, mostly large research
universities.[3] Among these institutions, the proportion of the student body

that is international tends to be far greater than the national median rate of 8.3 percent, and in some science and technology (S&T) departments, over half of all graduate students are international (Wendler et al. 2010).[4]

These recent growth rates point to a rebound from modest declines seen earlier this decade. The largest exception to recent growth came in the wake of September 11, with a marked drop in the number of incoming international students due to tightening of screening procedures for student visas and a concern among international students that they were no longer welcome in the United States (U.S. Government Accountability Office [U.S. GAO] 2008). The rate of growth flattened in 2002/2003, and the total population of international students actually decreased by 2.4 percent in 2003/2004—the largest rate of decrease seen in over three decades. The impact was felt in varied degrees from different sending countries and in different types of host institutions. For example, U.S. graduate schools— which often rely heavily on international students and scholars as teaching and research assistants, particularly in science, technology, engineering, and math (STEM) fields—saw much larger drops than other institutions. On a national level, attention was drawn to global perceptions of the United States as an unwelcoming destination and steps were taken by the U.S. government and by host institutions to counter these misconceptions.

Since that time the number of international students has rebounded, partly due to committed institutional efforts to reach out to students and partly due to the U.S. government's streamlining of student visa review

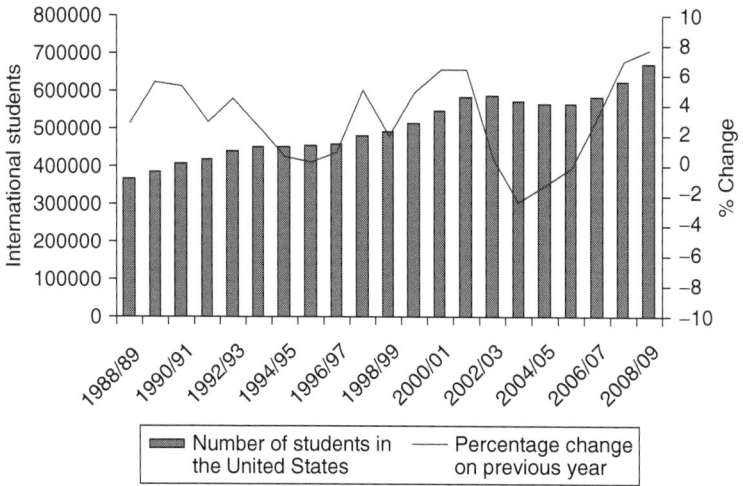

Figure 5.1   International Students in the United States, 1987/1988 to 2008/2009.
Source: IIE, *Open Doors Report on International Education Exchange*, 1987/1988 to 2008/2009.

procedures, expanded investment in EducationUSA advising services globally, and vigorous public diplomacy efforts to assure international students that the United States welcomes them. The most recent enrollment data (2008/2009) saw a strong positive increase in international student enrollments of 7.7 percent over the previous year, the largest rate of growth since the early 1980s (*Open Doors* 2009). The importance of this growing level of academic exchange between the United States and other countries was reaffirmed by President Obama in a speech given in Cairo in 2009 promising that "we will expand exchange programs and increase scholarships, like the one that brought my father to America." This commitment signals growth in exchange and mobility in both directions.

The International Student Profile in the United States

As with other top destination countries that receive large numbers of international students, growth over the past decade is largely attributed to the vast numbers of students from South and East Asian countries who seek an overseas education, especially in the United States. Indeed, approximately 41 percent of the total U.S. international student population in 2009 came from just three countries—India, China, and South Korea—that have comprised the top three places of origin for the past seven years and have been in the top five over the past two decades (table 5.1).

Despite the dominance of these three key sending countries, it is also worth highlighting a few countries among the top 20 that have recently become active in sending international students to the United States. For example, the number of students from Nepal, Saudi Arabia, and Vietnam increased dramatically in 2009, building on several years of growth (table 5.1). Each country experienced double-digit gains over the previous year: Vietnam (up 46 percent), Saudi Arabia (up 28 percent), and Nepal (up 30 percent). In each case, there was a mix of different factors driving the growth: limited capacity in the sending country's institutions, new scholarship initiatives by the Saudi government, increased recruitment by U.S. campuses (especially in Vietnam), and political instability in Nepal.[5]

In terms of academic level, about 42 percent of the international student population in the United States studied at the graduate level in 2008/2009, while slightly less (40 percent) studied at the undergraduate level. The remainder pursued non-degree studies including English language programs or Optional Practical Training (OPT) related to their degree studies. As international graduate students represent a growing segment of the overall international student population in the United States, they have come to play a key role in areas of research and teaching at many institutions. The

Table 5.1   Leading Places of Origin of International Students in the United States, 2007/2008 and 2008/2009

Rank	Place of Origin	2007/2008	2008/2009	2008/2009 % of Total	% Change
	World Total	**623,805**	**671,616**	**100**	**7.7**
1	India	94,563	103,260	15.4	9.2
2	China	81,127	98,235	14.6	21.1
3	South Korea	69,124	75,065	11.2	8.6
4	Canada	29,697	29,697	4.4	2.2
5	Japan	29,264	29,264	4.4	−13.9
6	Taiwan	28,065	28,065	4.2	−3.2
7	Mexico	14,850	14,850	2.2	0.1
8	Turkey	13,263	13,263	2	10.2
9	Vietnam	12,823	12,823	1.9	46.2
10	Saudi Arabia	12,661	12,661	1.9	28.2
11	Nepal	11,581	11,581	1.7	29.6
12	Germany	9,679	9,679	1.4	8.7
13	Brazil	8,767	8,767	1.3	15.7
14	Thailand	8,736	8,736	1.3	−3
15	The United Kingdom	8,701	8,701	1.3	4
16	Hong Kong	8,329	8,329	1.2	0.5
17	Indonesia	7,509	7,509	1.1	−2.4
18	France	7,421	7,421	1.1	5.3
19	Colombia	7,013	7,013	1	5.3
20	Nigeria	6,256	6,256	0.9	0.5

Source: IIE, *Open Doors: Report on International Educational Exchange*, 2007/2008–2008/2009.

National Science Foundation (NSF) reports that the proportion of foreign graduate student enrollments in science and engineering fields increased from 20 percent in 1985 to 25 percent in 2005 (NSF 2008).

International students in the United States are concentrated in a few fields. Business and management as a field of study consistently attracts the greatest share of international students (21 percent), though the combined fields that make up the STEM disciplines account for 41 percent of all international students in the United States. Among international students at the graduate level, the focus on the STEM fields is even more pronounced with 54 percent enrolled in these programs.

Growth Relative to Increasing Global Mobility

The expansion in the international student population in the United States reflects the broader global trend in the growing number of students worldwide who leave their home countries to pursue their education and degrees abroad. In 2007, some 3 million students comprised the internationally mobile student population worldwide, an increase of approximately 50 percent since 2001 (UNESCO/OECD 2009). Using this time period as a point of comparison, available data reveal that the global growth in this population outpaced international student growth rates in the United States, which increased by 6 percent between 2001 and 2007.

In light of this rapid growth on a global scale, many have questioned whether the United States has lost "market share" to other countries. Some have examined the extent to which this might even have an impact on the country's competitive edge in research and development, as studies have shown that international students who graduate from the STEM fields contribute their knowledge and talents to industry and innovation in the United States after they graduate (Galama and Hosek 2008). Although it is true that other top host countries—including the United Kingdom, Germany, France, Australia, China, and Canada—continue to see strong rates of growth in their international student enrollments, the global search for talent is not a zero-sum game in which one country's gain is another's loss.

Rather, the "global pie" of mobile students is continuing to expand: instead of being attracted to just a handful of countries, more international students are studying in a larger variety of countries (Bhandari and Blumenthal 2008). Moreover, in absolute numbers, the United States still attracts the largest number of globally mobile students to its institutions, even if its rate of growth is modest due to its large base of international students. Galama and Hosek note that competition from other countries does not necessarily signal a threat to the United States as much as it may point to increased educational capacity within the sending country or region. This may allow a growing number of students entering higher education—in developing countries especially—to stay closer to home due to expansion in the local higher education sector/region and the emergence of new host destinations.

Meanwhile, recent events and changes in host country policies governing student mobility may soon lead to a decline (at least temporarily) in international student enrollments in some traditional leading host country destinations. In the United Kingdom, for example, new visa regulations requiring students to establish proof of financial means and submit biometric information, besides other time-consuming procedures, have slowed the process of students gaining entry into the United Kingdom, so much so that some in the higher education sector anticipate up to a 20 percent decline in enrollments, placing a financial strain on the operation of U.K. universities since international students pay much higher fees than U.K. or European Union (EU) students (*The Guardian* 2009).

Even though immigration and visa policies directly impact inflows and outflows, other important push and pull factors involving international students in the local higher education sector also come into play. An important one is the extent to which a country is seen as "welcoming" toward international students. Although an index for a "welcoming" factor has yet to be devised, it would likely take into account the ease with which students can procure a visa, entrance policies both in embassies and at the border, the level of acceptance and integration into community and campus culture, and the safety and security of international students while in the host country, just to name a few. The opportunity to work in the destination country after a period of study would also no doubt register on this welcoming scale.

The issue of how hospitable a country is to its visitors plays an increasingly critical role in the market for attracting international students. Australia, the fifth largest host country, has rapidly drawn significant numbers of students to its institutions, but it has recently had to deal with the backlash from recent isolated events involving attacks against Indian students on and off campuses. Whether these events will signal an overall drop in future Indian student tallies remains to be seen. Still, the media honing in these events can significantly influence public and global perception of the extent to which a country is seen as "welcoming" toward international students. The United States knows this all too well after applications and enrollments from students in the Islamic world (and other top sending countries) declined for a few years following September 11.

U.S. Students Going Abroad: Shifting Course

After a brief overview of the current landscape of international students in the United States, we now turn our attention to their counterparts, the U.S. students abroad—who hardly resemble the international students in the United States. Any form of comparison—in population size, duration of study, academic profile, or even gender—between international students in the United States and U.S. students abroad produces quite a different profile.

The most noteworthy comparison is the size of the two populations: whereas there are over 670,000 international students in the U.S. higher education subsector, outbound mobility by U.S. students represents only a small proportion of total higher education enrollment in the country with about 262,000 U.S. students studying abroad in 2007/2008.[6] United Nations Educational, Scientific and Cultural Organization (UNESCO) calculates an outbound mobility ratio for various regions and countries of the world, and the United States has consistently ranked as the country with the lowest ratio (UIS 2006).[7] Understandably, countries with less capacity and an inadequate higher education infrastructure will send a greater percentage of their students abroad, and the U.S. higher education subsector certainly offers countless options and reasons for U.S. students to pursue their studies in their own country.[8] However, many higher education leaders in the United States feel that the imbalance in flow of students (figure 5.2) especially with respect to the number of U.S. students studying abroad, needs to be rectified and that a greater number of U.S. students would benefit from an education abroad experience, particularly U.S. students who have been historically underrepresented in study abroad such as those from minority groups, community colleges, and most students in the STEM fields.

Despite the relatively small number of U.S. students taking part in study abroad as compared to the number of inbound international students (and certainly against the backdrop of total U.S. higher education enrollment), growth in study abroad participation in recent years has been strong, averaging about 8 percent per year for the past several years (figure 5.3). Over the past decade, U.S. student participation in study abroad has increased by 130 percent. Despite a low participation rate nationally, the 262,000 students who did participate in study abroad in 2007/2008 comprised the largest population ever to do so, and among undergraduates at BA-granting institutions specifically, 10 percent of this cohort studied abroad.

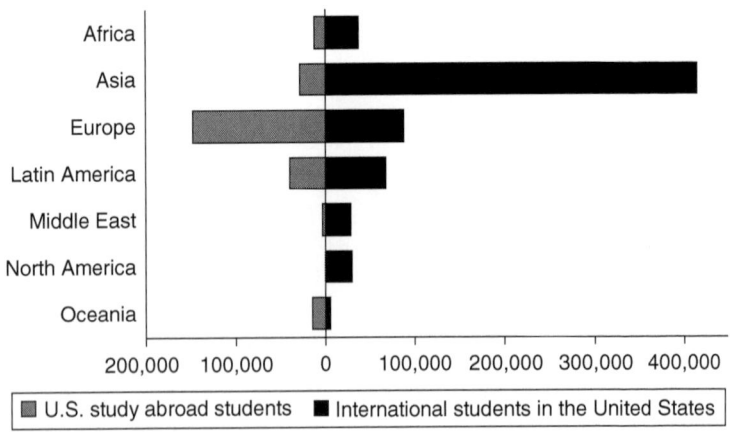

Figure 5.2   U.S. International Exchange Balance, 2007/2008.
Source: IIE (2009).

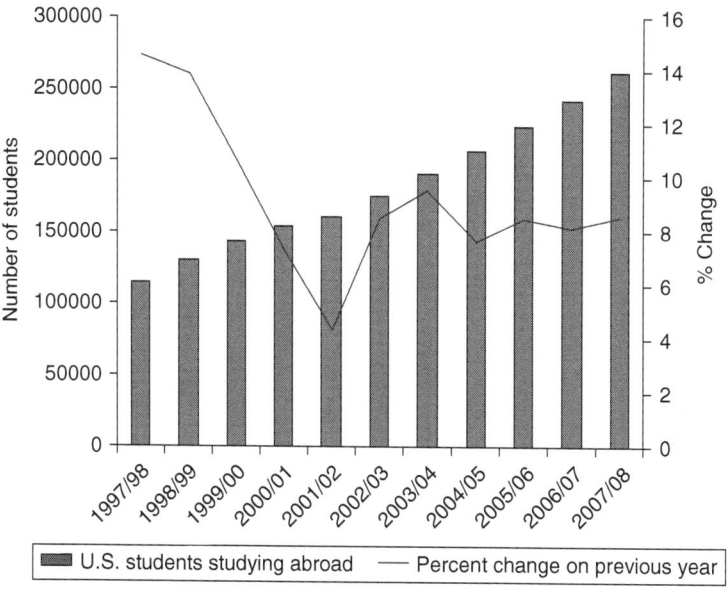

Figure 5.3   U.S. Study Abroad Students, 1997/1998 to 2007/2008.

Source: IIE, *Open Doors: Report on International Educational Exchange*, 1997/1998 to 2007/2008.

It is important to note that the annual rate of growth in U.S. study abroad, which saw double-digit increases in the late 1990s, dropped in 2001/2002 due to the SARS epidemic and rose again in 2002/2003—it has, since then, leveled off and remained fairly consistent at about 8 percent (figure 5.3). The rate has not fluctuated as sharply as it has for international students in the United States over the past two decades. In addition to recent positive growth rates, there is a strong push in the U.S. international education subsector to increase the capacity of U.S. institutions not only to send a greater number of students abroad but also to expand the diversity of the students' profile and their destinations. This goal has been accompanied by an increase in policy research, national debate, advocacy efforts, and legislative initiatives, all of which aim to increase opportunities for U.S. students to participate in study abroad. These efforts constitute a response to what can be described as the historical status quo of study abroad—the mostly unchanged profile of the typical U.S. study abroad student who continues to be a Caucasian female from the social sciences and humanities backgrounds. It is well known and documented that this profile has hardly changed over the past two decades (Obst et al. 2007).

Although U.S. institutions may not be on track to reach the initial goal put forth in 2005 by the Lincoln Commission of sending 1 million students abroad by 2017—roughly four times the current number—many institutions are launching strategic initiatives to expand opportunities for their students.

Besides increasing the overall numbers, there is also a strong push to expand participation in nontraditional destinations—which, in a U.S. context, generally implies countries outside of Western Europe. These include places as diverse and globally dispersed as China, Argentina, South Africa, Ecuador, and India, all of which factored into the top 20 destinations for U.S. students in 2009 and which showed double-digit percentage increases in terms of student participation over the previous year.

In terms of field of study, the majority of U.S. students who study abroad come from either the social sciences (22 percent), business and management (20 percent), or the humanities (13 percent). Study abroad participants pursuing their degrees in the STEM fields account for only 16 percent of the population, which is in stark contrast to the 41 percent of international students in the STEM fields in the United States. By academic level, participation in study abroad occurs mostly at the undergraduate level—again counter to the trend of higher rates of foreign graduate students studying in the United States (though it is important to note that graduate-level participation and other forms of education abroad, including internships and service learning, is not fully captured in *Open Doors*, as only academic credit-bearing study is counted). In general, U.S. students in the STEM fields face similar challenges as all other students related to financing an education abroad experience, but their specific degree and course sequencing requirements often present an additional constraint to participating in an education experience abroad.

Another key factor that distinguishes international students in the United States and U.S. students abroad has to do with duration of study. U.S. students tend to participate for shorter durations through programs that do not lead to a full degree from a foreign institution. In recent years, programs defined as "short-term"—those lasting eight weeks or less—have become increasingly popular for U.S. students. In 2008, 11 percent of those who studied abroad for academic credit chose to do so as part of a program that lasted eight weeks or less during the academic year, a percentage that represents a dramatic increase from just a decade ago when it was close to just 4 percent. It has been noted that although not ideal for allowing a prolonged cultural immersion experience—a primary goal acknowledged by many in the study abroad community in the United States—these short-term programs can provide opportunities for a wider array of students who normally would not be able to participate (Gutierrez et al. 2008).

With the increase in participation in short-term programs, participation in long-term programs, such as the traditional academic year abroad, has waned. About 4 percent of students participated in academic year-long programs in 2007/2008, compared to the 10 percent who did so ten years ago. Interestingly, semester-long study had historically been the most popular mode up until 2006, when a greater proportion of students participated in summer term programs (39 percent) than those who participated in a semester-long program (36 percent).

This may signal an interesting trend: as U.S. institutions continue to offer new programs in nontraditional destinations around the world, the United States may continue to see an increase in participation in shorter-term programs. It is difficult to predict, however, whether these short-term programs, which in many cases can be exploratory programs led by individual faculty members, will eventually expand into longer-term programs. In addition to institutions offering more program choice with respect to duration and destination, the growing number of third-party providers will further increase the capacity of U.S. institutions to provide more opportunities for students (Whalen 2008). The Forum on Education Abroad's recent work in this area to document standards for programs of varying lengths has helped guide many institutions and providers in developing and offering quality programs.

Drivers of Mobility Into and Out of the United States

There are a number of push and pull factors that contribute to mobility into and out of the United States, some of which have already been briefly discussed; the others will be explored in greater detail in this section.

The U.S. Higher Education Subsector: Large and Diverse

The diversity and size of the U.S. higher education system without a doubt plays a significant role in attracting international students and scholars to the United States. Indeed, the large imbalance between the inflow of international students into the United States and the outflow of U.S. students to other countries—a ratio of approximately 2.6 to 1—is not as much a reflection on a generalized U.S. student lack of interest in other parts of the world but points more to the ability and sizable capacity of the U.S. higher education subsector to draw much larger numbers of students to its institutions. The dominance of the United States in terms of its higher education capacity has been cited in a recent report as the key factor contributing to the United States' leading position (Becker et al. 2009).

At the same time, key sending countries that send many of their students to the United States are facing challenges related to the capacity of their higher education systems.

India, for example, which sends the largest group of students and the second largest group of scholars to the United States, has a significant higher education capacity shortage with its college-educated population accounting for only about 11–12 percent of the college-age population. This has been highlighted in news reports that have noted India's willingness and efforts to internationalize after India's minister of human resources development recently announced plans to open up India's higher education subsector to foreign institutions (Anand and Hechinger 2009). If U.S. institutions in particular take up this opportunity to establish a U.S. presence (presumably either through branch campuses or by forming collaborative partnerships with Indian institutions), this might help address India's current challenge of supply not meeting demand among its tertiary age population.

The reputation and prestige of an institution holds considerable weight in a student's decision to leave her home country and pursue study in the United States. The United States has a significant share of some of the world's top universities and colleges, according to international rankings systems such as those developed by Shanghai Jiao Tong University and the *Times Higher Education*.[9] The proliferation of these world rankings and the frequently updated (and debated) methodologies to improve upon such measurements have in some ways further impelled institutions to race toward becoming a "world-class university" (Salmi 2009). Indeed, many U.S. institutions rely on these types of ranking systems, specifically the *U.S. News and World Report*, as they serve as a marketing tool in addition to being a resource that allows institutions to benchmark themselves against one another. Despite the limitations of rankings and even classifications, which in many ways also can assume a certain level of bias,[10] these resources provide students overseas who are looking toward the United States with a greater understanding of the types of institutions available and the relative advantages of each.

Often receiving high marks in various ranking indices, certain fields of study at U.S. institutions, particularly the sciences and business and management fields, remain popular among international students. The natural sciences in the United States receive significant funding from national agencies such as the National Institutes of Health and the NSF and the result of this support can be seen in some of the most well-equipped and state-of-the-art U.S. laboratories and research facilities in the world. The opportunities to engage in cutting-edge research in science and technology fields present a further incentive for international students and scholars.

Business and management as a field also attracts large numbers of students from other countries. Information communication technologies have served as an innovation that has helped expand and drive global business, and students are well attuned to industry's demand for language and intercultural skills that can be obtained in the United States. Within the business and management fields especially, students learning a U.S. model of business also increases the likelihood of continued business ties to the United States and expansion of U.S.-style models of business (de Wit 2008). In the short-term and in the wake of a global economic downturn with origins in the United States, adoption of westernized modes of business may not be altogether ideal, as critics may likely point out. After all, the effects of the downturn were exacerbated by practices carried out by business leaders trained in the United States. However, it can be said that the site of a crash tends to provide the most clues, and U.S. business schools would do well to strategically rethink how global business will act in a recovery by incorporating in the classroom the lessons learned from the missteps of Wall Street.

Business and management as a field of study remains popular, and unsurprisingly, intensive English language course offerings are other options that remain highly attractive to international students in the United States. IIE's *Open Doors* project includes a separate survey of institutions in this specific area; it reports that in 2008 participation was up by more than 20 percent with approximately 54,500 students enrolled in intensive English language programs. As Asian countries (in particular East and Southeast Asian countries) continue to send increasing numbers of students abroad while at the same time serving as a growing hub for intraregional student mobility, the top host countries will likely continue to see increased enrollments both in higher education and in English language courses. Australia alone attracts over 115,000 students into its English Language Intensive Courses for Overseas Students (ELICOS) programs, many of whom come from the surrounding North and South Pacific region.

Gaining relevant work experience through Optional Practical Training presents another incentive for a greater number of international students to come to the United States. Sanctioned by the U.S. government, the OPT program allows an international student to work in the United States for up to 12 months in a job related to the academic program. Beginning in 2008, this time limit was extended to 29 months for eligible foreign students graduating from the STEM fields, highlighting the growing recognition of the value of these students' continued support to the U.S. economy, research, and academia.

Other top destinations such as Canada and Australia have also made significant strides in opening up the labor market to foreign talent with increasingly flexible national immigration policies and incentives that allow foreign students and workers into the country. Such policies in the United States, although deemed critical for keeping the United States at the forefront of research and innovation, tend to come up against greater challenges related to broader national immigration reform. However, the government, which has increased efforts to streamline international student and scholar entry into the United States, has been further pushed into action by more recent vocal support for reform from industry along with academia and the nonprofit sector (U.S. Congress 2008).

Economic Drivers

Closely linked to higher education capacity is the issue of economic drivers of mobility. In major sending countries such as China, India, South Korea, and more recently Vietnam, the emergence of a middle class has helped drive up the number of globally mobile international students attending U.S. institutions. In the short-term, there do not seem to be signs of these top sending countries seeing reduction in their capacity to send students to the United States, especially as families become more financially capable of sending their children abroad for higher education pursuits. Students coming from Vietnam, especially, have ranked the United States as their most preferred destination of choice well ahead of Australia and the United Kingdom, citing high favorable perceptions of the U.S. higher education subsector and the United States as a destination country in general (Chow 2009).

Other current economic drivers, including the global economic downturn, have at least in the short term not had a substantial impact on mobility into the United States and some countries continue to report growth in the number of students they are sending abroad. A stronger currency in China, for example, has potentially made it more affordable for more Chinese students to study abroad, thus a greater number of Chinese undergraduates may be pursuing their degrees abroad over the next few years, representing a departure from historical trends in Chinese graduate student outflow (Toh 2009).

Certainly, each country faces its own challenges in responding to the global economic crisis. Despite signs of the recession coming to an end, recovery will certainly take longer, as the United States for at least the next decade will still need to address and alleviate the negative effects of the recession and its taking on of more debt.[11] Moreover, the immediate outcomes of the crisis—the collapse of the financial sector, historically high level of unemployment, falling home prices, decreasing purchasing power of wages, and looming inflation—will certainly have some impact on higher education in the near future.

In light of these economic challenges, it remains to be seen whether the record-high number of U.S. students participating in study abroad and the positive rates of growth seen in recent years will continue to increase. Even though the U.S. higher education subsector is financed from a variety of sources, including the federal government, state and local governments, private organizations and institutions, and through charitable giving, the ability of families to pay has an impact not only on study abroad participation but, to a broader extent, also on enrollment patterns in higher education.[12] Even with these external forms of support, the high costs of pursuing higher education trickle down directly to families and students, as it has been noted that over the past decade tuition and fees have accounted for an increasing share of general revenues in both public and private institutions (Wellman et al. 2008). According to faculty and staff on U.S. campuses, rising cost remains the number one constraint limiting the number of students who participate in study abroad (Gutierrez et al. 2009). From the U.S. perspective of mobility, more funding opportunities for study abroad would reduce the financial burden associated with an international study experience for students.

U.S. Institutional Impetus toward Internationalization

Much of the country's ability to successfully attract and recruit students depends on the resources available to its institutions and the activities that are carried out at the institutional level. These efforts to attract international students have contributed largely to the rebound in the overall numbers. Despite modest changes in internationalization efforts between 2001 and 2006, an American Council on Education study found that most U.S. institutions are increasing their recruitment and support of international students, with approximately two-thirds of all institutions providing specific levels of funding for international student recruitment or admissions (Green et al. 2008).

At the same time, U.S. institutional efforts to create "global-minded" citizens, which in part has to do with students acquiring particular knowledge, skills sets, and experiences from studying and living in a different culture than one's own, are apparent at many levels of academia, from the redefining of institutional missions to the revision of core curricular and language requirements.[13] For a number of U.S. institutions, these efforts signal closer alignment with the internationalization objectives and goals that were once seen as relevant only to an international or study abroad office.

As globalization continues to drive U.S. institutions toward becoming more "global" in scope, the number of students participating in study abroad will likely continue to increase. However, there remain barriers to participation, largely related to external (non-U.S.) capacity issues, including the issue of the quality of providers and programs abroad, the physical capacity of overseas institutions to absorb a greater number of U.S. students, and perceptions of safety and security abroad. These and other areas also can limit the extent to which U.S. institutions will work with other institutions overseas in creating partnerships and establishing programs to increase outbound mobility from the United States.

Still, the availability of instruction in the English language in a growing number of institutions outside the United States will encourage more U.S. students to study abroad, and for longer durations up to full-degree study periods overseas. Within a U.S.-European context, for example, an increase in joint and dual degrees between the United States and Europe, accompanied by progress toward standards and policies articulated by the Bologna Process, has also allowed English to become the lingua franca for many degree programs at many European institutions, as these institutions are now offering full graduate-level courses and degree programs taught in English. However, language of instruction is not the only determinant of where students from the United States study. In many cases, most of these unique and innovative degree programs are moving toward English as the primary mode of instruction in order to appeal to all international students to enroll in their institutions.

Support from U.S. Government

Various forms of federal government support act as a key driver of student mobility in and out of the country and help advance foreign diplomacy through higher education. Initiatives that the government invests in include scholarship and fellowship programs such as the Fulbright Program, the national flagship international exchange initiative that aims to increase mutual understanding among nations through educational and cultural exchange. As a vehicle for national leadership development, the Fulbright Program includes initiatives benefiting students, scholars, and young professionals in a range of academic and professional fields, including the arts.

Other examples of government-supported activities include the Gilman International Scholarship and Boren Scholarship and Language Flagship Programs, the operation of EducationUSA offices and its global network of advisers, and training of U.S. visa consulate officers to streamline student visa applications, all of which may suggest that the country is moving toward a broader international education policy (Obst 2007). Despite programs such as these, there is no centralized national body that is charged with coordinating these separate initiatives—the U.S. Departments of State and Education both have international education on their agenda but work largely on separate issues both domestically and internationally. Adopting and applying a coordinated national policy for all higher education institutions would need to be reconciled with the large and complex nature of the U.S. higher education system itself, one that remains decentralized across national, state, and local levels, with a wide array of private and public institutions each having an equal stake in the international student sector (de Wit 2008).

Although the United States may not have a single coordinated national policy, the current system has provided U.S. institutions with autonomy to set their own internationalization agendas and policies, even though a more coordinated national approach has the potential to bring about other benefits as well. Australia, the United Kingdom, and Canada are three large host countries that have made significant strides over the past decade in shaping policies that have helped attract students by way of large-scale government programs, including support for scholarships and incentives to retain highly skilled students in the workforce.

The motivations for the U.S. government to continue creating paths for international students and scholars largely reflect the same historical motives that supported educational exchange when these initiatives were first put in place: to promote public diplomacy between U.S. and international students and for development and capacity-building goals (U.S. GAO 2009). A U.S. taskforce on immigration noted in a recent report by the Council on Foreign Relations that there is an ongoing need for further reducing the complexities and restrictions caused by quotas and delays in processing in the U.S. student visa program, which "has been an enormously important channel for attracting young, highly skilled individuals who often end up living permanently in the United States" (Council on Foreign Relations 2009). Since September 11, 2001, the U.S. Department of State has made laudable improvements in this area and continues to prioritize the streamlining of the visa process to ensure that students are able to continue pursuing their education in the United States.

The Impact of Scholars on Mobility

Forces such as government policies, economic factors, and institutional activities drive mobility, but the dynamics are also influenced by key actors and individuals. At the institutional level, U.S. scholars stand apart; it has been noted that those who participate in international experiences themselves—including academic sabbaticals abroad, Fulbright fellowship programs, or other programs—not only enhance their own academic careers and knowledge but also contribute to broader internationalization efforts at the home campus. Research has shown that the impact is significant on institutions opening up programs and creating new pathways for students after a faculty member has initiated a program or relationship with a foreign institution (O'Hara 2009). Many Fulbright scholars, for example, play an important role in facilitating institutional partnerships between their home institution in the United States and institutions overseas at which they either conducted research or taught courses. O'Hara further highlights the significant multiplier effect in these scenarios and how a scholar's participation abroad has the potential to create opportunities for U.S. students participating in study abroad in the long term.

The positive impact of scholar mobility is felt in both directions: the strong presence of international scholars in the United States has had a significant influence on the institutions where they teach and conduct research. *Open Doors* reports that the number of international scholars in the country increased by 61 percent in the past decade alone and the total currently stands at over 113,000 scholars.[14] Similar to international students, a large majority of these scholars (71 percent) predominantly take up their post in the STEM disciplines at U.S. institutions. In 2008, those in the biological and medical sciences accounted for 23 percent, while 18 percent were in the health sciences. Spread across various STEM fields, most of these scholars (71 percent) were primarily conducting research and only 12 percent were solely involved in teaching.

The drivers of mobility that attract international students are equally, if not more, applicable to international scholars and post-doc students. The reputation of the sciences and engineering fields at U.S. institutions and the opportunity to conduct research at some of the world's top laboratories and institutes position the United States as a major draw for international scholars and researchers. China, India, South Korea, Japan, and Germany constituted the top five senders of international scholars in 2009. The research networks established between international scholars in the United States and their counterparts in these home countries have increasingly allowed for collaborative research leading to discovery and innovation.

Although there are limited data on the stay rates for international scholars (and students), the international scholar presence at U.S. institutions and in some of the country's top STEM industries is evident; as the NSF Science and Engineering Indicators would suggest, between 2002 and 2005, more than 90 percent of science and engineering doctoral students from China and 88 percent of those from India had plans to stay in the

United States, while 60 and 63 percent, respectively, reported accepting firm offers of employment or research (NSF 2008).

Implications of Mobility: Concluding Issues

Historically, student and scholar mobility into and out of the United States has provided significant advantages not only for the higher education subsector, as it is positioned as a major player in internationalization at the institutional level, but also for industry, research and development, science, and innovation. The trends across U.S. borders will likely see increased mobility in new forms as well, including the proliferation of distance learning, a growing number of joint and dual/double degrees offered between U.S. and overseas institutions, and branch campuses, all of which present new challenges for understanding who is defined as "international" when physical borders and location of educational delivery become less defining factors. These more recent developments present new opportunities for students and scholars to exchange and move in ways that will require those in the field to continuously rethink how mobility is defined and how flows are documented, although they will also require ramped-up efforts to measure and hold accountable the rapidly growing international education field and industry.

Another developing issue that will still require attention with regard to U.S. mobility includes how higher education is increasingly viewed as a commodity, as there are few signs that international trade will abate worldwide (Altbach 2002). Where the United States stands to gain is based more on its recognition of the talent and skills international students provide and less on the revenue through tuition and fees they pay, which tends to be more important for other leading host countries where the differential income from international and home country students is wider. Even so, the economic impact of international students' presence on the U.S. economy—estimated around US$18 billion—is drawing more focus to the value of these students who typically pay the highest tuition rates.

A more formidable challenge for the international education community will be working with multiple stakeholders across the public and private sectors to create improved opportunities and access for students who wish to pursue their higher education in another country. A better understanding of mobility flows and the factors behind these trends will help, and certain initiatives at regional and global levels, such as the EURODATA (www.aca-secretariat.be/index.php?id=417) and Atlas projects (www.atlas. iienetwork.org), have made progress in reporting on comparable data and mobility patterns across countries.

The recent UNESCO world conference on higher education made the following point on the importance of mobility for the global higher education subsector:

> Institutions of higher education worldwide have a social responsibility to help bridge the development gap by increasing the transfer of knowledge across borders, especially towards developing countries, and working to find common solutions to foster brain circulation and alleviate the negative impact of brain drain... Partnerships for research and staff and student exchanges promote international cooperation. The encouragement of more broadly based and balanced academic mobility should be integrated into mechanisms. (UNESCO World Conference 2009 Communiqué, 5)

The United States will continue to increase its public and private sector support for the exchange of students and scholars as there is significant capacity for enhancing this type of mobility. This will also require the nation to strive toward continued openness to mobility and immigration, and to welcome the skills and talent that advance science, innovation, and learning. Progress in our society has been built upon such openness, and the country's position as a world leader in higher education and industry will continue to depend on it. The positive effects of mobility, moreover, pay dividends over a lifetime; fully one-third of all Nobel Prizes in science and medicine awarded to U.S. students were won by persons who started their lives and careers as citizens of another country.

The vision is as old as America itself. Reflecting on the budding identity of his young country in the 1780s, the essayist Hector St. John de Crèvecoeur in his *Letters from an American Farmer* described what he saw as the new American: one "who acts on new principles" and who "must therefore entertain new ideas and form new opinions." Then as now, new ideas come from different places and are strengthened by global perspectives. This essay was written at a time when the decennial census was being taken, a census that reminds us of how much migration continues to shape the country. Whether mobility is driven by negative or positive forces, from persecution and threat to economic advancement and education, it will continue to have a substantial impact on U.S. national policies and the way its citizens encounter and shape the world we share.

NOTES

1. Unless otherwise noted, figures for inbound and outbound student and scholar mobility for the United States are attributed in this chapter to Rajika Bhandari and Patricia Chow's (2009) *Open Doors: Report on International Educational*

Exchange. Open Doors is supported by the U.S. Department of State's Bureau of Educational and Cultural Affairs.

2. An international student according to *Open Doors* is defined as an individual who is enrolled for courses at an accredited higher education institution in the United States on a temporary visa, and who is not an immigrant, a citizen, an undocumented immigrant, or refugee.

3. The vast size of the U.S. higher education subsector, with some 4,000 institutions of higher learning and 18 million students enrolled, contributes to the relatively low ratio of international enrollment to total higher education enrollment as compared to other leading destinations. For a comparative view across various leading host countries, see *Open Doors 2009*, p. 46.

4. The 8.3 percent calculation is slightly inflated since OPT students are not counted in the overall higher education population enrollment, whereas they are counted among international students, according to *Open Doors*.

5. A more historical example of a surge from the Middle East came in the mid-1970s, when Iran was the leading sending country to U.S. institutions for nine consecutive years between 1975 and 1983. It is not surprising that the influx of Iranian students into the United States coincided with the mass exodus of middle-class and educated families from Iran in the years surrounding the country's revolution in 1979.

6. According to *Open Doors*, a student who participates in a study abroad experience is counted if academic credit is awarded by the U.S. home institution. Thus, the total number of U.S. students who participate in other forms of study abroad (including participation in full degree study, non-credit-bearing courses, experiential and service learning and internships) is likely far greater.

7. It is important to keep in mind that the outbound mobility ratio calculated by UNESCO likely underestimates the number of U.S. students abroad who earn academic credit for all durations of study.

8. On the opposite end of the spectrum, outbound mobility rates in Sub-Saharan countries in Africa are some of the highest in the world.

9. *The Times Higher Education* World Ranking reports that the United States had more than a quarter of the top-ranked institutions among the top 200 in the world, according to their ranking system. For more information, see http://www.topuniversities.com.

10. For an insightful description of how classification systems, generally thought to be more objective measurements than rankings, can be examined under the same lens of scrutiny as rankings, see Alexander McCormick (2008).

11. With the implementation of the fiscal stimulus, the country's predicted deficit for next year will be US$1.8 trillion, though it is expected to decrease to US$1.2 trillion in ten years, while federal debt will grow to US$11.7 trillion, according to the Congressional Budget Office (*The Economist* 2009).

12. However, this does not take into account the potential increases in enrollment in certificate programs, master's and professional programs, and graduate school that usually accompany a low unemployment market in the United States.

13. There is now a host of literature on defining and assessing "global citizenship" in a U.S. context. For a thorough and recent discussion on the topic, see "Understanding the Challenges of Assessing Global Citizenship" (Deardorff 2009).

14. The total number of international scholars in the United States reflects only those reported to *Open Doors* by U.S. higher education institutions and does not include international scholars based in industry, at non-profit organizations, at other types of educational institutions or in the national and federally funded research laboratories.

BIBLIOGRAPHY

Altbach, Philip G. 2002. "Knowledge and Education as International Commodities: The Collapse of the Common Good." *International Higher Education* 28 (Summer): 2–5.

Anand, Geeta, and John Hechinger. 2009. "Indian Minister Seeks to Ease Limits on Foreign Schools." *The Wall Street Journal*, June 11, A6.

Atlas of Student Mobility. 2009. *Global Destinations for International Students at the Post-Secondary (Tertiary) Level, 2001 and 2008*. New York: Institute of International Education (IIE). Available online at: http://www.atlas.iienetwork.org.

Australian Education International. 2009. *International Student Enrollments in Higher Education in 2008*. Canberra: Australian Education International. Available online at: http://www.aei.gov.au.

Becker, Rosa. 2009. *U.K. Universities and Europe: Competition and Internationalisation*. London, U.K.: U.K. Higher Education International Unit and the U.K. Higher Education Europe Unit.

Bhandari, Rajika, and Patricia Chow. 2009. *Open Doors: Report on International Educational Exchange*. New York: IIE.

Bhandari, Rajika, and Peggy Blumenthal. 2008. "Global Student Mobility: Moving towards Brain Exchange." In *The Europa World of Learning 2008, Volume 1*, ed. Anthony Gladman. London: Routledge.

Chow, Patricia. 2009. Attitudes and Perceptions of Prospective International Students from Vietnam: An IIE Briefing Paper. New York: IIE.

Council on Foreign Relations. 2009. *Task Force Report No. 63: U.S. Immigration Policy*. New York: Council on Foreign Relations Press.

Deardorff, Darla. 2009. "Understanding the Challenges of Assessing Global Citizenship." In *The Handbook of Practice and Research in Study Abroad: Higher Education and the Quest for Global Citizenship*, ed. Ross Lewin. New York: Routledge.

de Wit, Hans, and Laura E. Rumbley. 2008. "The Role of American Higher Education." In *The Dynamics of International Student Circulation in a Global Context*, ed. Hans de Wit, Pawan Agarwal, Mohsen Elmahdy Said, Molatlhegi T. Sehoole, and Muhammad Sirozi. Rotterdam: Sense Publishers.

The Economist. 2009. "Falls the Shadow." *The Economist*, July 25, 25–26.

Galama, Titus, and James Hosek. 2008. *U.S. Competitiveness in Science and Technology.* Santa Monica, CA: RAND Corporation.

Green, Madeleine. F., Dao Luu, and Beth Burris. 2008. *Mapping Internationalization on U.S. Campuses: 2008 Edition.* Washington, DC: American Council on Education.

The Guardian. 2009. "International Students May Spurn U.K. Because of New Visa Rules." *The Guardian* (online), September 1. Available online at: http://www.guardian.co.uk.

Gutierrez, Robert, Rajika Bhandari, and Daniel Obst. 2008. Meeting America's Global Education Challenge: Exploring Host Country Capacity for Increasing U.S. Study Abroad. New York: IIE.

McCormick, Alexander. 2008. The Complex Interplay Between Classification and Ranking of Colleges and Universities: Should the Berlin Principles Apply Equally to Classification. In *Higher Education in Europe: University Rankings: Seeking Prestige, Raising Visibility, and Embedding Quality* 33 (2/3), ed. Melanie Seto, and Peter Wells. Abingdon, U.K.: Routledge Taylor and Francis Group.

National Science Foundation. 2008. *Science and Engineering Indicators—2008.* Arlington, VA: National Science Foundation. Available online at: www.nsf.gov.

Organisation of Economic Co-operation and Development (OECD). 2009. *Education at a Glance 2009: OECD Indicators.* Paris: OECD.

Obst, Daniel. 2007. "National Policies for International Education." *IIENetworker* (Fall): 23.

Obst, Daniel, Rajika Bhandari, and Sharon Witherell. 2007. Meeting America's Global Education Challenge: Current Trends in U.S. Study Abroad & The Impact of Strategic Diversity Initiatives. New York: IIE.

O'Hara, Sabine. 2009. Internationalizing the Academy: The Impact of Scholar Mobility. In *Higher Education on the Move: New Developments in Global Mobility,* ed. Rajika Bhandari, and Shepherd Laughlin. New York: IIE.

Salmi, Jamil. 2009. "The Emergence of Rankings of Higher Education Systems." Paper presented at the IREG-4 Annual Conference, Astana, Kazakhstan, June 15, 2009.

Toh, Elgin. 2009. "College Abroad Becoming a Bargain." *China Daily.* July 13.

UNESCO. 2009. UNESCO World Conference on Higher Education: The New Dynamics of Higher Education and Research For Societal Change and Development. Communiqué. Paris: UNESCO.

UNESCO Institute for Statistics. 2006. Global Education Digest 2006: Comparing Education Statistics across the World. Montreal: UNESCO Institute for Statistics.

UNESCO Institute for Statistics. 2009. Global Education Digest 2009: Comparing Education Statistics across the World. Montreal: UNESCO Institute for Statistics.

U.S. Congress. 2008. "Written Testimony of William H. Gates." Hearing of the Committee on Science and Technology. Washington, DC: United States House of Representatives. Available online at: http://democrats.science.house.gov.

U.S. Government Accountability Office (GAO). 2008. "Higher Education: United States' and Other Countries' Strategies for Attracting and Funding International Students." GAO-08–878T. Washington, DC: US GAO.

US GAO. 2009. "Higher Education: Approaches to Attract and Fund International Students in the United States and Abroad." GAO-09-379. Washington, DC: US GAO.

Jane Wellman V., Donna M. Desrochers, and Colleen M. Lenihan. 2008. *The Growing Imbalance: Recent Trends in U.S. Postsecondary Education Finance*. Delta Project on Postsecondary Education Costs, Productivity and Accountability. Available at: http://www.deltacostproject.org/resources/pdf/imbalance20080423.pdf.

Wendler, Cathy, Brent Bridgeman, Fred Cline, Catherine Millett, JoAnn Rock, Nathan Bell, and Patricia McAllister. (2010). *The Path Forward: The Future of Graduate Education in the United States*. Princeton, NJ: Educational Testing Service.

Whalen, Brian. 2009. "Assessment and Improvement: Expanding Education Abroad Capacity and Enhancing Quality Through Standards of Good Practice." In *Meeting America's Global Education Challenge: Expanding Study Abroad Capacity at U.S. Colleges and Universities*. New York: IIE.

Chapter 6

International Education in Australia: From Aid to Trade to Internationalization

Tony Adams, Melissa Banks, and Alan Olsen

International Education Background

Australia's Education Minister and Deputy Prime Minister Julia Gillard opened the Australian Education International Industry Forum in 2008 with remarks on the contribution that international education makes to Australia's education system and national prosperity, and to cross-cultural understanding and international relationships, and commented on related trade pay offs and skilled migration benefits. She stated that its significance is much broader than economics and, reflecting the intrinsic nature of education itself, contributes to diplomacy and cross-cultural understanding and produces global citizens who can contribute to global understanding as well as to economic and cultural development. She also noted the importance and benefits that flowed to Australian students through experiences overseas. This chapter explores the development of international education in Australia, its history, the major forces of aid and export that influenced it, and its growth and importance in Australia today.

The History of International Education in Australia

Sixty years ago, there was no concept of international education in Australia's universities. According to Back, Davis, and Olsen (1996), internationalization was largely an outward flow with higher degree study and study leave by Australian scholars undertaken in the United Kingdom, the United States, or Canada, with very little reciprocity. The need stemmed from Australia's geographical remoteness from centers of learning in Europe and North America and the recognition that its academic work must meet international standards.

Phase 1: Bilateral Aid

It was through the establishment of the Colombo Plan for Cooperative Development in South and Southeast Asia in 1951 that many Australian institutions commenced the processes of internationalization (Cuthbert et al. 2008). In 2005, Australia's then minister for foreign affairs, Alexander Downer, captured the spirit of Australia's participation in the Colombo Plan. He described its prominence in the development of Australia's relationship with Asia, its influence on the Australian community that had to that time little contact with its near neighbors, and how it established the notion of international students in Australian universities.

The Colombo Plan marked the formal entry of the Australian government into direct sponsorship of overseas students for study in Australia, with universities hosting increasing numbers of students, both sponsored and private, the latter being admitted to the universities on the same fee conditions and entry requirements as Australian students (Back et al. 1996).

An important change was made in 1979 with the introduction by the Australian government of a "visa fee" for private overseas students, later called the Overseas Student Charge (OSC). This represented about 10 percent of the national full cost of a university place (from 1982 the level of the OSC was increased annually reaching a peak of 55 percent of the cost of a place by 1988), and thus the private students were "subsidized" by the Australian government and the education of private overseas students was a component of Australia's aid program.

Phase 2: From Aid to Trade

The next major shift in policy followed the release in 1984 of the reports of two substantial reviews—the Committee to Review the Australian

Overseas Aid Program (Jackson) and the Committee of Review of Private Overseas Student Policy (Goldring). Jackson's view was that education should be regarded as an export industry whereas Goldring rejected the market-based approach to the education of overseas students.

Jackson's view prevailed and in 1985 an Overseas Student Policy was introduced by the Australian government whereby overseas students previously not accommodated within the quota of private students partly subsidized from the aid program could be enrolled, without limits, provided they met entry requirements and paid full costs of their programs. This was followed by the *Policy on Export of Education Services*, to facilitate the recruitment of fee-paying students. A key element in these policies was that institutions could accept an international student only if there was no displacement of an Australian student.

The shift from a philosophy of educational aid to educational trade had commenced: the education of private overseas students had been a component of Australia's aid program, but the move from aid to trade in 1985 ended implicit subsidies of private students previously subsidized from the aid budget for whom Australian aid would not normally have been targeted and enabled more effective targeting of education aid through scholarships in a fee-paying environment.

Australia has continued to provide education as development assistance through targeted scholarships. From 1998, the Australian Development Scholarships (ADS) scheme became the mechanism for Australia's provision of scholarships for individuals from developing countries (Australian government 2005). With approximately 1,000 students receiving awards each year, there were 2,500 ADS enrollments per year from 34 countries.

In April 2006 Australia announced a doubling of the number of scholarships for the Asia Pacific region, reviving the spirit of the Colombo Plan. A new program, Australian Scholarships, provides nearly US$1 billion in funding over five years for more than 19,000 scholarships.

The government argued that scholarships have a proven record in promoting political and economic reform and enabling regional leaders to develop enduring connections with Australia. The initiative demonstrated the high value placed on building relationships with countries within the region and also enhanced Australia's reputation as a provider of high-quality education for international students (Downer and Bishop 2006).

Current Inbound Mobility in Australia

From the mid-1980s, consistent with the shift from the aid phase to the trade phase, Australian universities actively recruited international students, with income as a key driver. Numbers onshore grew from 21,000 in 1989 to 83,111 in 1999. Numbers of international students in Australia's universities onshore grew a further 95 percent between 1999 and 2004, or 15 percent per year. In comparison the growth in global student mobility was 43 percent over the same period, from 1.75 million students to 2.5 million (UNESCO 2006). During this period, Australia was increasing its global market share as well as benefiting from the growth in the total stock of globally mobile students.

In 2008, 543,900 international students studied in Australia, up from 455,000 in 2007 (AEI 2008c), across all education sectors from schools and English language learning to vocational education and training (VET) and higher education. English Australia (2008), representing English language colleges, estimates that an additional 50,000 students were enrolled in ELICOS (English Language Intensive Courses for Overseas Students) programs on tourist and working holiday visas, while Australian Education International (AEI) estimates another 100,000 students were studying offshore in transnational education (AEI 2008d). Table 6.1 shows the 2008 percentages of international students by sector. Australia is a key destination for students from Asia, all top ten source markets being Asian.

The distribution of international students by level of study in Australia's higher education system has been shifting from a largely undergraduate

Table 6.1 International Students by Sector, 2008

International Students	Percentage
Australia's international students studying onshore on student visas were enrolled in higher education	33.6
Vocational Education and Training (VET) programs	32.3
English Language Intensive Courses for Overseas Students (ELICOS)	23.1
Schools	5.3
Enrolled in non-award programs including foundation programs for university study and study abroad and exchange programs	5.7
International higher education students from Asia	83.6
International higher education students from China	28.2
International higher education students from India	15.2
International higher education students from Malaysia	8.6
International higher education students from Hong Kong	4.7
International higher education students from Singapore	4.1

Source: AEI (2008c).

student population to one where half the commencing students in 2008 were undergraduates and half were postgraduates, with the greatest growth occurring in master's and doctorate programs.

By broad field of study 44.5 percent of Australia's international students enrolled in higher education in 2008 studied business administration and management, 9.6 percent Computer Science and Information Systems, 8.2 percent Engineering and Surveying, and 6.5 percent Arts, Humanities, and Social Science. The fastest growth disciplines included Education, Health and Community Services, Nursing, and Language Studies.

According to the Department of Education, Employment and Workplace Relations (DEEWR 2008), in 2006 19.1 percent of all students studying onshore in Australia's universities were international students. This is in line with the proportion of overseas students in the Australian community. According to the 2006 Australian census, 22.2 percent of Australian residents were born overseas and 21.5 percent spoke a language other than English at home (Australian Bureau of Statistics 2006).

In June 2009, AEI's most recent market update (AEI 2009) reported continued growth across all sectors in first semester 2009 with numbers up 19.6 percent from a year earlier. Higher education enrollments grew from 147,150 to 166,566 (11.6 percent), while commencements increased 16 percent indicating little impact to date of the global financial crisis.

During this period, a number of incidents involving violence against Indian students and the collapse of a small number of private vocational education colleges with significant Indian enrollments caused a great deal of adverse publicity in both Australia and India. Anecdotal reports from universities suggest that Indian enrollments may be down in 2010, but for semester two (July 2009) there has been a 20 percent growth in Indian commencements on the same semester in 2008. Overall growth in higher education international student enrollment is unlikely to be adversely impacted.

Transnational Education

The World Trade Organization provides a typology of four modes of supply of services for exports, described here in terms of education exports (Davis et al. 2000):

- Consumption abroad: the student crosses national borders in order to obtain education; this on-campus mode is the predominant mode for trade in education services.

- Commercial presence: the education institution establishes a commercial presence (such as an offshore campus) either as a standalone entity or as a partnership.
- Cross-border supply: the education institution remains in one territory and the student remains in another territory, receiving education by distance education or online.
- Presence of natural persons: the producer (a teacher on behalf of an education institution) travels to another country to produce and/or deliver the service for the purchaser (the student) in another country.

Australian education providers have used all four modes for supply of education services to other countries, the most significant development being that consumption abroad accounted for 96.8 percent of international student spending on fees, goods, and services (AEI 2008e). The three modes outside Australia were grouped together as transnational education and accounted for 3.2 percent of all international student expenditure in 2006–2007.

Australia's Industry Commission had explored the notion of transnational education as early as 1991.

Exports of education services are most commonly thought of as students coming to Australia to study but they can also include correspondence programs for overseas students, the electronic transmission of lectures and programs overseas, and Australians traveling overseas personally to provide various forms of education. (Industry Commission 1991)

Twinning programs represented the model that typified Australia's early involvement in transnational education. According to McBurnie and Pollock (1998) they are as follows:

- fully taught programs
- following the same syllabus and timetable as the home campus program
- use the same materials, lectures, and examinations as their peers in the home institution
- academic staff are usually locally engaged but selected or approved by the home institution

Within the Australian system, twinning normally means that part of the program is carried out in the host country and part in the provider country; typically this has been important in Malaysia with two years in Malaysia followed by two years in Australia.

Most transnational programs operated by Australian institutions have been partnerships with host country organizations such as professional associations, private providers, and universities. Generally these have been small in scale with attributes similar to those of twinning programs, often with full program completion in the host country and a balance of local and home teaching staff.

More recently there has been a move away from these "small-scale" often unincorporated partnerships to full-campus operations. These include the following:

- RMIT University—Vietnam
- Swinburne University of Technology—East Malaysia
- Curtin University of Technology—East Malaysia, Singapore
- Monash University—Malaysia, South Africa
- James Cook University—Singapore
- University of Wollongong—Dubai

These operations take on the attributes of a full campus in terms of range of services and programs and have an onsite senior academic administrator linked back to the management structure of the home university. Monash has been notable in moving toward transparency of fee levels and mobility of students between its campuses.

Following quality concerns as a result of audits and media reports, education ministers across Australia agreed in 2005 to a Transnational Quality Strategy framework to protect and promote the quality of Australian education delivered transnationally. The strategy focused action in three areas: (1) communication and promotion of Australia's quality arrangements to stakeholders, (2) increased access to data and information about Australia's transnational education, and (3) a strengthened national quality framework (AEI 2008a).

Also, Australia's education minister in April 2008 announced the AusLIST initiative as a quality-control mechanism, an online directory of Australian providers who deliver programs offshore to a standard comparable to those in Australia (Gillard 2008). Through AusLIST, students and potential employers are able to determine the standing of Australian providers and their courses offshore (AEI 2008b).

In 2007, Universities Australia (the peak body of Australian university vice chancellors) surveyed Australian universities on their offshore programs. The number of programs, 307 in 1996, grew to 1,009 in 2001, peaked at 1,569 in 2003, and fell back to 1,002 in 2007 (Universities Australia 2007).

There may have been consolidation in the number of offshore programs (particularly in terms of small non-viable programs), but demand overall has continued to increase. IDP Education Pty. Ltd. (IDP) undertakes a biannual survey of students enrolled in Australian universities in full degree, study abroad or exchange, and transnational programs. In second semester 2008, IDP reported that 59,590 students enrolled in transnational programs at Australian universities: 50,830 in programs conducted on offshore campuses, and 8,760 in distance education or online programs (IDP 2008). Numbers enrolled in transnational higher education had reached an all-time high a semester earlier.

Education as an Export for Australia

International education plays a large role in Australia's tertiary education system with fee income providing 15 percent of revenue to Australian universities. It is Australia's third largest export, its largest service export contributing US$12 billion to the Australian economy in 2008 (Australian Bureau of Statistics 2009). The economic value of education exports has grown at a rapid pace, at an average annual rate of 15 percent between 1996 and 2006/2007 (AEI 2008e). A recent report into the economic impact of international students estimated that over 126,000 jobs are directly attributable to international education (Access Economics 2009).

International graduates represent a valuable source of skilled human resources sought after by Australia's labor market; 21.5 percent of international higher education students who completed their studies in 2005 are living and working in Australia today providing skilled labor for Australia's economic development (Banks and Olsen 2008).

A market-led approach to international education has driven Australian providers to innovate in the development of channels and pathways to improve preparedness and enhance access to Australian higher education for international students. Benchmarking studies carried out annually since 2002 by the Australian Universities International Directors Forum (AUIDF) identify the following key recruitment channels used by Australian universities: university pathways, university offices offshore, private education agents, and IDP (as an agent and directly with no agent). With the exception of university offshore offices, these channels may operate both on and offshore (AUIDF 2009).

The largest recruitment channel is via education agents (private agents and IDP), operating both on and offshore and supplying up to 60 percent of each commencing cohort. Using AEI data it can be estimated that some 45 percent of commencing undergraduates come via pathway programs conducted in Australia. Besides English language programs and schools in Australia as pathways to higher education, Australia has many foundation or access programs. Typical examples are those operated by Navitas, a for-profit company listed on the Australian stock exchange that operates university-level diploma programs that include the partner university's first year syllabus, with successful students who meet specified academic requirements normally guaranteed entry into the partner university's second year. These programs provide for lower entry levels than the partner university and employ small classes and greater numbers of teaching hours to achieve exit levels similar to those of the partner university. Navitas operates predominately in Australia but also runs similar pathway programs in the United Kingdom and Canada.

A further development of these "private-public" partnerships has been the undertaking of full campus degree issuing operations, particularly in downtown Sydney by organizations such as Navitas. For example, Navitas operates Sydney campuses for Curtin University of Technology (a Perth-based university), Macquarie University (a Sydney suburban university), and Latrobe University (a Melbourne-based university), as well as the Singapore campus of Curtin.

The Australian International Education Framework

Australian government policy has provided the basis of a unique framework for quality assurance and growth in international education in Australia. This framework, which is a private-public partnership of governments, institutions, private providers, and service providers, is a significant factor in Australia's success. The Department of Education, Employment and Workplace Relations (DEEWR), largely through Australian Education International (AEI), promotes and regulates Australia's international student program.

The *Education Services for Overseas Students Act* (ESOS) and the accompanying *National Code of Practice* are intended to protect Australia's reputation for delivering education and the interests of international students by setting standards for student services and support along with providing consumer protection, stipulating obligations of providers, and giving tuition and financial assurance. The *ESOS Act* and *National Code* framework administered by the Australian and state governments include the following:

Commonwealth Register of Institutions and Courses for Overseas Students (CRICOS). It is a database of more than 1,200 Australian education institutions (DEEWR 2008). All institutions that recruit, enroll, or teach international students must be registered on CRICOS, as must each program.

Provider Registration and International Students Management System (PRISMS). All CRICOS-approved providers and programs are listed on the Provider Registration and International Students Management System (PRISMS), as is each student studying in Australia on a student visa. The system interfaces with the Department of Immigration and Citizenship (DIAC) visa data. DIAC regulates Australia's international student visa policy and skilled migration policy for international graduates. Through PRISMS, providers notify DIAC of each student's acceptance into a program, prior to the student applying for a student visa. This information generates an electronic Confirmation of Enrolment (e-CoE) as evidence of admission to a registered, full-time program. The e-CoE enables a prospective student to obtain a student visa and is proof of their acceptance into a CRICOS-registered institution and program. Education providers also use PRISMS to notify DIAC of students who may have breached the terms of the student visa.

The ESOS Assurance Fund. The ESOS Assurance Fund was established to protect the interests of current and intending overseas students enrolled with registered providers, by ensuring that students are provided with suitable alternative programs, or having their program monies refunded if the provider cannot offer the program(s) that the student has paid for. Private providers are required to contribute to the fund a proportion of their international student income. Providers take ESOS responsibilities very seriously. Typical university responses involve a staff position for monitoring ESOS compliance—encompassing marketing of publications (print and electronic); framing procedures for appointment; monitoring of agents; registering under CRICOS of new and changed programs; setting international fee structures; monitoring student performance; and reporting on PRISMS, fee refund policies, and grievance procedures and critical incident policies.

In mid-2009, the Australian government announced a review of the ESOS Act in 2009–2010 to ensure that Australia meets world's best standards before it becomes the responsibility of a new TEQSA (Tertiary Education Quality and Standards Agency). TEQSA also will replace the Australian Universities Quality Agency (AUQA), an independent agency jointly owned by Australian national and state governments that audits and reports on quality assurance in Australian higher education. All international activities, on and offshore, are subject to audits.

A student visa is required for all non-Australian residents seeking to study in Australia for more than three months. On July 1, 2001, major changes to Australia's student visa assessment procedures came into effect to streamline visa processing. The restructured student visa system consists of the following:

- Visa subclasses: Australia's student visa program has seven subclasses linked to education sectors
- Country assessment levels (CALs): each education sector in each country is ranked according to one of five assessment levels. The assessment levels relate to the extent to which students are likely to comply with their visa conditions; these levels are determined based on experience with previous students. Assessment level 1 represents the lowest risk, level 5 the highest. The higher the assessment level, the more evidence is required for students to support their visa application
- Evidentiary standards: these visa requirements include English language proficiency and proof of financial status and are increasingly stringent from level 1 through to level 5.

Applications for student visas may be made online for students in level 1 countries as well as for students located in China, India, Indonesia, and Thailand, or for students already located in Australia who need to renew their visas.

Key Choice Factors

Australia is a destination of choice due to a range of attractive attributes. AEI's International Student Survey (AEI 2008) shows that the key reasons for choosing Australia as a study destination include the following: the desirability of studying and living in an English-speaking country; perceptions of safety and security; a desire to experience a different culture/lifestyle (with Australians generally perceived as easygoing and friendly); comparatively lower costs of living and tuition; relative close proximity to home for students from Asia; and a pleasant climate. Australia is generally characterized as value for money offering affordable, quality education.

Other factors include opportunities for skilled migration, access to part-time work, and opportunities to gain relevant work experience to improve career prospects. Since 2001 international students have been able to apply for permanent residence on completion of their studies. The selection criteria for skilled migration favor graduates with skills and qualifications that are in short supply in Australia's labor market. A desire to gain qualifications that enhance skilled migration and global employment prospects is driving demand for specific programs of study in Australia.

International Research Students and Internationalization of Research and Development

The global competition for high-quality research students (doctoral or masters) is intensifying. In a paper to the European Association for International Education in 2007, Forbes suggested four main drivers:

> research students make a significant contribution to current research and development activities, either through their original contributions of intellectual property, or through the support they provide to the overall research groups to which they belong; after graduation research students provide essential expertise for knowledge economies; research students provide the next generation of academic and research staff in universities; and research students can help facilitate collaboration among research groups. (Forbes 2007, 1)

The U.K. International Unit in 2008 presented a popular but misleading view of Australia's competitiveness in this global market for research students:

> Australia has been the most successful country at international student recruitment over the last ten years or so. Its main strength, however, has been in undergraduate recruitment from East and South East Asia. Australia has not been as successful at the postgraduate research level. This relative underperformance is being addressed and more focused strategies for PGR students are emerging. (Kemp et al. 2008, 61).

The International Unit report points out that U.K. universities have been very successful in recruiting international postgraduate research students and numbers have grown consistently at the rate of over 4 percent per year.

Over the nine years from 1998 to 2007, the number of international postgraduate research students in Australian universities grew on average 10 percent per year. In 1998, 4,047 international postgraduate research students made up 11.4 percent of Australia's 35,577 postgraduate research students. In 2007, after a growth of 10.3 percent per year, the number of international postgraduate research students had more than doubled to 9,836 or 19.7 percent of Australia's 49,819 postgraduate research students (DEEWR 2008).

Australia's competitiveness in the market for international postgraduate research students is demonstrated by universities' commitment of funds to scholarships. In an unpublished survey of universities, 29 universities reported spending in aggregate in 2008 the equivalent of 4.1 percent of total revenue from international student programs on scholarships and stipends for commencing international postgraduate research students.

The Bradley Review of Australian Higher Education identified research as an area where the Australian higher education subsector would need to build on its success. The report included the following recommendations (Bradley et al. 2008):

- more diverse international student body
- bigger proportion of higher degree research students
- greater focus on international research collaborations
- effective connections to global innovation and research networks

Universities Australia (2007), the peak body of universities, in 2007 surveyed universities on their formal links with higher education institutions overseas. The number of formal links for the purpose of collaboration in academic and/or research projects had grown from 2,198 in 1999 to 3,421 in 2007.

The International Student Experience in Australia

International Student Performance

International students perform academically just as well as Australian students. This has been the consistent finding in three studies conducted over 12 years across Australian universities.

Most recently, Olsen (2008a) used student progress rates to compare the academic performance of 200,000 students, in cooperation with the Group of 8 (Go8), a coalition of leading Australian universities, intensive in research and comprehensive in general and professional education. Within this group, 195,694 students in 2007 passed 91.8 percent of what they attempted. The 46,812 international students on campus in Australia passed 91.6 percent and did just as well as the 140,903 Australian students, who passed 92.0 percent. The 7,939 transnational international students, that is, those residing outside Australia but studying at a Go8 university, passed 89.2 percent. In terms of student progress rates international students on campus in Australia did as well as Australian students and did better than international students offshore.

Retention and Attrition

In the same paper, Olsen reported on student completion, in cooperation with the Australian Universities International Directors Forum (AUIDF), and found that international students were more likely to continue with or complete their programs than Australian students. The study examined 485,983 students in 32 Australian universities in 2006. Overall, including both domestic and international students, the retention figure was 89.5 percent. Conversely, the attrition figure was 10.5 percent. The reasons for international students having higher retention rates may be the requirement to study full time, the strict performance requirements to avoid termination of visa, and enrollment in programs with well-defined professional outcomes. In staying the course, international students did better than Australian students: 7.6 percent of the 102,686 international students dropped out, staying the course better than the 383,297 Australian students (11.3 percent).

Student Satisfaction

Overall, the vast majority of international higher education respondents were satisfied with their study experience (AEI 2008):

- 85 percent were very satisfied or satisfied with studying in Australia
- 88 percent would recommend studying in Australia to friends and family
- 83 percent were either very satisfied or satisfied with the program
- 67 percent would recommend the program to friends or family

International respondents generally regarded Australia as a safe country with plenty to see and do and the majority felt that Australia offered suitable accommodation. However, Australia did not perform as well on cost of living and factors relating to finding part-time employment. The Survey concluded that

> to retain high satisfaction levels among students (both international and Australian), it is imperative that perceptions about costs are addressed to

better explain the benefits of the program relative to costs. Another driver of international respondents' Overall Stay Satisfaction was Australian students' attitudes toward them...the findings show that social integration aspects such as Australian attitudes towards international students, as well as forming close friendships between international and Australian students, were potential areas for improvement. (AEI 2008, ix)

Following concerns related to international student safety and exploitation, the Victorian government established in 2008 the Overseas Student Experience Taskforce. This taskforce recommended a number of changes, including greater attention to student orientation and housing, and expressed concerns about exploitation of international students in the workforce.

The taskforce did reflect growing community concern for issues around safety and social inclusion. In May–June 2009, Indian students clashed with the Lebanese community and the police in Melbourne and Sydney, largely around issues of racism and alleged assaults on students. Acknowledging these issues and the importance of the quality of Australian international student experience, the education minister announced a review of the ESOS Act and invited international student representatives to participate on a continuing basis in a roundtable to discuss issues affecting their study experience such as accommodation, welfare, and safety. In addition a number of ministerial missions to India were planned for the 2009 period.

Outbound Mobility

Outbound student mobility has become increasingly important to Australian universities (Adams 2007) and is seen as a key part of preparing graduates for professional life in a global society of the twenty-first century. International offices set up in the late 1980s and early 1990s for recruitment of international students soon took on the responsibility of developing bilateral exchange linkages and administering student exchange and other forms of mobility.

Australian universities enthusiastically developed exchange agreements with their counterparts predominately in North America and Europe and took part in the work of international networks such as the International Student Exchange Program (ISEP) and the Australian Exchange Network, a grouping of Australian universities connected to the European Utrecht network.

The task of sending Australian (and international) students out on mobility experiences, however, proved difficult with the lack of a mobility culture in universities and the cost of traveling long distances leading to imbalances of exchange numbers and complaints from partner universities that while they could send students easily to Australia, it was harder to attract Australian students.

Over time, this scenario has changed with universities being more strategic and proactive in marketing opportunities for their students, developing significant mobility infrastructures in universities, arranging for university and Australian government financial support, and designing leadership programs (e.g., Macquarie University's Global Leadership Program [GLP]).

University student mobility staff as a group have for several years coordinated an Australian exchange fair circuit, encouraging partner universities to come to Australia and take part in on-campus activities across the country, thus promoting mobility nationally. An outgrowth of this has been the establishment of Australia's first outbound mobility company to provide principally short program mobility opportunities for Australian students.

The 2008 AUIDF research on student mobility in 37 Australian universities (Olsen 2008b) provides an understanding of the Australian context that can be compared internationally. It showed that in 2007, there were 10,718 international experiences (at all academic levels), both for-credit and non-credit, for students in those universities compared with 7,282 in 2005 when a similar study was carried out.

Using a comparable methodology that estimates the proportion of U.S. students studying abroad, the study took the number of international study experiences (10,718) as a percentage of the graduating cohort of the 37 participating universities. It showed that 4.8 percent of completing students (all levels) had one of the above international experiences, and that there were several universities that reached above 10 percent (one at 18 percent). At the undergraduate level it showed that 5.8 percent of completing undergraduates had one of the above international study experiences.

The study also showed that 57.5 percent of these experiences were undertaken by women and that 16.3 percent were undertaken by international students (up from 13 percent in 2005). The higher proportion of women undertaking mobility has also been a feature of U.S. study abroad. The figure of 16.3 percent of international students represents just under the proportion of international students in the university cohort across Australia and suggests that international students have a similar propensity to travel as Australian students.

When looked at in terms of length of the experience, 45.9 percent went for a semester (down from 47 percent in 2005), 16 percent for a year, and 40 percent for less than a semester (up from 36 percent in 2005). This includes a number of categories: short-term programs (23.2 percent), placements or practical training (7.8 percent), and research (14.6 percent). Nationally, 93 percent were for credit and the remainder for developing international or discipline skills.

The study also reported that 60 percent of the experiences had university financial support (up from 56 percent in 2005), 4 percent were supported by the Australian Government University Mobility in the Asia Pacific (UMAP) funding program and 13 percent by OS HELP, the Australian government mobility loan scheme. The amount of financial support provided by universities was US$10 million. In terms of field of study, 20.3 percent were in management and commerce and 19.6 percent in society and culture. In terms of destination, 38.6 percent traveled to Europe, 31 percent to Asia, and 24.7 percent to the Americas.

The figures are likely to be accurate for the exchange category but may understate other categories, most particularly those programs under a semester in duration. This is because, in many universities, there is little known centrally about short programs as they are often study tours or similar programs organized by academics for their classes, or work placements as part of a professional program. A conservative estimate is that if these additional experiences were included then it would probably add another 2,000 international experiences. If this is correct then the actual percentage of undergraduate students who have an international study experience is likely to be in the order of 8 percent and is directly comparable with the 9.4 percent in the United States in 2006/2007 as reported in *Open Doors* (Bhandari and Chow 2008).

Most of the growth in mobility is occurring in programs of less than a semester's duration, for example, summer programs that run for three to six weeks, or short work placements. According to the study, short-term mobility experiences in Australia grew from 32.6 percent of all outbound international experiences from Australia in 2005 to 35.1 percent in 2007.

Educators may argue that the experience gained is not the same as an immersion six or twelve months long, and although this may be true, the shorter time periods seem consistent with what has been observed or is known anecdotally about the millennial or Y Generation. The shorter periods fit in well with their lifestyle and economic capacity. Australian universities have been slow to recognize this trend and to deal with it in a strategic fashion.

Data for the period 2002–2007 show the growth of student exchange over the period and the narrowing of the gap between incoming and

Table 6.2 Mobility Growth Statistics 2003–2007

Year	2003	2004	2005	2006	2007
Universities	29	34	33	36	36
Dedicated Staff	52.5	65.4	71.9	82.5	93.3
Total Students	6,676	8,469	8,780	9,566	11,755
Inbound	3,815	4,860	4,690	4,970	5,943
Outbound	2,861	3,609	4,090	4,596	5,812
Caseload	127	129	122	116	126
Outbound Growth		21%	12%	11%	21%
Total Growth		21%	4%	8%	19%

Source: Olsen (2008c).

outgoing students (Olsen 2008c). Inbound exchange is no longer out of balance with outbound exchange. AUIDF benchmark data show that by 2007 inbound and outbound exchanges were approximately equal (table 6.2). The balance between inflow and outflow of students is likely to improve further given a recent Australian government budget statement in which it was announced that the loan fee attached to OS HELP would be removed to provide more support to Australian students who choose to study abroad (Gillard 2009a). Table 6.2 shows the significant changes that have occurred between 2002 and 2007 as well as the caseloads of staff. It also shows the increase in staff resource that Australian universities have provided for student exchange.

In terms of outgoing international student mobility, a 2008 study of 37 Australian universities found that in 2007 women dominated all types of international study experiences. The 37 universities reported that in 2007 57.5 percent of students with international study experiences were women (Olsen 2008b). This is similar to the gender gap in the United States, where 65.1 percent of all study abroad students in 2006/2007 were women.

Looking Forward

International education has grown rapidly to become a significant part of the Australian higher education system, a major contributor to Australian economic growth, and a highly effective "soft power" means of building alliances, enhancing Australian influence and creating cultural understanding between Australia and Asia. The private-public partnership that comprises the Australian international education framework has been a key factor.

The outlook for the international education industry continues to be positive. Forecasting work suggests that the high growth rates seen in education exports over the past two decades will decrease to reach moderate levels, due to increasing competition from other countries that are providing places to both international and domestic students. The expectation is that growth in Australian international student numbers will continue at a sustainable pace. There is a limit, at around one quarter of the total student population, to a university's appetite and capacity for international students (Banks et al. 2007). The emergence of private providers such as the Navitas operations in Sydney may provide considerable additional capacity.

The global economic crisis may affect the short- to medium-term outlook for education exports. It is too early to gauge the impact of the crisis except to note that education exports initially withstood the international economic conditions better than other export industries. Families in countries such as China and India, lacking facilities to provide quality education to their most capable young people, do not see education as discretionary spending and continue to focus on an overseas education.

Beyond the aid phase and the trade phase, Bradley and colleagues' (2008, 87) *Review of Australian Higher Education* suggested that it is time for a third phase:

> The higher education subsector needs to capitalize on its considerable strengths in international education and focus on developing a long-term sustainable strategy for global engagement. There is a need to move to what is being called a "third phase" of internationalization characterized by a more holistic approach which would include:

- maintaining a sustainable "trade" agenda with a more diverse international student body and a greater proportion of higher degree research students;
- better supporting students (both domestic and international) to improve their experience on campus and ensure their work readiness in the global environment;
- improving coordination across government to ensure an alignment of policies to support industry development, regulation and skilled migration; and
- focusing more on international research collaborations.

Amidst a global financial crisis, increasing concerns for student safety and social inclusion, and university concerns about their capacity to enroll increasing numbers of international students, the outlook remains vibrant. The challenge will be for Australia to continue to develop new approaches to the business of international education, while maintaining quality.

Bibliography

Access Economics. 2009. The Australian Education Sector and the Economics Contribution of International Students. Melbourne: ACPET.

Adams, Tony. 2007. "International Education in Australia." *Journal of Studies in International Education* 11 (3–4): 410–420.

Australian Education International (AEI). 2007. *2006. International Student Survey: Higher Education Summary Report.* Canberra: Australian Government.

AEI. 2008. 2007 Follow-up International Student Survey: Higher Education. Canberra: Australian Government.

AEI. 2008a. *Transnational Quality Strategy.* Canberra: Australian Government. Available online at: http://www.transnational.deewr.gov.au.

AEI. 2008b. *AusLIST.* Canberra: Australian Government. Available online at: http://www.transnational.deewr.gov.au.

AEI. 2008c. *International Student Statistics.* Canberra: Australian Government. Available online at: http://aei.gov.au.

AEI. 2008d. Evidence to Servicing Our Future: Inquiry into the Current and Future Directions of Australia's Services Export Sector. Canberra: Australian Government.

AEI. 2008e. "Export Income to Australia from Education Services." *Research Snapshot* 34. Available online at: http://www.aei.dest.gov.au.

AEI. 2009. *Australia YTD March 2009: Monthly Summary of International Student Enrolment Data.* Canberra: Australian Government. Available online at: http://www.aei.dest.gov.au.

Australian Bureau of Statistics. 2006. *Census Data.* Canberra: Australian Bureau of Statistics. Available online at: http://www.abs.gov.au.

Australian Bureau of Statistics. 2009. *5302.0 Balance of Payments and International Investment Position, Australia Dec 2008.* Canberra: Australian Bureau of Statistics. Available online at: http://www.abs.gov.au.

Australian Government. 2005. *Education without Borders: International Trade in Education.* Canberra: Department of Foreign Affairs and Trade, Australian Government.

Australian Universities International Directors Forum (AUIDF). 2009. *AUIDF Benchmarking 2008.* Melbourne: AUIDF.

Back, Kenneth, Dorothy Davis, and Alan Olsen. 1996. *Internationalisation and Higher Education Goals and Strategies.* Canberra: Australian Government Publishing Service.

Banks, Melissa, and Alan Olsen, eds. 2008. Outcomes and Impacts of International Education: From International Student to Australian Graduate, the Journey of a Lifetime. Melbourne: IDP Education Pty. Ltd.

Banks, Melissa, Alan Olsen, and David Pearce. 2007. *Global Student Mobility: An Australian Perspective Five Years On.* Canberra: IDP Education Pty. Ltd.

Bhandari, Rajika, and Patricia Chow. 2008. *Open Doors 2008: Report on International Educational Exchange.* New York: Institute of International Education.

Bradley, Denise, Peter Noonan, Helen Nugent, and William Scales. 2008. *Review of Australian Higher Education: Final Report*. Canberra: Australian Government.

Cuthbert, Denise, Wendy Smith, and Janice Boey. 2008. "What Do We Really Know About the Outcomes of Australian International Education? A Critical Review and Prospectus for Future Research." *Journal of Studies in International Education* 12 (3): 225–227.

Davis, Dorothy, Anthony Böhm, and Alan Olsen. 2000. Transnational Education Providers, Partners and Policy: Challenges for Australian Institutions Offshore. Canberra: IDP Education Pty. Ltd.

Department of Education, Employment and Workplace Relations of Australia (DEEWR). 2008. *Higher Education Statistics Collections*. Canberra: DEEWR. Available online at: http://www.dest.gov.au.

DEEWR. 2008. *Selected Higher Education Statistics*. DEEWR. Available online at: http://www.dest.gov.au.

Downer, Hon. Alexander. 2005. "Launch of Australia and the Colombo Plan 1949–1957." Speeches, Australian Minister for Foreign Affairs, Canberra. Available online at: http://www.foreignminister.gov.au.

Downer, Hon. Alexander, and Hon. Julie Bishop. 2006. "Australia Doubles Number of Scholarships to the Asia—Pacific Region." Joint Media Release AA 06 15, Australian Minister for Foreign Affairs, and Minister for Education, Science and Training, Canberra. Available online at: http://www.australian-scholarships.gov.au.

English Australia. 2008. *Survey of Major ELICOS Regional Markets in 2007.* Sydney: English Australia.

Forbes, Dean. 2007. "Research Student Mobility in a Competitive Global Knowledge Economy." Paper presented at the European Association for International Education Conference, Trondheim, September 12–15, 2007.

Gillard, Hon. Julia. 2008. *Speech: Globally Connected*. Canberra: Ministers' Media Centre. Available online at: www.mediacentre.dewr.gov.au.

Gillard, Hon. Julia. 2009a. *Speech: International Education—Its Contribution to Australia*. Canberra: Ministers' Media Centre. Available online at: www.deewr.gov.au.

Gillard, Hon. Julia. 2009b. *Media Release: More Support For Students*. Canberra: Ministers' Media Centre. Available online at: www.deewr.gov.au.

Higher Education Policy Institute (HEPI). 2009. Male and Female Participation and Progression in Higher Education. Oxford: HEPI.

IDP. 2008. International Students in Australian Universities National Survey Results Semester 2, 2008. Melbourne: IDP Education Pty. Ltd.

Industry Commission. 1991. *Exports of Education Services*. Canberra: Australian Government Publishing Service.

Kemp, Neil, William Archer, Colin Gilligan, and Christine Humfrey. 2008. *The U.K.'s Competitive Advantage: The Market for International Research Students*. London: U.K. Higher Education International Unit.

McBurnie, Grant, and Anthony Pollock. 1998. "Transnational Education: An Australian Example." *International Higher Education* 10 (Winter): 12–14.

Olsen, Alan. 2008a. "Impacts and Outcomes for Students in Banks." In *Outcomes and Impacts of International Education: From International Student to Australian Graduate, the Journey of a Lifetime,* ed. Alan Olsen and Melissa Banks. Canberra: IDP Education Pty. Ltd.

Olsen, Alan. 2008b. *Outgoing International Mobility of Australian University Students 2007.* Melbourne: SPRE. Available online at: www.spre.com.hk.

Olsen, Alan. 2008c. *Yearly Benchmarks from 2002 to 2007.* Melbourne: AUIDF.

Scott, David. 2005. "Retention, Completion and Progression in Tertiary Education in New Zealand." *Journal of Higher Education Policy and Management* 27 (1): 3–17.

UNESCO. 2006. Global Education Digest 2006: Comparing Education Statistics across the World. Montreal: UNESCO Institute of Statistics.

Universities Australia. 2007. *Offshore Programs of Australian Universities.* Canberra: Universities Australia. Available online at: http://www.universitiesaustralia.edu.au.

Chapter 7

Student Mobility Trends in Latin America

Isabel Cristina Jaramillo and Hans de Wit

Student mobility has become one of the most important activities for the higher education subsector worldwide. The number of students moving around the world has more than doubled over the past twenty years and it is expected to grow even more in the next decade. Global competition for top talent in the present knowledge economy is an extremely important factor, especially considering the shortage of local talent in developed societies and in emerging economies such as Brazil.

The flow of Latin American students out of the region is increasing but not approaching levels that represent mobility in other regions in the world. Even fewer students choose to come to pursue studies in the region than leave it. What is the participation of Latin America as a region in this global scenario? What are the challenges it faces? These are some of the questions addressed in this chapter, not an easy task given the heterogeneity of the higher education systems and the lack of transparent information that the governments and the institutions themselves provide.[1]

Characteristics of Higher Education in Latin America

Latin America is a diverse and complex region. It refers to those countries where the Spanish and the Portuguese languages prevail and is normally identified by the countries that span from Mexico all the way to Argentina, including Cuba and the Dominican Republic. Latin America and the Caribbean are, therefore, one big region composed of nearly 8,910 institutions of higher education. Of these, only 1,231 (13.81 percent) are universities (IESALC/UNESCO 2008).

Although we must speak of a diverse region, it has also some common historical factors that provide opportunities that until recently have been underused due to lack of a common regional approach to higher education. Latin American universities inherited several of such common characteristics that distinguish them from universities elsewhere.

The first institutions of higher education were established in Santo Domingo in 1538 and in Mexico and Peru in 1551. At the time, the Old World had only 16 such institutions, and there were none in what is now the United States. The establishment of these institutions responded to the need to evangelize and to offer educational opportunities that were more or less equivalent to those in Spain. The organization of national universities in Latin America was inspired by the tradition of the University of Salamanca, while the university Alcalá de Henares can be considered as a model of the Catholic university. This coexistence of national and private universities of a primarily Catholic character dominated the higher education landscape in the region for a long time. The current organization of higher education in the region is primarily influenced by Spanish and French models. The basic one is the Napoleonic model, which can be described as vocationally oriented and national and nationalistic in nature (de Wit et al. 2005, 3412).

A second common factor, related to the historical link to the Old World, is that the region has only two main languages of instruction, research, and communication: Spanish and Portuguese, which should allow for much more cooperation and interaction.

Another important common factor was the influence of a liberal movement in Argentina in 1918, the so-called Cordoba Reform, which gave Latin American higher education one of its main characteristics, university autonomy, introduced student participation in university administration, and gave the universities an active role in social development. These three features still play a key role in public higher education all over the region.

From the end of the nineteenth century one can see the first signs of active mobility of students and scholars to Europe and gradually also to the United States. Due to lack of a substantive middle class, this remained limited to a small economic and social elite. In the post–World War II period, international cooperation did get a new dimension in the form of development cooperation. Capacity building for research and teaching and scholarships for graduate training became more important and for several decades influenced the development of higher education in the region.

These historical factors and common characteristics are important to understand present Latin American higher education, its international dimension, and mobility. Latin American universities, seen as key actors in the social and economic development of the region, face some global challenges for which they have to prepare if they want to play an active role in the global market: increased mobility and competition to attract the best talent, increased convergence of national higher education systems, increased liberalization and trade in educational programs, and increased competition for research funding (Holm-Nielsen 2009). Over the past decades, important improvements have taken place, which can be factors that help the region become a more relevant player in the global market for talent and higher education services.

Despite this progress, many problems still need to be addressed. Some facts reveal the current status of key aspects of higher education in the region. It is under these conditions that Latin American higher education institutions and the subsector have to face the challenges and opportunities that the knowledge economy and globalization have to offer (IESALC/UNESCO 2008; Balán 2008).

- Enrollment has increased significantly in the last four decades. Countries such as Chile, Argentina, and Uruguay are among the leaders. The participation rate in those countries is now 30 percent, while the Organization for Economic Cooperation and Development's (OECD) average rate is currently at 56 percent.
- A group of only ten countries (Brazil, Mexico, Argentina, Venezuela, Colombia, Peru, Cuba, Bolivia, Chile, and Ecuador) contribute 93.5 percent of the tuition in higher education in Latin America and the Caribbean.
- Expansion has been pushed forward in different ways, from the creation of new public universities (Argentina, Mexico, and Venezuela) to the appearance of a strong private sector, including for-profit and nonprofit institutions, that has accounted for most of the 40 percent increase in higher education enrollment in countries such as Colombia, Chile, and Brazil. At present there are more students in the region studying at private universities, which are predominantly teaching institutions, than at public universities, which have a strong research base.
- Graduate education has seen impressive growth throughout the region, but Latin American countries still produce a small number of PhDs compared to developed countries. Brazil is the leader (100,000 graduate students, 38,000 of them in doctoral programs). Mexico is second (100,000 students enrolled in master's programs in 2005, but only 13,000 registered as doctoral students). Argentina ranks third, with almost 25,000 master's and 8,000 doctoral students. Chile, a

smaller country, currently enrolls 13,000 master's and almost 3,000 doctoral students. Colombia lags behind with less than 12,000 master's and 1,000 doctoral students.

- National governments have set up scholarship schemes for study abroad to increase the number of graduate students. A recent example is the US$6 billion "Bicentennial Fund for the Development of Human Capital" in Chile. Some US$250 million in annual earnings from the fund is expected to be used to finance overseas scholarships to enable students to study in a range of other countries.
- Program and institutional accreditation and quality assurance mechanisms have become central parts of the governments' agendas. National agencies have been created in Argentina, Bolivia, Chile, Colombia, Mexico, and Nicaragua, to mention a few; these agencies include external peer reviewers for both undergraduate and graduate programs
- At the national level, the region is starting to see more emphasis being placed on creating regulatory and policy frameworks along with institutional policies that give shape to a more sophisticated way of internationalizing the higher education subsector. This is achieved through quality assurance, accreditation, and credit transfer via increased and diversified inter- and intra-regional mobility programs.

Specificities of Student Mobility

Latin American student mobility within the higher education subsector is still very limited and accounts for only 5 percent of the world's mobility (figure 7.1).[2] Around 130,000 Latin-American students study abroad, but only 15 percent of them study in the region, 60 percent go to the United States, and the rest to Europe, particularly to Spain, Great Britain, France, and Germany. Pull factors that induce students to move to other countries include opportunities to improve English skills, enhance career opportunities, experience new/different environments and cultures, and enhance personal development, as well as reputation of the foreign higher education system (JWT Education 2008).

Main Destinations

The United States remains the top destination for international students around the world, and the same is true for Latin American students, with

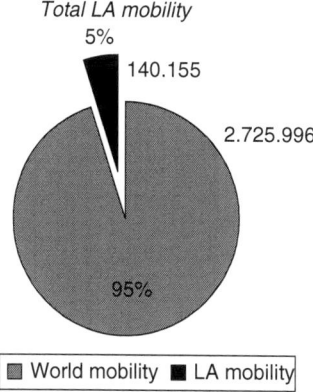

Figure 7.1 Total Latin American Outward Mobility, 2005.
Source: OECD (2007).

64,473 students studying in a variety of programs ranging from English as a second language courses to graduate programs. According to the *Open Doors 2008 Report on International Educational Exchange*, the top sending countries from Latin America are Mexico (14,837 students), Brazil (7,578 students), and Colombia (6,662 students). The majority of students fund their U.S. studies through personal or family resources. Several mobility programs have been created since the establishment of the North American Free Trade Agreement (NAFTA) between Mexico, Canada, and the United States, such as the Program for North American Mobility in Higher Education (PROMESAN) and the Consortium for North American Higher Education Cooperation (CONAHEC), but they have not attracted a large number of students.

European countries, particularly Spain and France, have become increasingly popular destinations due to their linguistic and cultural links with Latin America. A total of 22,656 students studied in Spain and 7,866 went to France, which—like Germany (5,437)—has witnessed a significant increase in Latin American students on its campuses as a result of international cooperation funding programs, scholarships, and reputable higher education systems (UNESCO 2007).

The EU and national governmental funds, as well as scholarships by universities themselves, have fostered Latin American student mobility. Programs such as Alfa and Alban, and scholarships offered by the Spanish Agency for International Cooperation (AECI), the German Academic

Exchange Service (DAAD), Campus France, Nuffic in the Netherlands, and the British Council have all been decisive mechanisms to facilitate mobility between these two regions.

Students from Central American countries[3] tend to favor the United States as their main foreign destination, with 7,075 students studying in the United States in 2007 (UNESCO Institute for Statistics 2007). The second most popular destination is Cuba (3,558 students), followed by Spain (2,057), France (451), Costa Rica (432), and Germany (382). Students from Central America are also attracted to neighboring countries such as Costa Rica, Honduras, and El Salvador because of the proximity, the common Spanish language, and similar social and economic conditions.

Students from South American countries[4] present a somewhat different pattern in their student mobility. The United States has received up to 35,676 South American students. Spain is also an attractive destination due to its European location, language, and cultural background. Up to 17,399 students have pursued some type of academic program in Spain while France (5,979), Germany (5,055), and Cuba (3,232) have climbed to third, fourth, and fifth place respectively. They have recently surpassed England, which for many years was considered one of the top destinations for international and Latin American students. Intraregional mobility is increasing among the countries that are part of the *Mercado Común del Sur* (MERCOSUR) agreement (Argentina, Bolivia, Chile, Brazil, Uruguay, and Paraguay).

Mexico, though Latin American, is part of the North American region and sends large numbers of students to the United States (13,644) due to its geographical proximity and its membership in NAFTA. Spain is the second leading destination (3,200), followed by the United Kingdom (1,843), France (1,440), and Canada (1,435).

Other nontraditional destinations such as Australia, China, and Japan have seen a rise in numbers. Australia is the most active of these in recruiting Latin American students to come to study, with more than 17,676 students from Latin America enrolled in 2007 at universities, technical and further education institutes, and English language colleges across the country, up from just 6,914 in 2002 (GlobalHigherEd 2007).

Intraregional Mobility

Though one can observe in some regions of the world the emergence of regional hubs where students from neighboring countries go to study (Singapore and Malaysia in Asia, and South Africa in Sub-Saharan Africa, for instance), they do not exist in Latin America. In the past Argentina, and to a lesser extent Venezuela, played a similar role in attracting students from neighboring countries because of its stronger economy, but more recently this has no longer been the case. At present, Cuba is the only regional receiver, but this is more a result of its special political position than its economic status. Over the past eight years, though, a revised trend is observed by UNESCO. The 2009 Global Education Digest (UNESCO 2009) noted that the share of mobile students within the region rose from 11 percent in 1999 to 23 percent in 2007. This reflects the gradual development of a middle class in the region and of a common Latin American higher education area.

Many actors and programs have appeared over the past decade. They are a reflection of the increased connectivity of the region. These programs are developed within the region and for the region: some are Ibero-American, others respond to governmental alliances between the European Union and Latin America, some are part of NAFTA (in which Mexico participates).

Most of these programs have to do with mobility of students, faculty, and programs across national borders with a variety of actors that include science and technology organizations, university associations and rectors conferences, student mobility and exchange groups, development assistance agencies, student recruitment bodies, quality assurance agencies, graduate organizations, international relations networks, research and development entities, export agencies, and cultural cooperation bodies.

An important trend is the attention being given to student mobility, at both the undergraduate and graduate levels. Mobility programs such as the *Programa Interamericana Estudiantil* (PIMA), PROMESAN, and the interregional program of the *Centro Interuniversitario de Desarrollo* (CINDA) are good examples. The emphasis on providing scholarships for graduate students and junior faculty members is still strong (good examples are the programs provided by Mercocyt). The Inter-American Organization for Higher Education and other regional university associations remain active in management training, but this does not appear to be a key area of growth (table 7.1)

The total participation in these programs as of 2007 totaled 2,368 students. Although not necessarily Latin American, mobility programs between Mexico with North America (the United States and Canada), which moved 1,808 students between 1995 and 2006, need to be mentioned. Worth mentioning as well is the CINDA program that between 2003, the year of its creation, and 2007 moved 284 students, within some Latin American and with some Belgian and Italian universities. Other Latin American and Ibero-American mobilities take place in the context of bilateral institutional agreements.

Table 7.1   Undergraduate Mobility within Latin America

Program	Participant Countries	Number of Participant Universities	Year of Creation
ESCALA- ESTUDIANTIL	Argentina, Brasil, Chile Paraguay, Uruguay	18	2000
PME (CRISCOS)	Argentina, Bolivia, Chile, Perú	21	1998
PAME (UDUAL)	Argentina, Bolivia, Brasil Colombia, Ecuador, Mexico, Nicaragua Panama, Peru, R. Dominicana, Uruguay	24	2003
JIMA	Argentina, Mexico	18	2005
MARCA	Argentina, Bolivia, Brazil, Chile, Paraguay, Uruguay	17	2006

Source: SEGIB (2007).

The increase in intraregional mobility is due to the establishment of subregional academic agreements, participation of national and regional university associations, and intraregional cooperation by foreign and national agencies. Examples of national agencies that act as donors are *El Consejo Nacional de Ciencia y Tecnología* (CONACYT) in Mexico, *Instituto Colombiano de Crédito y Estudios Técnicos en el Exterior* (ICETEX) in Colombia, *Coordenação de Aperfeiçoamento de Pessoal de Nível Superior* (CAPES) in Brazil, and *Consejo Nacional de Investigaciones Científicas y Técnicas* (CONICET) in Argentina.

National and regional university associations have become active in the region promoting and supporting student mobility as well as creating programs on a relatively small scale. That is the case with the Union of Latin American Universities (UDUAL), which sponsors a mobility program known as PAME-UDUAL among its 24 university members. More than 200 students have participated in the program (SEGIB 2007). The Latin American and the Caribbean Macro Universities Network, created in 2002, which brings together the largest number of public universities, seeks to strengthen academic cooperation through mobility and research.

Student mobility within MERCOSUR countries is the best model for subregional mobility. The University Association of the Montevideo Group's ESCALA program, for example, facilitated the exchange of over 1,300 students between 2000 and 2006. Similarly, IME/CRISCOS facilitated the exchange of 763 students among 21 universities from Argentina, Bolivia, Chile, and Peru from 1998 to 2006, and the Council of University Presidents for the Integration of the West-Central Sub-Region of South America's Student Mobility Program creates study abroad opportunities for undergraduate students. The Academic Mobility and Exchange Program (PIME), established by the Spanish Agency for International Cooperation (AECI) and the Organization of Ibero-American States for Education, Science and Culture (OIM) during the 1990s and the early years of this century, facilitated connections between participating Latin American universities and institutions in Spain. These programs had a significant influence on international education and promoted the creation of international offices in the universities throughout the region (table 7.2).

Recent interregional agreements with the European Union and among Ibero-American countries—such as the Pablo Neruda Program, and the Program *Ventana para la Cooperación Exterior* of the Education, Audiovisual and Culture Executive Agency (EACEA) of the European Commission—seek to enhance student mobility within the region and countries in Europe. These agreements intend to create a common space to facilitate educational collaboration, similar to the European, Latin American and Caribbean Common Space for Higher Education and the Ibero-American Space for Knowledge.

Table 7.2   Ibero-American Mobility (2007)

Program	Participant Countries in Mobility	Number of Students
PIMA/OEI	Spain, Portugal, 18 countries in Latin America	Mobility: 1105
Carolina Foundation	Spain and the Ibero-American Community of Nations	Mobility: 1475
MAEC-AECI Scholarships	Spain, Latin America, Puerto Rico, Barbados, Belize, Haiti, Jamaica, Trinidad, and Tobago	Mobility: 960
Ibero American Association of Postgraduate Universities, AUIP	Universities from Spain, Portugal, Latin America, and the Caribbean	N/A

Source: SEGIB (2007).

Since mobility represents a very important manifestation of the international process within the Latin American higher education institutions, several aspects should be examined if the region is to play an important role in the knowledge economy and the talent circulation in the global scenario:

- The academic terms vary depending on the country. In general, there are two semesters per year; some, such as Mexico, Honduras, or Nicaragua, have four terms; in Uruguay there is one year-long term; some institutions start in January, others in March or in September.
- The criteria for admission differ substantially. Some require a higher education diploma, others a written exam, while still others (e.g., Colombia) are obliged to present a national exam.
- Grades are a sensitive issue and they need to be interpreted since they vary significantly from country to country.
- In the majority of cases, the higher education subsector is regulated by the Ministry of Education, as in Colombia, Mexico, and Cuba, while in Guatemala, it corresponds to the San Carlos University, the biggest and most important public university. In other cases, it corresponds to the university associations as in Peru with its National Association of Rectors.
- Migratory policies differ from country to country making it difficult to issue student visas.
- In general, higher education institutions are granted great autonomy, but in some cases recognition of professional qualifications may be in the hands of the State and in others in the hands of professional colleges.
- Whether a higher education institution is public or private causes confusion as regulations and control on the part of the State vary accordingly. In countries such as Colombia, both types are under the surveillance of the Ministry of Education. In Venezuela and Uruguay, public universities are very autonomous, while private institutions are very regulated.
- The variety of study terms throughout the region makes the systems difficult to comprehend.

The Future

Despite the differences and challenges to meet, mobility has become an important strategy for any university that considers itself internationalized.

This important activity has turned out to become a criterion for selecting a program or an institution due to the value given to study abroad. In this demanding scenario in higher education, new critical issues—quality assurance, accreditation, mutual recognition, financing, information-sharing, and language barriers—arise and should, therefore, be addressed by the governments and the higher education institutions in the context of both horizontal and vertical mobility. This is true for higher education in both Latin American and elsewhere.

Latin American universities are becoming more and more conscious of the changes derived from several convergences around the world as a response to a greater global interdependence and understand the need to implement structural modifications and respond quickly to the challenges. They urge for regional actions that finally overcome the differences and facilitate the process. A progressive harmonization of the divergent higher education systems is a must if the region wants to see a meaningful increase in intra and inter mobility. It requires transparent information from the governments and the institutions themselves. In an attempt to promote a "one voice, one language" system that represents the traditional and the new potential actors and programs, universities, governments, multilateral banks and organizations, university associations, and networks, among others, would help to increase the performance of the region, an attempt that in essence would benefit the quality and the pertinence of the subsector.

Latin America looks to Europe and its Bologna Process as an example of how to build a regional higher education and research area. Subregional cooperation agreements, as in the case of MERCOSUR, are positive signs. Countries such as Argentina, Brazil, Colombia, and Mexico are starting to position themselves not only as senders but also as potential receivers of students from the rest of the world. The strong presence of private institutions in the region will present challenges and opportunities, as would the increased presence of foreign providers such as Apollo, Kaplan, and Laureate along with regional providers such as Monterrey Tech University in Mexico.

The above analysis makes it clear that higher education in Latin America is experiencing major changes: increasing participation rates, an expanding private sector, and attempts to harmonize and regionalize systems. At the same time, in the global market for international students and scholars its role is still minor compared to that of North America, Europe, and the Asia-Pacific region, as well as the Middle East. The comparative advantage of having a common popular language and culture still has not paid off. The building of a common Latin America Higher Education Area has begun, but there is still a long way to go before Latin America becomes an attractive and recognized higher education destination for its own students and students from other parts of the world.

NOTES

1. For a more detailed analysis of the international dimension of Latin American Higher Education see Hans de Wit et al. (2005).
2. Information taken from different studies supported by the World Bank and the Institutional Management in Higher Education, IMHE/OECD, the European Commission through its Alfa Program, and the UNESCO Global Education Digest and SEGIB.
3. Central America includes Costa Rica, Cuba, Dominican Republic, El Salvador, Guatemala, Honduras, Nicaragua, and Panama.
4. South America includes Argentina, Bolivia, Brazil, Chile, Colombia, Ecuador, Paraguay, Peru, Uruguay, and Venezuela.

BIBLIOGRAPHY

Balán, Jorge 2008. "Graduate Education in Latin America: The Coming of Age." *International Higher Education* 50 (Winter): 9–11.

Bhandari, Rajika, and Patricia Chow. 2008. *Open Doors 2008: Report on International Educational Exchange.* New York: Institute of International Education.

de Wit, Hans, Isabelle Christina Jaramillo, Jocelyne Gacel-Avila, and Jane Knight. 2005. *Higher Education in Latin America: The International Dimension.* Washington, DC: The World Bank.

Holm-Nielsen, Lauritz. 2009. Foro internacional de investigación "investigar para innovar." Bogotá: Ministerio de Educación Nacional.

IESALC/UNESCO. 2008a. Conferencia Regional de Educación Superior. Cartagena.

IESALC/UNESCO. 2008b. Mapa de la Educación Superior de América Latina y el Caribe– MESALC.

Jaramillo, Isabelle C., Julio Theiler, and Francisco Sánchez. 2007. Sistema Iberoamericano de movilidad de estudiantes y docentes–SIMEP. Secretaría General Iberoamericana, SEGIB.

JWT Education. 2008. "An Update on the Latin American Market." Paper presented at the 6th Washington International Education Conference, Washington, DC, January 28–29, 2008.

OECD. 2004. Internationalisation and Trade in Higher Education: Opportunities and Challenges. Paris: OECD.

Olds, Kris 2007. *Latin American Students "Flood" into Australia (and Away from the USA)*, October 10, Global Higher Education. Available online at: http:// globalhighered.wordpress.com.

Organisation for Economic Co-ordination and Development (OECD). 2007. Number of Foreign Students in Tertiary Education, by Country of Origin and Destination (2005) and Market Shares in International Education (2002, 2005). Paris: OECD.

UNESCO Institute for Statistics. 2007. *Global Education Digest 2007: Comparing Education Statistics across the World*. Montreal: UNESCO Institute for Statistics.

UNESCO Institute for Statistics. 2009. *Global Education Digest 2009: Comparing Education Statistics across the World*. Montreal: UNESCO Institute for Statistics.

Chapter 8

Student Mobility Trends in Africa: A Baseline Analysis of Selected African Countries[1]

Roshen Kishun

Introduction

The movement of African students within the continent or of those from outside seeking opportunities to study in Africa is not new. Nor is the movement of African students to study at overseas higher education institutions, especially during the colonial period and during the era when most African countries lacked university-level institutions. African students studied in the United States as early as the 1870s. Between 1896 and 1931, 22 black South Africans studied in the United States at Lincoln University (Menell-Kinberg 1991). Many of the educated African elite who provided leadership for the nationalist movements throughout Africa received their education at overseas higher education institutions (Lulat 2003).

While Africa was realigning its higher education system to meet the challenges of the new millennium, international student mobility around the world increased markedly. Between 1999 and 2004, the number of international students worldwide surged by 41 percent from 1.75 million to 2.75 million, according to UNESCO (2006a).

The analysis of student mobility trends in Africa presented in this chapter is based primarily on data collected by the authors of 11 country case studies included in the book *Higher Education in Africa: The International Dimension* (Teferra and Knight 2008). This seminal publication on the internationalization of higher education in selected African countries builds on the extensive work and experience gleaned from the *African Higher Education: International Reference Book Handbook* (Teferra and Altbach 2003), conferences/seminars organized by Association of African Universities on Cross-Border Education (AAU 2004), and the regional comparative studies on internationalization done in Latin America, Asia Pacific, Europe, and North America (Knight and de Wit 1997, 1999; Knight 1999, 2000; de Wit et al. 2005).

The baseline analysis is premised on the fact that the Teferra and Knight book is the only publication to have undertaken in-depth country case studies by authors who have a wide array of expertise, several institutional affiliations, and many levels of experience with the process of internationalization of higher education. The authors come from Botswana, Egypt, Ethiopia, Ghana, Kenya, Mauritius, Mozambique, Nigeria, Senegal, South Africa, and Tanzania. They provide an understanding of the challenges facing their countries in a manner that will allow for in-depth understanding of those factors that impact on international student mobility of African students and provide the foundations for further research to begin the task of examining the flow of these students in a more systemic manner.

This chapter is divided into three broad sections. The first section attempts to analyze trends in African student mobility with a special focus on the following: developments within the African continent and the rest of world; trends prevalent among African students from a selected group of countries who study in other African countries; regional trends in parts of Africa; and trends in the number of students who come from outside the continent to study in the selected countries. The primary focus in this section is mainly limited to Botswana, Egypt, Nigeria, and South Africa. The second section of the chapter offers a more in-depth analysis of the remaining seven countries as case studies examining some of the challenges in understanding mobility patterns in and from these countries. The third and final section focuses on the broader unique historical and current challenges that shape the movement of African students, the paucity of data, and the lack of mechanisms to collect and record data for research purposes.

Trends in Student Mobility in Africa

The purpose in the first part of this section is to describe student movement in Africa in a wider context and to appraise its importance to individual countries by using "external data"[2] on outbound mobility, which is expressed as the number of students from a given African country or region who are studying in another country, both within the African continent and outside it.

The second and third parts of this section examine internal[3] data available in four identified African countries on (a) students who are pursuing their studies outside of their countries but within the continent, and (b) students coming to these countries from outside of the continent. And finally, the chapter examines regional trends that are influenced by unique historical and local factors in the African continent.

"External Data" on African Student Mobility

Agencies such as UNESCO, the Organisation for Economic Co-operation and Development (OECD), and the Institute of International Education (IIE), through its *Open Doors* project, have data on African students studying abroad. Table 8.1 displays data on the numbers and destinations of outbound students from 12 African countries: Botswana, Egypt, Ethiopia, Ghana, Kenya, Mauritius, Mozambique, Nigeria, Senegal, South Africa, Tanzania, and Uganda. These statistics provide a glimpse into the extent of key mobility of African students. According to UNESCO, France is the dominant receiving country with about 109,000 from Sub-Saharan Africa. South Africa is the only African country with more than 36,000 students coming to study at its universities.

Research by the Observatory on Borderless Education (2007) also finds that France is a much more attractive destination of choice for Francophone African countries as evidenced by the numbers of students from the following countries who were studying in France in 2005: Morocco, 25,782; Algeria, 21,552; Tunisia, 9,593; and Senegal, 9,019. The United States also attracts students from most countries, as shown in figure 8.1. The countries identified sent at least a thousand students each.

Several countries in Sub-Saharan Africa have many students abroad, some even more than the number enrolled at home, often because access to domestic institutions is severely limited. Yet some of these students abroad are rarely counted in national statistics on higher education enrollment. For example, in Cape Verde, just 6 percent of the university-age population is reportedly enrolled in higher education institutions. But this figure would double if students abroad were also counted. Similarly, in Mauritius the gross enrollment ratio would rise from 17 percent to almost 24 percent and in Botswana from 6 percent to 11 percent (UNESCO 2006b).

Student mobility, although growing rapidly, has not fully kept up with the region's rapid expansion of tertiary education. Between 1999 and 2004,

Table 8.1 Numbers and Destinations of Students from Select Sub-Saharan African Countries, 2004

Country of origin	Destination (Ten Key Receiving Countries)											
	France	United States of America	South Africa	United Kingdom	Germany	Portugal	Australia	Morocco	Canada	India	Other Countries	Total
	1	2	3	4	5	6	7	8	9	10	11	
Botswana		488	7,012	700			792				479	9,471
Egypt	849	1,822		799	566					225	1,883	6,545
Ethiopia		1,060		263	1,192						1,208	3,322
Ghana		3,288		2,798	744				222		1,096	8,148
Kenya		7,381		3,083			1,115		341	521	1,707	14,123
Mauritius	1,893		1,732	1,646			860			366	727	7,224
Mozambique		93	815	71		1,066	67				254	2,366
Nigeria		6,140		5,942	630						2,426	15,138
Senegal	8,329	805			256			435	246		606	10,677
South Africa		1,971		1,408	196		643				1,401	5,619
Tanzania		1,471	283	1,053	115		119				866	3,907
Uganda		696		885	121					93	659	2,454
Other Countries	97,856	12,273	26,444	6,841	18,450	7,470	1,455	2,782	2,096	28	35,299	2,11,014
Total	1,08,927	37,488	36,286	25,489	22,270	8,536	5,051	3,217	2,905	1,233	48,611	3,00,013

Source: UNESCO-UIS/OECD (2005).

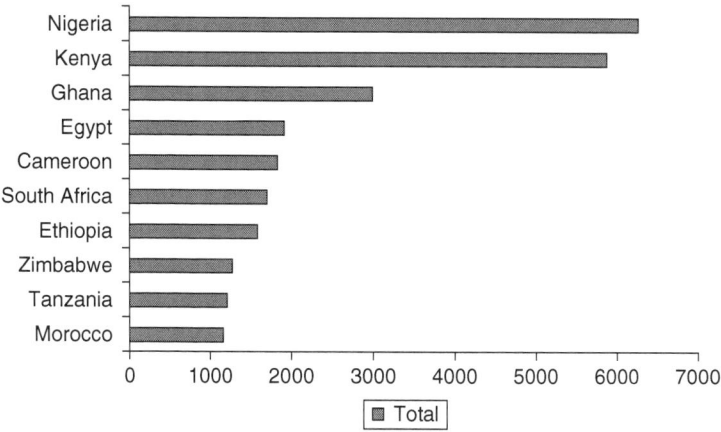

Figure 8.1 African Students in the United States by Countries that Send at Least 1,000 Students, 2009.

Source: Bhandari and Chow (2009).

enrollment in higher education institutions in the region grew by 53 percent, while the number of international students from the region grew by 48 percent. With 194,000 outbound international students, Sub-Saharan Africa accounts for 8 percent of the global total. The Sub-Saharan African countries that send the most students abroad are Zimbabwe (17,000), Nigeria (15,000), Cameroon (15,000), and Kenya (14,000); 51 percent go to Western Europe. Their second most important destination is Sub-Saharan Africa (21 percent) followed by North America (20 percent). Nine out of ten international students who stay in the region go to South Africa, especially those from the following Southern African countries: Botswana, Malawi, Namibia, Swaziland, Zambia, and Zimbabwe (UNESCO 2006b). In addition to South Africa, Ghana and Egypt have also emerged as major recipients of international students, particularly from within Africa.

Internal Data on Inbound Students

Using data generated by a national-level agency and/or the higher education system of the country under study, the analyses in this part focuses on incoming students to Egypt, Nigeria, Botswana, and South Africa during the 1995–2005 decade.

Figure 8.2 shows that the Egyptian practice of giving scholarships to students from other African countries has been institutionalized by the

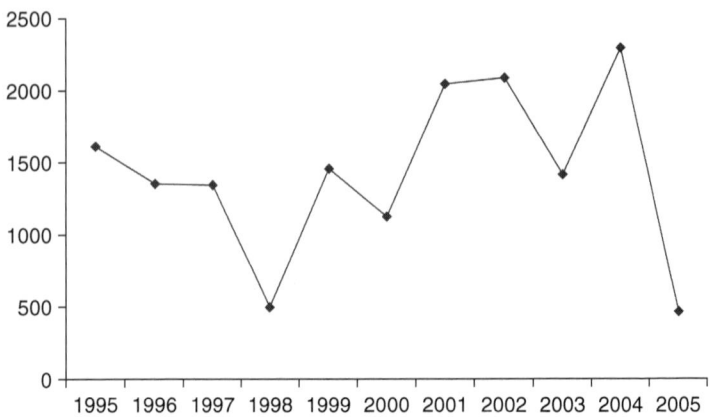

Figure 8.2 Students from Other African Countries Studying in Egypt, 1995–2005.

Source: General Administration of Foreign Students at the Islamic Research Academy, Al-Azhar Al-Sharif, in Egypt (2006). In Said, Mohsen Elmahdy, and Maha Moustafa Kamel (2008).

Egyptian Ministry of Education and Al-Azhar Al-Sharif University.[4] The number of scholarships available has been generally stable except for 1998 and 2005, when the Egyptian authorities reduced the awards owing to budgetary constraint. Egypt awarded 468 scholarships in 2005 and peaked in 2004 with 2,294 scholarships. The fluctuation shows that funding is a critical element in student mobility within Africa, particularly for those aided by scholarships.

Nigeria has a policy of attracting international students, although it has not been pursued systematically with Nigerian universities being "considerably less international in terms of academic staff diversity, student composition and even curriculum offering than in the incipient days in the early 1960s" (Jibril and Obaje 2008). As figure 8.3 shows, the annual enrollment of international students in Nigeria for 1997–2005 did not exceed 400; the data available also does not distinguish between African and non-African students. The country may need to reshape its policy of attracting African students to ensure that it benefits maximally from the gains that can be derived from an increased inflow of international students.

While the higher education subsector in Botswana reserves a percentage of its enrollment slots for international students, the numbers are small in relation to total enrollments. Figure 8.4 shows that between 1995 and 2005 the number of international students fluctuated between a minimum

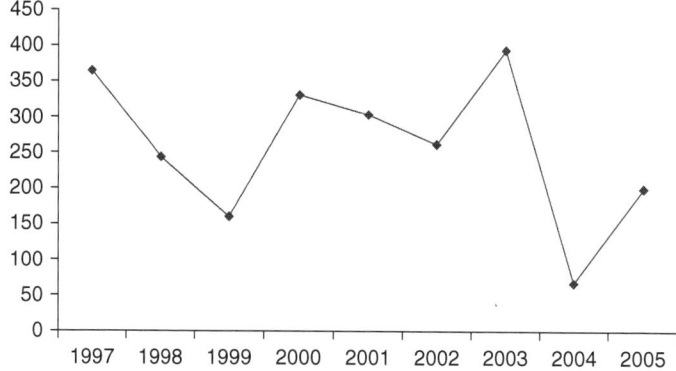

Figure 8.3 Number of International Students Studying in Nigeria, 1997–2005.
Source: Jibril et al. (2008).

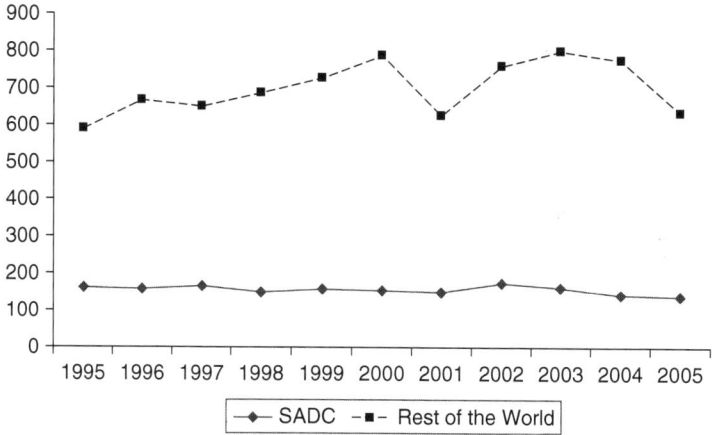

Figure 8.4 International Students from SADC and Other Countries in Botswana, 1995–2005.
Source: Tertiary Education Council (2006). In Molutsi and Kobedi (2008).

of 750 and a maximum of 960. Interestingly, the number of students from the "rest of the world" outnumbers those from the Southern African Development Community (SADC), of which Botswana is a member; but it is not clear whether African students from non-SADC countries are included among those from the "rest of the world." Botswana attracts more students from the "rest of the world" than its African neighbors do. Still, as Molutsi and Kobedi (2008) observe, "Foreign students do not seem to be a significant factor in the internationalization of tertiary education in Botswana."

South Africa has witnessed the most dramatic increase in the numbers of students coming to study at its institutions. In the short period since gaining democracy in 1994, South Africa has reconnected with the global higher education community and the number of international students in South Africa has more than quadrupled—from around 12,500 in 1994 to nearly 53,000 in 2005, constituting more than 7 percent of the total enrollment of 730,000 (Kishun 2006).

As figure 8.5 shows, there has been a dramatic increase in incoming students among those of SADC countries, of which South Africa is a member. These results mirror the South African government's demonstrated commitment to support the SADC's Education and Training Protocol that mandates increased access to higher education and mobility of students from other member countries.

Students from Outside Africa

African universities have typically not received large numbers of full-time, degree-seeking students from outside the continent. Students come mainly for short courses as study-abroad or as exchange students for one or two semesters. Many students are drawn to Africa because of the "exotic"

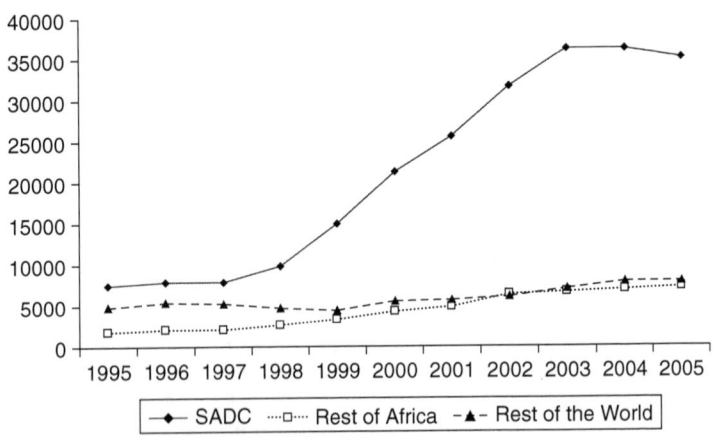

Figure 8.5 International Students Studying in South Africa, 1995–2005.
Source: South Africa Department of Education (2006).

experience and not necessarily for academic reasons. However, although research is sparse and reliable data on students coming from outside the continent is almost nonexistent, it is safe to assume that most countries in Africa have, in fact, had some experience with hosting non-African students.

According to Said and Kamel (2008), during academic year 2006–2007, 14,854 international students were enrolled at Al-Azhar Al-Sharif University in Egypt. This number does not differentiate African from non-African students. The majority of foreign students enroll in Islamic studies, with Indonesia having the highest enrollment rate among male students (2,799, 25.6 percent) and Malaysia (1,933, 52.7 percent) among female students.

In 2005 South Africa was the recipient of almost 7,800 students from outside the continent, an increase from the 4,800 it attracted in 1995 (figure 8.5). This increase of over 61 percent coincides with the establishment of democracy in South Africa in 1994 when the first free elections took place. The number of international students from the SADC and the "rest of Africa" also grew quite substantially.

Regional Mobility Trends

One of the striking features of student mobility on the African continent is its regional character, in particular how intercountry mobility reproduces patterns of colonization. The colonial influence seen in Southern and Eastern Africa comes from the United Kingdom, while in West Africa it is largely from France, and Central and North Africa draw upon France and Germany. Maringe and Carter (2007) confirm that African students tend to migrate to countries formerly included as colonies of the same European power under which their own country was in the past, largely because of derived cultural capital, language facility, and a somewhat shared history. Thus, postcolonial associations are a significant influence on international student mobility.

There are, of course, exceptions to the colonial pattern, such as Cameroon, Eritrea, Ethiopia, and Somalia. But France, the region's single most important host country, and Belgium are the preferred destinations for francophone students from Benin, Gabon, Comoros, Congo, Democratic Republic of the Congo (DRC), Ivory Coast, Madagascar, and Senegal. Each of these countries sends more than 2,000 students abroad every year across the entire world. Students from Lusopohone countries, such as Angola, Cape Verde, and Mozambique, tend to go to Portugal. After South Africa, the United States is the main destination for students from Anglophone Sub-Saharan countries, including Ghana, Kenya, Nigeria, and South Africa, each of which sends more than 1,900 students abroad annually.

Many students from West African countries go to Nigeria, Ghana, Cameroon, and Senegal; students in East Africa come mostly from neighboring countries such as Uganda, Kenya, Rwanda, and Tanzania; students from Southern African countries go mainly to South Africa. Historically, many of the higher education institutions established during the colonial period were set up to serve more than one country, capitalizing on common heritage, language, closer trade relations, and political stability. For example, before independence, Botswana, Lesotho, and Swaziland had a joint university based in Lesotho that served the higher education needs of these three countries. Makerere College (conceived as the University of East Africa) was set up to serve the three East African countries of Uganda, Kenya, and Tanzania. The same arrangement would have happened in West Africa but for Ghana's resistance to a university based in Nigeria that would serve all of British West Africa. These colonial institutions had affiliated colleges that nearly always developed into self-governing universities after independence. However, most of the original universities maintain a collaborative relationship with their affiliates, a relationship that has, in some cases, been built over many years. These collaborations usually take the form of student and faculty exchanges and collaborative research.

In the case of Southern Africa, SADC, consisting of 14 countries, signed the SADC Education and Training Protocol in 1997. This important instrument requires member countries to allot at least 5 percent of their enrollment to students from the region. The political changes of the region since the early 1990s and South Africa's good educational infrastructure meant that most SADC students found South Africa an attractive destination after 1994.

Case Studies of Select Sub-Saharan African Countries

In this second section of the chapter case studies of the following countries highlight the historical, political, and other factors that determined both inbound and outbound mobility of students from these countries. These cases demonstrate clearly the challenges in data collection and the difficulties in extracting information from different and disparate sources.

Ethiopia

Mobility is not a new phenomenon for Ethiopian higher education students (Semela and Ayalew 2008). In 1973, about 700 students were pursuing higher education in the United States (Zewde 2002). In 1974, when the military dictatorship replaced Haile Selassie 1, opportunities for scholarship shifted to the Soviet Union and its allies. The change of regimes had no immediate effect on study abroad for Ethiopian students and staff supported by government scholarships. Although the data available indicate that between 2000–2001 and 2004–2005 the total number of those receiving government scholarship did not exceed 233 per year, the number of those returning from study abroad exceeded 500 annually except for 2001–2002. This suggests that other sources of scholarships, not included in the official statistics, account for this larger figure of returned students and staff.

Table 8.2 lists countries in which Ethiopian graduate students studied between 2002 and 2004. Ghana, Russia, Ukraine, Israel, Turkey, Kenya,

Table 8.2 Ethiopians Returned from Abroad with Postgraduate Qualification by Destination Country

Country	Academic Year						Total	Percent
	2002–2003		2003–2004		2004–2005			
	Master's	PhD	Master's	PhD	Master's	PhD		
Austria	3	5	4	10		9	31	2.58
Belgium	–	2	12	1	19	2	36	2.99
China	8	–	4	–	13		25	2.08
England	47	3	36	5	45	11	147	12.24
France	8	3	3	4	2	11	31	2.58
Germany	21	16	22	29	31	22	141	11.74
Ireland	7	–	13	1	9	1	31	2.58
India	72	6	23	9	45	2	157	13.07
Italy	7	3	5	4	2		21	1.75
Japan	4	1	2	4	3	1	15	1.25
Norway	20	9	24	6	30	7	96	7.99
South Africa	10	14	19	26	7	3	79	6.58
Sweden	9	10	11	8	3	8	49	4.08
The Netherlands	58	18	63	11	108	4	262	21.82
Thailand	1	1	–	16	6	10	34	2.83
The United States	10	5	11	10	8	2	46	3.83
Total	285	96	252	144	331	93	1,201	100

Source: Compiled based on data obtained from Semela and Ayalew (2008).

Egypt, Tanzania, and the Philippines attracted relatively few advanced students while the Netherlands, Germany, Norway, Sweden, and England attracted larger numbers.

Ghana

The outward mobility of Ghanian students dates back to the colonial period. Between 1948, when the University College of the Gold Coast (UCGC) was established, and independence in 1957, a conscious effort was made to develop human resource skills amongst the locals to assist in the nation's development. A number of students who graduated from UCGC were provided opportunities to further their studies in the United Kingdom. After independence, because of the socialist inclination of the government, many students were sent to the Soviet Union and Eastern Europe, a substantial number of whom did not return (Effah and Senadsa 2008).

Government scholarships continue to be available for skills development and capacity building: in 2005/2006, 88 such scholarships were awarded. The majority of the scholarship awardees (72 percent) go to the United Kingdom thus continuing the "the colonial legacy" of mobility. The United States emerges as the second most important destination for government scholarship holders. The number of Ghanaian students studying in the United States has been steadily increasing since 1998–1999 (figure 8.6). Effah and Senadsa (2008) acknowledge the fact that

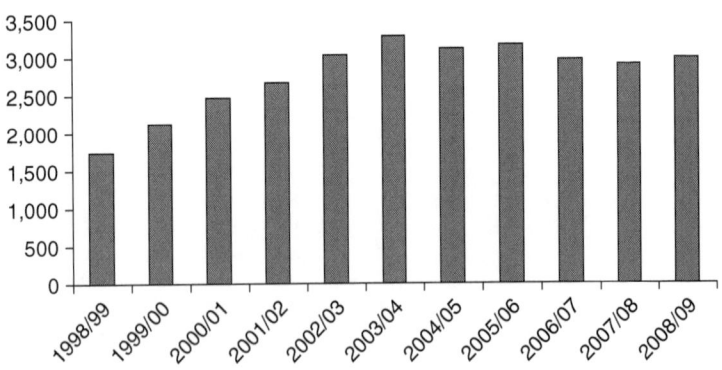

Figure 8.6 Ghanaian Students in the United States, 1998–2009.
Source: Bhandari and Chow (2009).

obtaining accurate figures for all Ghanaian students studying outside or for international students inside the country is difficult.

Kenya

Otieno and colleagues (2008) map out the Kenyan student mobility patterns that mirror the colonial legacy movement imperatives. The difference being that Kenyan nationalists "organized massive airlifts to train young Kenyans in American universities and the former Union of Soviet Socialist Republics (USSR) respectively" (249). The first group of 81 students left for studies in 1959, becoming pioneering academics and civil servants upon their return to Kenya (Mboya 1963). By 1991, it was estimated that about 10,000 Kenyan students were studying abroad. With 30,000 students abroad by 2001, Kenya had the highest number of African students studying in universities abroad and was the only African country listed among the top 20 countries sending students to the United States in 2005.

Otieno and colleagues (2008) note that only 2 percent of students at Kenyan universities are designated as international. Most of them are refugee students from neighboring countries and, in the strict sense, may not be considered as international students. It would seem that students from outside the continent mainly take part in short courses and are not necessarily counted. Key host institutions of international students in Kenya include the following: the University of Nairobi, Kenyatta University, Moi University, Egerton University, Jomo Kenyatta, and the U.S. International University.

Mauritius

According to Mohamedbhai (2008), every year over 2000 students leave Mauritius to study overseas, and this figure has been steadily increasing in the past decade. In 2005, there were 7,357 students pursuing tertiary education studies abroad. This is a very significant figure, representing 34 percent of Mauritian students, and is greater than the number of students studying at the University of Mauritius. Table 8.3 shows the students by countries of destination.

Looking next at international students, Mohamedbhai (2008) cites figures that indicate the very low numbers of foreign students at Mauritian institutions, whether public or private. Only about 0.6 percent of total enrollments in public-funded institutions were international students. The majority of these students, estimated at between 400 and 500, were

Table 8.3   Mauritian Students Studying Outside of the Country, 2005

Country of Study	Number of Students
Austria	1,572
Canada	62
China	34
CIS (Russia & Ukraine)	253
France	1,968
India	1,333
Madagascar	41
Pakistan	84
Singapore	26
South Africa	258
The United Kingdom	1,522
The United States	97
Others	107
Total	7,357

Source: Mohamedbhai (2006a).

studying at SSR Medical School and Mauras College of Dentistry and came mainly from India.

Mozambique

Examining the numbers of students going out to study, Brito and colleagues (2008) report the lack of official data on Mozambican students studying abroad. All the data were collected by the authors by approaching representatives of countries with a Mozambican student population.

Table 8.4 summarizes data available for students studying in Mozambique and outside. The number of those studying in OECD countries was recorded as over 1,400 for 2003 and 2004. The spike in 2000 was caused by missing data for 2001–2002 about Mozambicans studying in Portugal, which was estimated at 1,000 students. The most impressive increase has been among students who study in South Africa, increasing from 385 in 2000 (the first year data was available) to 887 in 2004. However, it is noted that 41–51 percent are enrolled at the University of South Africa (UNISA), a distance education provider.

While more than 2,500 Mozambicans are studying outside of the country the authors noted that no more than 350 students from abroad are studying at local universities. The study does not provide any breakdown regarding exactly what these students study or the level of their study. The

Table 8.4 Comparison between the Number of Mozambicans Studying in the Country and those Registered Abroad in Selected Countries

	1998	1999	2000	2001	2002	2003	2004
Moz. Students in Mozambican institutions	10,227	12,447	13,423	14,375	17,320	17,225	22,565
To OECD Countries[*]	373	460	1,318	404	449	1,475	1,433
Brazil[†]	–	–	60	65	120	105	86
South Africa[‡]	–	–	385	437	580	764	887
Asia[§,**]	–	–	–	5	10	10	56
Total Abroad	413	500	1,803	951	1,199	2,394	2,502
For/(Int+For)	4%	4%	12%	6%	6%	12%	10%

[*] OECD statistics database

[†] Estimates based on figures regarding yearly admission of BSc and Licenciatura programmes of the Centro de Estudos Brasileiros in Maputo

[‡] Unpublished data from the Ministry of Education of South Africa

[§] Estimates solely on the basis of scholarships of the Petronas University (five per year) in Malaysia for 2001–2003

[**] Figure for 2004 based on the Petronas University Scholarship and an extrapolation from data for 2005 for India and China provided by the Ministry of Foreign Affairs of Mozambique

Source: Data from Brito et al. (2008).

Ministry of Education does not have the data because of the relatively small number of international students and also since institutions do not record such information.

Senegal

According to Mbaye (2008, 373), the "fundamental rationale for internationalization in Senegal is related to colonial history." Mobility data is available for outbound Senegalese students only. Africa (including North and Sub-Saharan Africa) is the primary source for international students, accounting for 84.9 percent of enrollment in Senegal. European and American students make up less than 2 percent of the international student population. It should be noted that official statistics do not recognize a significant number of "foreign" students, mainly from the United States, who come to Senegal for short-term language study or other purposes. Table 8.5 provides the nationalities of the international student population in Senegal.

Table 8.5   Foreign Students in Senegal by Selected Country of Origin

Country of Origin	Percentage
Morocco	19.4
Mauritania	15.7
Cote d'Ivoire	6.7
Burkina Faso	6.6
Congo	6.3
Benin	5.7
Gabon	5.3
Cameroon	5.2
Togo	5.1
Chad	3.3
Republic of Guinea	2.5
Mali	2.2
Central African Republic	1.3
Tunisia	1.2

Source: Mbaye (2008).

Tanzania

The primary catalyst for supporting international student mobility in Tanzania is the Ministry of Education, Science and Technology (MHEST), through the Directorate of Higher Education, which arranges scholarships through bilateral and cultural exchange agreements. Table 8.6 shows the number of graduates and undergraduates studying in various countries in the 2005–2006 academic year.

As table 8.6 shows China provided the most scholarships (30.9 percent), followed by Russia (20.1 percent), India (16.1 percent), Algeria (12.4 percent), Uganda (10.5 percent), and South Africa (4.1 percent). The large numbers of Tanzanian students in China, Russia, India, and Algeria are explained by the fact that these countries have been Tanzania's traditional allies since independence.

Interestingly, Uganda was the most popular destination for Tanzanian students in the years 2004–2005. Ishengoma (2008) cites South Africa as another important African destination for Tanzanian students. In all, according Ishengoma, a total of 3,041 Tanzanians students were studying abroad under various arrangements in 2007 (table 8.7), while only 275 students from outside the country were studying in Tanzania. From the information provided it is not clear whether the 3,041 were funded by government or financed privately.

Table 8.6 Tanzanian Undergraduate and Graduate Students Studying Abroad through MHEST Scholarships, 2005–2006

Country	Undergraduate Students			Postgraduate Students		
	Male	Female	Total	Male	Female	Total
China	124	30	154	21	5	26
Russia	91	23	114	3	0	3
Poland	11	1	12	0	0	0
Cuba	6	2	8	0	0	0
Czech Republic	3	0	3	0	0	0
Algeria	51	32	83	0	0	0
South Africa	12	12	24	0	0	0
India	51	43	94	0	0	0
Uganda	51	10	61	0	0	0
Total	400	153	553	24	4	29

Source: Adapted from Ishengoma (2008, 15–17).

Table 8.7 Tanzanian Students Studying Abroad, 2007

Country	Number of Students	Percentage
The United States	1,471	48.3
The United Kingdom	1,053	34.6
South Africa	283	9.3
Australia	119	3.9
Germany	115	3.8
Total	3,041[a]	100.0

[a] GUNI (2007) gives a total of 3,907. However, adding up the reported figures yields 3,041, a discrepancy of 860. This source reports that 275 foreign students were studying in Tanzanian higher education institutions.

Source: Adapted from Ishengoma (2008).

Challenges that Shape the Movement of African Students

This third section of the chapter discusses broader questions around African student mobility. In the African context one can ask whether the mobility of students is truly "an international experience." The data reveal that the movement of African students may not necessarily be tied to the romanticized and idealistic definitions of internationalization.[5] In fact, African student mobility may be more directly linked to the geopolitical struggles of the past and to the colonization of many parts of the African continent. This can be easily demonstrated by African countries that send large numbers of their students to countries that colonized them, as identified in this chapter.

The movement of African students is impacted by the General Agreement on Trade in Services (GATS) of the World Trade Organization and the European Union Bologna Process, both of which have implications for international education. GATS could potentially open the way for a more global market in higher education as well as for a burgeoning of cross-border and private provision and could also place public higher education in many (especially developing) countries under threat. The Bologna Process, however, covers 45 countries and is the largest and most substantial higher education grouping in the world. Its agenda is much broader than creating common course structures and quality assurance systems, as it includes higher education reforms and the projection of "European higher education area" more emphatically onto the world stage (Huisman and van der Wende 2005). The Bologna Process now reaches (or will soon reach) countries far from Europe—for example, Francophone and Anglophone countries in Africa—and the Bologna-linked Erasmus Mundus program is designed to promote far greater student mobility between Europe and the rest of the world. How the higher education subsector in Africa will engage with these worldwide developments is a question that African policymakers will need to address.

What is apparent in the data presented is the fact that more students leave to study outside than come into Africa. South Africa in the only African country that has more international students studying in the country than South African students going out for their studies. At the same time South Africa is also seen as encouraging qualified academics and highly skilled personnel from other African countries to work in South Africa. Similarly, knowledge-hungry and rich industrialized countries seeking to increase their economic and scientific competitiveness are attractive destinations, especially when the quality of life in the home country is undesirable or dangerous for any number of reasons. Given this dynamic, Africa is extremely vulnerable to sophisticated recruitment strategies by industrialized countries' governments and private sectors.

There is some reason to believe that the Third World becomes a cheap source of skilled labor in the First World's search for "knowledge workers." In effect, the exodus of students and qualified people from some of the poorest countries to some of the richest may be an unmitigated tragedy unless steps are taken to reverse the flow. Competition for international students should be examined in the broader context of mass skilled labor mobility that is a central global feature of the twenty-first century (Kishun 2006). While the major African initiatives such as New Plan for Africa's Development (NEPAD) require highly qualified and skilled personnel, the global market demands the very same people.

Of great concern for the higher education subsector in Africa is the fact that the scientific and well-resourced research system in industrialized countries fuels the brain drain from developing countries. Countries with highly advanced infrastructure, attractive salaries, and advanced research facilities tend to be the most attractive destination for students, who bring along with them international experience and who also serve as a source of revenue for the institutions. Advanced countries consciously target students through attractive offers and immigration regulations that make it easier to stay.

But perhaps of greater concern, as Crush and colleagues (2006) point out in their study of six SADC countries, brain drain attacks not only the existing skills base but also the potential skills base. Although most SADC students are proud of their countries, have a strong sense of national identity, desire to help build their countries with their talents and skills, and want to play a role in their country's future, there is a high risk of a continued brain drain from all six countries in the research sample. About 36 percent of the students said it was likely they would emigrate within six months of graduation, with the proportion rising to about 52 percent within two years of graduation. The findings identified the low levels of satisfaction with personal and national economic conditions as powerful "push" factors.

In the African context, the monetary value of international students has not been researched. Rhee and Sagaria (2004), summarizing reasons why American universities attract international students, included the fact that international students are a valuable source of revenue, contributing over US$13 billion to the U.S. economy annually (this figure has now increased to US$17.7 billion according to the 2009 *Open Doors* report). The United Kingdom and Australia also earn substantial income from "exporting" their education. While international student mobility may be seen as a form of education export, African countries may need to grapple with whether this mobility is as profitable to Africa as people first thought.

The lack of a formal structure to support internationalization also means that African universities are unable to market themselves or position their institutions as global players. While geographic, historical, cultural, economic, political, and other factors are all critical, African universities must take active steps to be part of the global networks that will position them on the global landscape. African universities are usually not visible at major international education conferences and fairs where opportunities for institutional collaboration are showcased in terms of services, course offerings, and programs of interest to participants from around the world. For instance, Botswana was the only other African country besides South Africa that participated for the first time at the Association for International Educators (NAFSA) conference, held in Montreal, Canada, in 2006.

The mobility of international students is also influenced by the ability of the educational institutions to determine eligibility. International office personnel will be required to provide highly specialized services. For example, universities accept a wide diversity of international students with many different backgrounds and qualifications (many of them unknown) from partner institutions around the world. Credentials evaluation has thus become a topic of increasing concern to universities (Wenger and Frey 2006). High levels of expertise are required to determine the eligibility of the growing numbers of international students from almost all countries. It is critical not merely to recognize other education systems but also to understand, interpret, and equate different systems so that issues of access to higher education can be handled holistically.

Conclusion

The movement of African students is intertwined with colonial legacy, language, economics, imported educational systems, and geopolitical global factors. In the analyses of the data the first two challenges that became apparent were the lack of reliable data generated from African higher education institutions and the absence of a commonly accepted definition of mobility. The limited data available were in different formats, were not collected consistently, or were collected by different agencies for different purposes. Except in South Africa, the higher education regulatory agencies and universities themselves do not keep records of international student enrollment. Often even available data is not made accessible to researchers, which further hampers the task of researching mobility in Africa.

Caution must be exercised in reaching any definitive conclusions on the basis of the analyses. There are 53 countries in the African continent with an estimated population of 1 billion people, 50 percent of whom are under age 20. All of these countries have different languages and cultural backgrounds. There exists no single African language comparable to the English language that unites most Western countries. At the same time, the colonial languages that have replaced traditional local languages in

Africa such as French, Portuguese, Spanish, and German play a significant role in connecting countries to their colonizers.

There is a strong need for a systematic study of trends in African student mobility to provide the basis of developing educational policies, strengthening existing regulatory frameworks at both the national and continental levels, and generally developing an environment that will encourage international student mobility from both within and outside Africa. In meeting the challenges facing the higher education subsector in Africa, the Teferra/Knight book initiative led to the formation of two important organizations with the primary focus of engaging, promoting, and researching internationalization in the African context. The African Network for Internationalization of Education (ANIE) and its sister organization the Network of Emerging Scholars for Internationalisation (NESI) are key instruments in positioning the African continent as an integral player in the global world.

NOTES

1. The data in this Chapter is taken primarily from Chapter 16 ("International Student Mobility In and Out of Africa: Challenges and Opportunities") of the book titled *Higher Education in Africa: The International Dimension,* edited by Damtew Teferra and Jane Knight (2008). This Chapter provides a more comprehensive analysis of African student mobility trends and includes the seven countries that were not considered in the previous publication.
2. "External data" is sourced from organizations based outside of the African continent.
3. "Internal data" is sourced from universities and other organizations based inside the continent.
4. Mobility data for Egypt is available only for those students who received government scholarships.
5. For example, definitions that tend to include words such as "global education" and "multicultural education" or the process of adding these dimensions into education may not necessarily be the motivating factors for African student mobility.

BIBLIOGRAPHY

Bhandari, Rajika, and Patricia Chow. 2009. *Open Doors 2009: Report on International Educational Exchange.* New York: Institute of International Education.
Brito, Lidia, Roland de Brouwer, and Ana Menezes. 2008. "Mozambique." In *Higher Education in Africa: The International Dimension,* ed. Damtew Teferra and Jane Knight. Boston: Boston College.

Crush, Jonathan, Wade Pendleton, and Daniel S. Tevera. 2006. "Degrees of Uncertainty: Students and the Brain Drain in Southern Africa." In *The Internationalisation of Higher Education in South Africa: Progress and Challenges,* ed. Roshen Kishun. Durban: International Education Association of South Africa.

de Wit, Hans, Isabel C. Jaramillo, Jocelyne Gacel-Avila, and Jane Knight, eds. 2005. "Higher Education in Latin America: The International Dimension." In *Higher Education in Africa: The International Dimension,* ed. Damtew Teferra and Jane Knight. Boston: Boston College.

Department of Education. 2006. *Higher Education Management Information System (HEMIS).* Pretoria, South Africa: Department of Education.

Effah, Paul, and Bernardin Senadza. 2008. "Ghana." In *Higher Education in Africa: The International Dimension,* ed. Damtew Teferra and Jane Knight. Boston: Boston College.

Ishengoma, Johnson M. 2008. "Tanzania." In *Higher Education in Africa: The International Dimension,* ed. Damtew Teferra and Jane Knight. Boston: Boston College.

Jibril, Munzali, and Abdulkarim Obaje. 2008. "Nigeria." In *Higher Education in Africa: The International Dimension,* ed. Damtew Teferra and Jane Knight. Boston: Boston College.

Kishun, Roshen. 2006. "Introduction: The Internationalization of Higher Education in South Africa: Progress and Challenges." In *The Internationalisation of Higher Education in South Africa: Progress and Challenges,* ed. Roshen Kishun. Durban: Astro Printers for International Education Association of South Africa.

Lulat, Y. G-M. 2003. "The Development of Higher Education in Africa: A Historical Survey." In *African Higher Education: An International Reference Handbook,* ed. Damtew Teferra and Philip G. Altbach. Bloomington, IN: Indiana State University.

Marginson, Simon, and Marjik van der Wende. 2007. *Globalisation and Higher Education.* Education Working Paper, No. 8. Paris: Organization for Economic Co-operation and Development.

Maringe, Felix, and Steve Carter. 2007. "International Students' Motivations for Studying in the U.K. HE: Insights into the Choice and Decision Making of African Students." *International Journal of Educational Management* 21 (6): 459–475.

Mbaye, Ahmadou Aly. 2008. "Senegal." In *Higher Education in Africa: The International Dimension,* ed. Damtew Teferra and Jane Knight. Boston, MA: Boston College.

Menell-Kinberg, Monica E. 1991. "United States Scholarships for Black South Africans, 1976–1990: The Politicization of Education." PhD dissertation, Graduate School of Education and Information Studies, University of California, Los Angeles.

Mohamedbhai, Goolam. 2008. "Mauritius." In *Higher Education in Africa: The International Dimension,* ed. Damtew Teferra and Jane Knight. Boston: Boston College.

Molutsi, Patrick, and Kagiso Kobedi. 2008. "Botswana." In *Higher Education in Africa: The International Dimension,* ed. Damtew Teferra and Jane Knight. Boston: Boston College.

Otieno, James Jowi, Crispus Kiamba, and David K. Some. 2008. "Kenya." In *Higher Education in Africa: The International Dimension,* ed. Damtew Teferra and Jane Knight. Boston: Boston College.

Rhee, Jeong-Eun, and Mary Ann Danowitz Sagaria. 2004. "International Students: Constructions of Imperialism" *Chronicle of Higher Education. Review of Higher Education 28* (1): 77–96.

Said, Mohsen Elmahdy, and Maha Moustafa Kamel. 2008. "Egypt." In *Higher Education in Africa: The International Dimension,* ed. Damtew Teferra and Jane Knight. Boston: Boston College.

Scott, Peter.2006. "Internationalising Higher Education: A Global Perspective." In *The Internationalisation of Higher Education in South Africa: Progress and Challenges,* ed. Roshen Kishun. Durban, South Africa: Astro Printers for International Education Association of South Africa.

Semela, Tesfaye, and Elizabeth Ayalew. 2008. "Ethiopia." In *Higher Education in Africa: The International Dimension,* ed. Damtew Teferra and Jane Knight. Boston: Boston College.

Teferra, Damtew, and Jane Knight, eds. 2008. *Higher Education in Africa: The International Dimension.* Boston, MA: Boston College.

Teferra, Damtew, and Philip G. Altbach, eds. 2003. *African Higher Education: An International Reference Handbook.* Bloomington, IN: Indiana University Press.

UNESCO Institute for Statistics. 2006a. "African Students the Most Mobile in the World." Press Release: May 31, 2006. Montreal: UNESCO Institute for Statistics. Available online at: http://www.uis.unesco.org.

UNESCO Institute for Statistics. 2006b. *Global Education Digest 2006: Comparing Education Statistics across the World.* Montreal: UNESCO Institute for Statistics. Available online at: http://www.uis.unesco.org.

UNESCO Institute for Statistics. 2006c. *Global Education Digest 2005: Comparing Education Statistics across the World.* Montreal: UNESCO Institute for Statistics. Available online at: http://www.uis.unesco.org.

UNESCO Institute for Statistics. 2006d. *Global Education Digest 2006: Comparing Education Statistics across the World.* Montreal: UNESCO Institute for Statistics.

UNESCO-UIS/OECD. 2005. Education Trends in Perspective: Analysis of the World Education Indicators. Montreal: UNESCO Institute for Statistics.

Wenger, M., and Jim Frey. 2006. Basic Principles and Procedures of Credential Evaluation. In *The Internationalisation of Higher Education in South Africa: Progress and Challenges,* ed. Roshen Kishun. Durban: Astro Printers for International Education Association of South Africa.

Chapter 9

Structural Incentives to Attract Foreign Students to Canada's Postsecondary Educational System: A Comparative Analysis[1]

John McHale

Introduction

The idea that countries are competing for the world's top student talent has become a focus—and the source of some hype—in the globalization debate. As the number of foreign students enrolled in higher education fell for the first time in 2003/2004, leading figures in the scientific community in the United States worried that the country would lose its lead in cutting edge industries (National Science Board 2004a, 2004b). Observers look to the rapidly increasing graduate population in China and India—and the increasing competition for students from other countries—and worry that the United States is losing its status as the "world's greatest talent magnet" (Florida 2005).[2] In the United Kingdom, universities now depend on foreign students for roughly one-tenth of their revenues, and leading institutions such as the London School of Economics stay competitive for top research faculty by recruiting full-fee-paying students from outside the European Union (EU). In Australia, the number of foreign students increased more than sixfold since 1990.

A comparison of foreign student enrollment numbers across countries reveals that Canada lags key comparator countries in the market for foreign students. In an attempt to question all the hype surrounding this issue, this chapter looks at Canada's participation in the market for foreign students and explores the costs and benefits of foreign student recruitment.

In considering the merits of foreign student recruitment, my metric will be the costs and benefits to Canadians, especially would-be Canadian students. Of course, other considerations matter as well—for example, fostering mutual understanding between Canada and other countries or helping to build the institutional capacities of poorer countries—though they are outside the scope of the current chapter.[3] The most worrisome potential cost for *Canadians* is that domestic students are "crowded out" of higher education. The potential benefits are more subtle. I consider three main rationales for recruiting foreign students: revenue generation, knowledge production in higher education, and a more productive immigrant pool. My general conclusion is that there are significant benefits based on each of these rationales, and that it should be possible to devise an incentive structure that expands the scope for foreign student recruitment in a way that, rather than harming local interests, helps Canadian students and strengthens Canada's national innovation system.

Recruitment of foreign students has risen dramatically across the Organisation for Economic Co-operation and Development (OECD) since the early 1990s. Somewhat surprisingly for a country that has pioneered the use of skill-based immigration policies, Canada has been a relatively reluctant recruiter of foreign students until quite recently. This chapter provides a comparative and policy-focused examination of Canada's participation in the "market" for foreign students. It first documents how Canada's recruitment of foreign students compares with that of other countries and also how it has evolved over time. With a focus on the costs and benefits for Canadians, it then examines various rationales for recruitment, including revenue generation, improved knowledge production at Canadian postsecondary institutions, and complementarities with the system of skills-based immigrant selection.

The rest of the chapter is organized as follows. In the next section, Section 2, I describe both longer-term and also more recent trends in the recruitment of foreign students in Canada and its leading "competitors" in this market. Section 3 analyzes the revenue-raising potential of foreign student recruitment, notably by examining fees charged to foreign and domestic students at Canadian universities. Section 4 examines how foreign students affect knowledge production at Canadian institutions of higher education. One aspect is the way that foreign students alter the human capital acquisition of Canadian students, impacts that include the value of diversity and competition-induced changes in teaching practice. A second aspect is how foreign graduate students affect research productivity, and thus the level of knowledge spillovers from Canadian institutions.

In Section 5, I turn to important connections between foreign student recruitment and the ability to attract and select a pool of immigrants who will be successful in the Canadian labor market. The background here is that relative to the Canadian-born students recent cohorts of immigrants are performing less well than earlier immigrant cohorts. Part of the reason is that there is a low return to foreign education and experience. This underscores the value of recruiting from a relatively large pool of foreign students with Canada-specific human capital. Section 6 offers some concluding thoughts.

Canada and the Competition for Foreign Students

Canada has been a relatively reluctant recruiter of foreign students. Figure 9.1 shows that in 2006 Canada ranked sixth in terms of the number of foreign students in postsecondary education, far behind the United States, and also behind the United Kingdom, Germany, France, Australia, and Japan. Even more revealingly, Canada's ranking is even lower when we look at its share of foreign students in the total postsecondary-educated student body. In 2006, 15 percent of Canada's postsecondary-level student body was foreign, which compares with 18 percent in the United Kingdom and 21 percent in Australia. These two English-speaking countries are especially interesting because they are close competitors in the market for students seeking instruction in English.[4] Canada's relative lack of presence in this market is curious given its pioneering polices in recruiting permanent immigrants through its points system, and its sizable immigrant population (18 percent).

Figure 9.2 shows that a number of countries—Australia and the United Kingdom included—significantly scaled up the size of their foreign student populations after 1990. In the period up to 2001, Canada was next to last on this list of OECD countries, with only France having a lower rate of increase. However, Canada has been a much more active recruiter of foreign students in recent years, with overall growth rates in foreign student numbers that are just behind those of Australia and the United Kingdom.

Although it is somewhat simplistic to classify Canada with English-speaking countries for foreign students, table 9.1 shows that Canada's "market share" is low across all the regions considered. For example, in 2001 46 percent of all Asian students who were studying in an OECD country were in the United States, with a further 12 percent going to each of Australia and the United Kingdom. Canada had just 2 percent. Even from the share

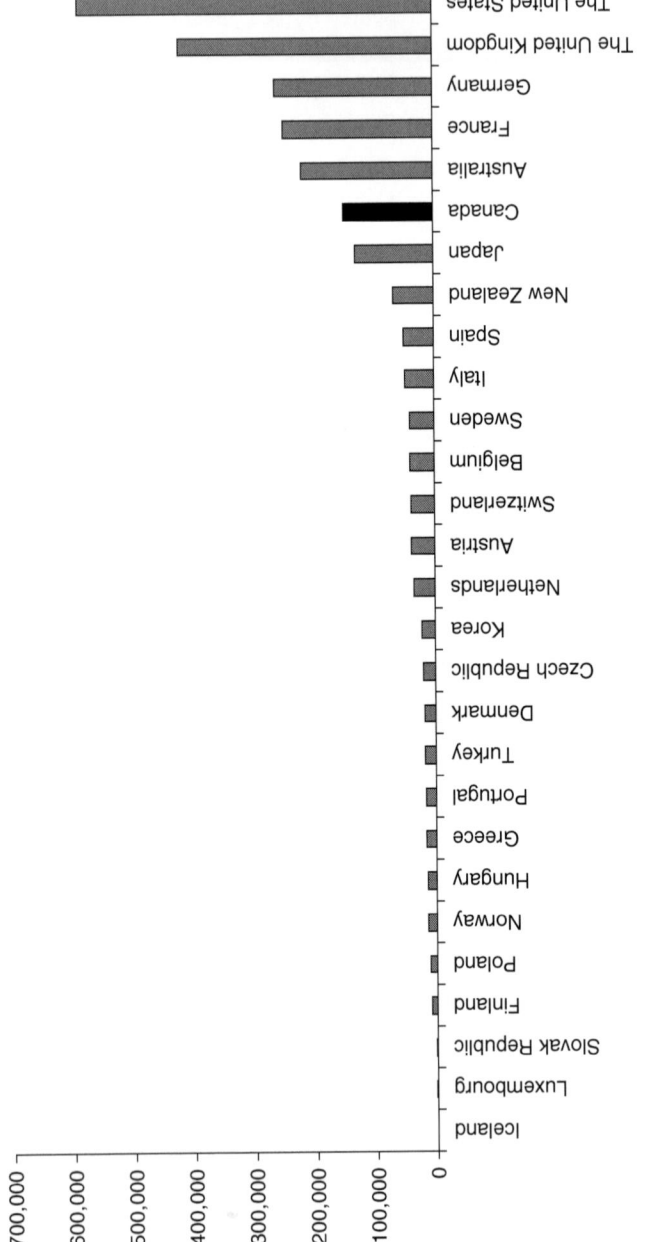

Figure 9.1 Number of Foreign Students in Tertiary Education in 2006.

Source: OECD, Education at a Glance Database, accessed June 19, 2009.

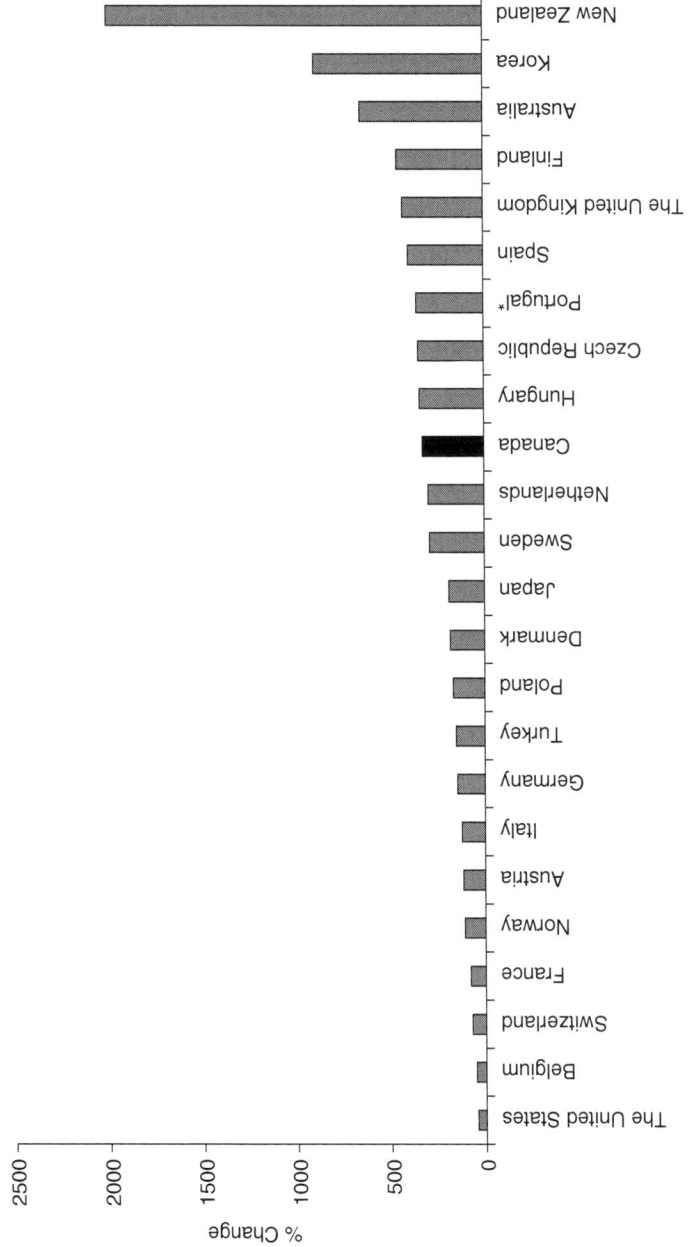

Figure 9.2 Percentage Change in Foreign Students in Tertiary Education, 1990 to 2006.

Source: OECD, Education at a Glance Database, accessed June 19, 2009.

Table 9.1 Shares of Foreign Tertiary Students in Selected English-Speaking Countries, 2001

World Region of Origin	The United States	The United Kingdom	Australia	Canada	Total
Asia	46	12	12	2	72
Oceania	26	12	43	3	84
South America	52	5	2	2	61
North America	50	19	6	7	82
Europe	13	21	2	2	38
All OECD Countries	30	14	7	3	54

Source: OECD (2004).

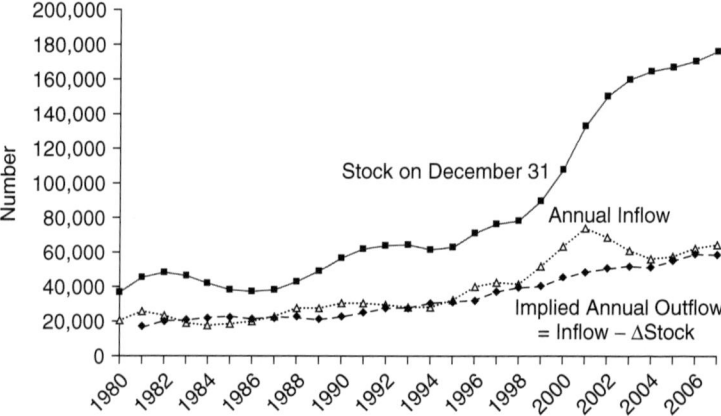

Figure 9.3a Stocks and Flows of Foreign Students in Canada, 1980 to 2007.

Sources: CIC (2003) *Foreign Students in Canada, 1980–2001*; CIC (2007), *Facts and Figures 2007*.

of North Americans studying outside their home country—a group primarily comprised of students from the United States—Canada hosted just 7 percent compared with the United Kingdom that attracted 19 percent.[5]

Figures 9.3a and 9.3b provide a rather different perspective on the changing importance of foreign students in Canada. The source here is Citizenship and Immigration Canada data on student stocks and flows. Figure 9.3a shows the evolving stocks and flows of foreign students at all education levels. Figure 9.3b shows the stocks and flows for just university students. Concentrating on university students, we see that the stock has grown rapidly since the mid-1990s. Interestingly, the stock continued to rise

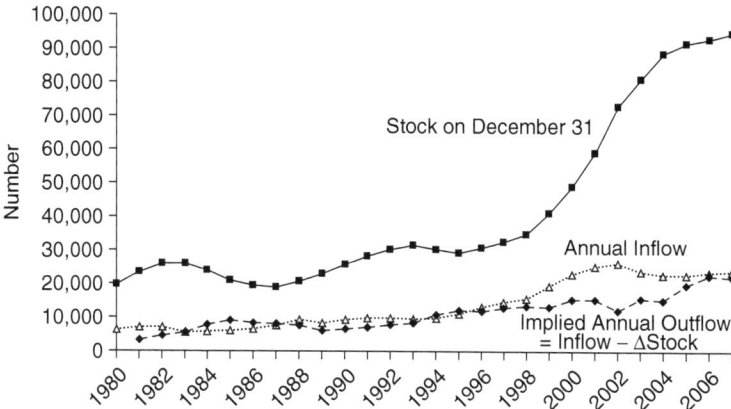

Figure 9.3b   Stocks and Flows of University Students in Canada, 1980 to 2007.

Sources: CIC (2003) *Foreign Students in Canada, 1980–2001*; CIC (2007), *Facts and Figures 2007.*

after 2001, even as the annual inflow declined from 2002 to 2004. The graph also shows the implied outflows given the inflows and the change in the size of the foreign student population. Assuming that the inflows and the stock are being measured correctly, the numbers imply that the outflow rate is lagging the inflow rate, which in turn suggests the lengthening of average durations in Canada. Eventually, however, the average duration must stabilize and stock will move in the same direction as annual inflows.

Table 9.2 provides additional information on the distribution of foreign students across levels of education in Canada based on the Citizenship and Immigration Canada (CIC) data. University students now account for just over half of all foreign students, a share that has been relatively stable since the late 1980s. There has been a marked decline in the share of students at the secondary and lower levels over this period, with the share falling from a peak of 39 percent in 1989 and 1990 to just 19 percent in 2007. There has also been a notable increase in the "other postsecondary" category—presumably colleges—since the mid-1990s, rising from 5 percent in 1993 and 1994 to 12 percent in 2007.

There is little doubt that the United States is Canada's closest competitor in the market for foreign students. September 11 and its aftermath have raised questions about the United States' interest in and attractiveness to foreign students. Reports abound of difficulties faced in getting a U.S. student visa in the years following September 11, although there is evidence that visa processing time has become considerably less more recently. Florida (2005) reports that the number of student visas dropped

Table 9.2   Shares of Foreign Students in Canada by Level of Study, 1980 to 2007

	Secondary or Less	Trade	University	Other Post-Secondary	Other	Total
1980	31	12	54	0	3	100
1981	34	11	52	0	3	100
1982	33	11	54	0	3	100
1983	31	10	56	0	3	100
1984	31	11	57	0	2	100
1985	33	11	54	1	2	100
1986	35	10	52	1	2	100
1987	37	9	50	2	3	100
1988	38	9	48	2	3	100
1989	39	9	47	3	3	100
1990	39	9	45	4	2	100
1991	38	9	46	5	2	100
1992	35	9	48	6	2	100
1993	33	10	49	5	3	100
1994	32	10	49	5	3	100
1995	31	13	46	6	3	100
1996	31	15	43	6	5	100
1997	30	15	43	7	6	100
1998	30	12	45	7	7	100
1999	27	13	46	8	7	100
2000	26	14	45	9	6	100
2001	24	13	44	13	6	100
2002	22	15	49	10	4	100
2003	19	15	52	10	4	100
2004	19	15	54	9	3	100
2005	18	15	55	9	3	100
2006	19	13	55	10	3	100
2007	19	12	54	12	3	100

Sources: CIC (2003), Foreign Students in Canada, 1980–2001; CIC (2007), *Facts and Figures 2007.*

by 20 percent in 2002 and by a further 8 percent in 2003. After a marginal increase in foreign-student enrollments in higher education for the academic year 2002/2003 (0.6 percent), enrollments actually fell in 2003/2004 for the first time since records began in the 1950s (−2.4 percent). Table 9.4 shows that the decline was not uniform across countries, with enrollments from India actually increasing by 19 percent, while those for most other Asian countries fell. A survey by the Council of Graduate Schools found a 6 percent decline in first-time foreign graduate student enrollment from

Table 9.3 Number of International Students in the United States by Country of Origin, 2003/2004 and 2007/2008

		2003/2004	2007/2008	% Change
1	India	79,736	94,563	18.6
2	China	61,765	81,127	31.3
3	Korea	52,484	69,124	31.7
4	Japan	40,835	33,974	−16.8
5	Canada	27,017	29,051	7.5
6	Taiwan	26,178	29,001	10.8
7	Mexico	13,329	14,837	11.3
8	Turkey	11,398	12,030	5.5
9	Thailand	8,937	9,004	0.7
10	Indonesia	8,880	7,692	−13.4
11	Germany	8,745	8,907	1.9
12	The United Kingdom	8,439	8,367	−0.9
13	Brazil	7,799	7,578	−2.8
14	Colombia	7,533	6,662	−11.6
15	Kenya	7,381	…	…
	World Total	572,509	623,805	9.0

Source: Bhandari and Chow (2009).

2003 to 2004. The reported declines were 8 percent for China and 4 percent for India. Where surveyed institutions indicated that the enrollments had declined, 40 percent noted visa troubles (both delays and denials) as the top factor contributing to the decline, while 20 percent noted a drop in applications. However, the number of students entering the United States has resumed its growth in recent years, with the total enrollment rising by 9 percent between 2003/2004 and 2007/2008 (table 9.3).

From Canada's perspective, the interesting question is how these changes affecting the United States should alter Canada's recruitment efforts in the market for international students. On the one hand, with the country's chief competitor becoming less welcoming, it could be argued that Canada can afford to be less aggressive in its efforts to attract top student prospects. On the other hand, if the United States has become a less attractive destination or is turning away highly qualified students without good reason, then Canada may have the opportunity to recruit top students who would previously have gone to the United States. Assuming that the optimal recruitment effort is positively related to the quality of the potential applicant pool, this suggests that Canada should be competing more aggressively for students rather than less.

Foreign Students and Revenue Generation

Perhaps the most obvious rationale for foreign student recruitment in the Canadian context is that it generates revenues for cash-strapped universities and colleges. Tuition at Canada's public institutions is typically set well below the total cost per student (though closer to the marginal cost per student); government subsidies to cover the short fall are only loosely linked to the number of students. It follows that schools have a strong revenue-raising rationale for expanding the number of foreign students paying full (or greater than full) tuition. Of course, since outside of professional schools—notably schools of business, law, and medicine—foreign graduate students typically receive subsidized tuition, this rationale mainly applies to the recruitment of foreign undergraduates.

Table 9.4 shows the foreign-student tuition levels at a number of Canadian universities for the 2004/2005 academic year. The recorded tuitions are for arts and science programs. These tuitions compare with typical subsidized tuitions charged to domestic students of C$4,000 to C$6,000,[6] so that foreign students typically pay two to three times what domestic students pay. The table also shows the shares of international students at each institution at both the graduate and undergraduate levels. At present, the shares of foreign students in the undergraduate body are quite low at most institutions. The highest share of foreign undergraduates is recorded at McGill at almost 18 percent, while the median share is just 4.7 percent.[7] The table suggests, however, that most institutions have a strong monetary incentive to increase the foreign share.

The implications of such revenue-driven foreign student recruitment for Canadian students depend on how this recruitment affects the quantity of slots and the quality of education provided. Take the case where there is a fixed number of undergraduate slots. The recruitment of a foreign student will then "crowd out" a domestic student. Domestic students may still gain overall to the extent that the increased revenues are used to increase the quality of education provided. It is clear that cash-strapped institutions receiving fixed government allocations have a strong monetary incentive to shift their student mix toward full-tuition paying foreign students.[8]

Take next the case where the number of slots is expanded to accommodate the newly recruited foreign students. The impact on domestic students depends now on how the larger student body affects the quality of their education. Putting aside for the moment any advantages of a more diverse student body or competition-induced effects on the quality of instruction (these will be taken up in the next section), one notes that the expanded student body may drive quality down as more students are

Table 9.4 Foreign Student Shares and Tuition Costs at Canadian Universities

	Percentage of First-Year Undergraduate Students from Outside Canada	Percentage of Graduate Students from Outside Canada	Tuition Fess 2004–2005 Undergraduate Arts and Science Programs
Undergraduate and Graduate			
Alberta	3.4	17.5	$12,161
Calgary	1.9	17.0	$12,032
Carleton	8.5	30.0	$11,438
Concordia	11.7	58.7	$10,592 to $14,941
Dalhousie	6.1	20.9	$10,440 to $11,190
Guelph	1.7	15.4	$10,221
Laval	11.5	24.9	$11,311
Manitoba	5.1	20.8	$6,847
McGill	17.9	29.3	$12,289 to $13,461
McMaster	6.8	22.8	$11,632 to $16,854
Memorial	4.6	20.6	$8,950
Montreal	12.8	26.4	$9,824
New Brunswick	6.1	21.3	$9,713
Ottawa	5.8	20.9	$12,176
Queen's	2.2	17.4	$15,136
Regina	4.6	20.3	$8,653
Saskatchewan	0.8	14.5	$11,811
Sherbrooke	1.4	16.6	$10,199 to $11,309
Simon Fraser	8.5	25.8	$14,759
Toronto	6.2	21.0	$12,405
UBC	8.6	23.6	$16,844 to $16,853
Victoria	7.1	25.4	$13,102
Waterloo	5.0	20.9	$15,763
Western	4.8	20.3	$13,346
Windsor	11.4	33.8	$10,612
York	3.0	16.8	$11,881
Primarily Undergraduate			
Acadia	17.0	...	$13,963
Bishop's	10.1	...	$10,642 to $11,752
Brandon	3.6	...	$5,249 to $5,779
Brock	6.8	...	$10,486
Cape Breton (UCCB)	8.4	...	$9,422
Lakehead	2.1	...	$9,908
Laurentian	4.7	...	$10,424
Lethbridge	9.4	...	$8,991
Moncton	4.0	...	$8,285

Continued

Table 9.4   Continued

	Percentage of First-Year Undergraduate Students from Outside Canada	Percentage of Graduate Students from Outside Canada	Tuition Fess 2004–2005 Undergraduate Arts and Science Programs
Mount Allison	7.3	...	$11,811
Mount Saint Vincent	5.5	...	$10,863
Nipissing	0.7	...	$9,293
Ryerson	3.9	...	$13,421
Saint Mary's	16.1	...	$10,706 to $10,806
St. Francis Xavier	2.8	...	$10,718
St. Thomas	4.8	...	$7,955
Trent	3.6	...	$11,851
UNBC	1.7	...	$12,962 to $13,149
UPEI	5.1	...	$8,357
Wilfred Laurier	1.0	...	$9,913 to $12,371
Winnipeg	4.6	...	$5,407.00

Source: Maclean's *Guide to Canadian Universities* 2005.

spread over fixed resources or it may drive quality up as extra resources are funded out of the additional revenues.

Of course, the effect of additional resources depends on how the money is spent. One obvious fear is that money is used just to increase faculty and administrator salaries and perks, and not for increased resources. While this fear is real, it is important to recognize that "quality" in part depends on the ability to recruit and retain world-class faculty. The internationalization of education also extends to the integration of markets for top teaching and research talent, with the United States clearly being the main competitor for Canada. Thus the funding of higher salaries need not be at odds with stronger institutions from the point of view of domestic students.

This brief discussion makes clear that the impact on domestic students of revenue-driven foreign student recruitment depends on the incentives and opportunities that institutions have to alter the number of student slots, the student mix, and the quality of education provided. In a primarily public-funded system, the government may not want to take a completely hands-off attitude to foreign recruitment. Instead, it must make sure that the incentives of the public institutions are well aligned with using foreign recruitment to maximize the benefit to domestic students.

A crude incentive structure with the right properties is to set a floor on domestic recruitment and allow unconstrained recruitment of fee-paying foreign students, with all the revenues going to the university or college. This provides the institution with a strong incentive to compete aggressively for foreign students while limiting their ability to crowd out domestic students. Drawbacks of this incentive structure include the loss of autonomy for institutions in determining the size of their domestic student bodies, and the possible decline in quality due to overcrowding or the lowering of standards to attract revenue-rich foreign students.[9]

The United Kingdom's experience with revenue-driven recruitment is instructive. Higher education is widely viewed to have been underfunded by successive governments, while institutions have (until recently) been prevented from raising tuition above nominal levels. The result has been lagging performance relative to top private and public universities in the United States. Revenue-strapped universities—particularly those with international reputations—have eagerly embraced fee-paying students from outside the EU, whose remittances now account for roughly 10 percent of total revenues. The London School of Economics has been a leader in the competition for foreign students. For the academic year 2003/2004, London School of Economics and Political Science (LSE) had 5,203 foreign students, comprised of 2,036 undergraduate students and 3,167 graduate students. The largest source country was the United States with 890 students, followed by China with 395 students. The total number of students at the LSE in 2003/2004 was 8,381. Of the 5,203 foreign students, the LSE reports, 1,184 were not paying the higher rate for overseas students, presumably because they came from within the EU. For the academic year 2004/2005, the fees for undergraduates originating in the United Kingdom or another EU country was £1,150,[10] which compares with a fee of £10,509 for non-EU students. The LSE example highlights the significant revenue implications of foreign student recruitment at an institution with a strong international reputation. It also underlines the risk that domestic students will get crowded out when institutions have a strong monetary incentive to recruit overseas.

Foreign Students and Knowledge Production

The second often-mentioned rationale for recruiting foreign students is that it improves broadly defined knowledge production at Canadian universities and colleges. I find it useful to distinguish between the impact of foreign students on the human (and possibly social) capital acquisition of domestic students, and the impact of foreign (primarily graduate) students on research output.

Human Capital of Domestic Students

There are two major channels through which the recruitment of foreign students is likely to affect the learning experience of domestic students. The first is the diversity effect—the costs and benefits of learning in a more diverse environment. The second is the competition effect—the way the learning experience of domestic students is affected by the need to compete with foreign students.

Diversity can be both good and bad for domestic students. On the one hand, a diverse student body allows for a greater frequency of interactions that lead to the sharing of non-redundant information. In contrast, when you interact with people who are very like you and tend to know the same things as you, much of the information exchange is likely to be redundant (see, for example, Burt 1992). On the other hand, highly variable capabilities and communication difficulties among a diverse student body may impede knowledge acquisition, forcing teaching to the lowest common denominator and slowing down the pace of instruction. This cost will be most apparent when the recruited students are not fluent in the language of instruction.

The conventional wisdom at elite universities in the United States is that diversity is a positive force in education. Terenzini and colleagues (2001, 510) quote former Harvard University president Neil Rudenstein as saying that the "fundamental rationale for student diversity in higher education [is] its educational value," and Lee Bollinger, former president at the University of Michigan, as asserting that "a classroom that does not have a significant representation from members of different races produces an impoverished discussion." Terenzini and colleagues note that these are not isolated examples. A statement published by the Association of American Universities and endorsed by the presidents of 62 research universities read, "We speak first and foremost as educators. We believe that our students benefit significantly from education that takes place in a diverse setting." These authors go on to report that the literature is broadly supportive of the hypothesis that diversity improves student outcomes; their own finding acknowledges a small but significant positive effect of diversity on student learning. These findings relate mainly to the representation of minority citizens in the student body, and much of the broader benefit for society in diverse learning environments is seen to come though the learned ability to thrive in such multi-ethnic environments. It is not obvious how applicable such findings are to international student diversity, especially where a large majority of the international students return home. On the one hand, cultural differences in an internationally diverse student body are likely to be large, increasing the potential for both non-redundant knowledge sharing and poor communication. On the other hand, interactions with international students do not necessarily make for a more cohesive multi-ethnic society, though it is likely to make students more comfortable working and living in an ever more integrated world.

Studies of the effects of diversity on economic performance in knowledge-intensive sectors outside of education are also revealing. In recent work by Ajay Agrawal, Devesh Kapur, and John McHale (2004) on Indian inventors in the United States and Canada, we have found that both co-ethnicity and co-location are each significant facilitators of knowledge flows between inventors (using patent citations as a proxy measure). However, co-ethnicity has little additional effect where inventors are co-located. This suggests that co-ethnicity and co-location are substitutes in overcoming barriers to knowledge flows. It also suggests that a location gains from having a more diverse inventor population. In effect, co-location is effective in facilitating knowledge flows between diverse inventors—in part because it provides opportunities for diverse individuals to form social relationships—and co-ethnicity-related links between non-co-located inventors help build location access knowledge from other locations. In a recent National Bureau of Economic Research working paper, Gianmarco Ottaviano and Giovanni Peri (2004) find that "cultural diversity" (based on country of birth) at the city level increases the productivity and earnings of the domestic population. In the Canadian context, Daniel Trefler and Michael Baker (in their work for the Ontario Institute for Competitiveness and Prosperity) find that urbanization—which is probably in part a proxy for diversity—increases the return to a university education, with the largest effect (10.4 percent) observed for advanced university degrees.

Turning now to the competition effect, the idea is that colleges and universities that must compete for foreign talent will be induced to improve their performance, and that improvement will also benefit domestic students. A useful way to think about this competition effect is in terms of Hirschman's distinction between "exit" and "voice" as mechanisms for improving performance in organizations. Poorly performing schools may be induced to improve performance if they fail to attract and retain high-fee-paying foreign students who effectively vote with their feet. This channel will be most important where competitive pressures are weak in the market for domestic students. Where fees are capped for domestic students, leading to an excess demand for places, the incentive to compete for students with better teaching and other services may well be attenuated. Of course, leading schools will still want to attract the best possible students to sustain and improve their reputations. Nevertheless, budgetary strains can be a very immediate motivator, and the absence of short-term financial gain from providing superior quality education to domestic students might impair performance. In contrast, allowing cash-strapped schools to compete for fee-paying foreign students—or even highly talented non-fee-paying applicants who have a vast array of options in the international marketplace—can provide very immediate motivation for improved performance.

Although there is little evidence of a competition effect in higher education, there is credible evidence of a significant competition effect at the pre-tertiary level. Hoxby (2000) shows that the greater the range of school choices available to parents the better the schools perform. In particular, she looks at what she calls "Tiebout choice" among districts. Parents effectively choose their schools by choosing where to live. Hoxby posits that natural geographic features (e.g., streams) affect the number of school districts and thus possibly provide exogenous variation in the availability of choices among schools.[11] Hoxby (2000, 1237) also concludes that choice needs to have "financial consequences if it is to produce the productivity effects described."

Securing net benefits for domestic students from competition for foreign students again requires that institutions are provided with an appropriate incentive structure. It is important that institutions do not face a binding ceiling on foreign recruitment and that institutions have a strong financial incentive for such recruitment. Moreover, it is equally important that a two-tiered price structure for foreign and domestic students is not matched by a two-tiered quality structure. This ensures that competition-induced quality improvements to attract foreign students work to the benefit of domestic students.

Research Output from Universities

I next turn to the contribution of foreign graduate students to the research output of universities. Such output is typically viewed as a key component of a country's "national innovation system." It is well known that knowledge tends to be "locally sticky" (Jaffe et al. 1993), so that local knowledge-based enterprises can gain competitive advantage from locally produced research.

One of the outstanding facts about the national innovation system in the United States is its ability to draw top talent to its universities from around the world. The National Science Foundation reports that of the 430,000 graduate students in science and engineering in 2001, 133,000 were foreign citizens on temporary visas (National Science Board 2004a). Moreover, the 2000 census revealed that the foreign-born comprised 22.4 percent of all tertiary-educated individuals working in science and engineering. The share of the foreign born amongst those with doctorates was 37.6 percent overall, and 51.3 percent of those with doctorates in engineering.[12]

There is concern in the U.S. scientific community over the recent drop in graduate enrollments, and the risk of losing its leadership in knowledge-intensive sectors. A recent paper released along with the National Science Board's Science and Engineering Indicators for 2004 expressed the concern as follows:

> If the trends identified in *Indicators* 2004 continue undeterred, three things will happen. The number of jobs in the U.S. economy that require science and engineering training will grow; the number of U.S. citizens prepared for those jobs will, at best, be level; and the availability of people from other countries who have science and engineering training will decline, either because of limits to entry imposed by U.S. national security restrictions or because of intense global competition for people with these skills. The United States has always depended on the inventiveness of its people in order to compete in the world marketplace. Now, preparation of the S&E (science and engineering) workforce is a vital arena for national competitiveness. (National Science Board 2004b, p. 1)

Table 9.4 reveals that leading Canadian research institutions are also heavy recruiters of foreign graduate students, with the median foreign share just below 21 percent. Thus foreign graduate students also play an important role in Canada's national innovation system. In this context, the fact that the inflow of foreign students has fallen over the last three years should be of some concern. As noted in Section 2, the recruitment difficulties faced by institutions in the United States should have provided an opportunity for Canadian institutions to capture a larger share of the market. Of course, both countries have been facing similar challenges, including security issues that prompted the need for greater vigilance in processing applications and the strengthening of domestic institutions in key markets such as China. Canada has also been put at somewhat of a competitive disadvantage of its own by the significant strengthening of the Canadian dollar vis-à-vis the U.S. dollar. On the other hand, although there are anecdotal stories of Canadian institutions taking advantage of the increased difficulty in getting and renewing visas in the United States, there has not been a concerted effort to capture a larger share of the internationally mobile graduate student market.

How should we think about the role of foreign graduate students in the national innovation system? At the most basic level, access to these students will increase the supply of researchers and help to lower the cost and increase the output of research. One unwelcome implication of the lower cost would be that earnings are held down for domestic graduates, leading to a partly offsetting contraction of domestic supply in terms of quantity. In a recent paper, Borjas (2005) provides evidence that the earnings of domestic researchers are adversely affected in the short run. A less pessimistic view is that foreign researchers complement domestic researchers, making them more productive and raising their earning potential.

Foreign Students and Immigrant Selection

The previous two sections examined channels through which foreign students impact the education system and the broader economy *while they are students*. In considering the long-term impact of recruiting foreign students, we need to recognize that some foreign students will want to remain in Canada. In contrast to its position as a reluctant recruiter of foreign students, Canada has one of the world's most developed systems for recruiting immigrants based on their skills. It is important, then, to take account of the links—or the absence of links—between foreign student recruitment and Canada's broader immigration regime.

Under the reformed points system that came into effect in 2002 under the Immigration and Refugee Protection Act, a substantial number of points (25) are available for educational attainment. Another category of points is based on indicators of adaptability to Canada.[13] The maximum number of points available under this category is ten and can be attained by some combination of spousal education (3–5), a year's worth of authorized work in Canada (5), two years of postsecondary education in Canada (5), arranged employment (5), and a family relationship in Canada (5). Thus, although there is some advantage to having obtained Canadian education, little differentiation is made between a Canadian and a foreign education.

Recent international evidence suggests that the value of education can vary greatly depending on where it was acquired. In an influential study of immigration to Israel, Friedberg (2000) found that education (and experience) acquired abroad are significantly less valuable than human capital acquired in Israel. She also found that the value of foreign education differs greatly depending on its quality and its comparability with what is provided domestically. An additional important finding is that education acquired in Israel has the additional benefit of increasing the value of education acquired abroad. It appears that getting additional education in the host country helps them apply their previously acquired knowledge.

In recent work using Canadian data, Alboim, Finnie, and Meng (2005) have also found evidence of heavy discounting of foreign university degrees compared with Canadian degrees. Their study uses a rich data set that allows them to distinguish based on where education is acquired. For "non-White" immigrants, they find that a foreign degree yields a proportionate increase in income that is less than one-third of what a Canadian degree yields to the native born. For "White" immigrants, however, foreign degrees have roughly the same yield as Canadian degrees. Interestingly, the value of Canadian degrees for both "White" and "non-White" immigrants is roughly equivalent to their value to the native born. This evidence suggests that immigrants from countries with education systems that are poorly adapted to the Canadian economy do much better if their degrees are obtained in Canada.[14] Ferrer, Green, and Riddell (2005) point to an important reason why foreign-acquired education is less beneficial in the Canadian labor market—literacy. Indeed, they find that once literacy is controlled for, foreign degrees are rewarded equally to domestic degrees in terms of wages in the Canadian labor market.

Empirical studies have also found that age at arrival is a strong predictor of success in the Canadian labor market (see, in particular, Schaafsma and Sweetman 2001). Immigrants arriving at younger ages tend to outperform those who arrive at older ages for given levels of measured education and experience. One explanation is that immigrants who arrive at younger ages tend to obtain more of their education and experience in Canada, and that these domestically acquired skills have greater value in the Canadian labor market (see also Sweetman 2004). Another factor is that younger immigrants are likely to "acculturate" better to Canadian society. Whether the greater success of younger immigrants stems from their higher domestically acquired human capital or their easier adaptation to their new home, these results underscore the value of recruiting immigrants prior to their completion of formal education.

A central motivation for looking for better ways to link foreign student recruitment and immigrant selection is the evidence that recent immigrant cohorts are doing poorly in the Canadian labor market (see, for example, Baker and Benjamin 1994; Green and Worswick 2004). One factor in this deteriorating performance is that the origin mix has been changing over time, with a greater proportion of immigrants coming from countries with educational and industrial structures that match less well with those in Canada. In addition, Reitz (2005) has argued that the underutilization of immigrant skills has worsened with the shift to a more knowledge-based economy and the attendant problems of credential recognition that tend to be associated with knowledge-based jobs. Reitz suggests a range of valuable policies to hasten the immigrant-integration process, including bridge-training programs to make foreign skills transferable to the Canadian labor market. Another part of the solution is better immigrant selection. McHale and Rogers (2005) explore methods for devising a more rational points system based on the best available evidence from earnings regressions on how immigrants with different bundles of human capital characteristics are performing in the Canadian labor market. The emerging econometric evidence on the differential value of Canadian and foreign degrees in terms of their impact on earnings suggests the need to differentiate between credentials in the points allocation process. At present, even graduates with PhDs from Canadian universities often do not qualify for permanent residency until they have acquired a number of years of experience.

The foregoing analysis considers how a better immigrant pool can be selected by taking better advantage of a given pool of foreign students. Probably just as important is the opportunity to recruit a higher-quality student pool by offering a package to prospective student recruits that provides a predictable path to permanent residency. In the United States, employment-based permanent residency is quite difficult to obtain. A Canadian system that offers student visas plus a clear path to permanent residency could help Canada secure a greater share of the world's best mobile student talent. Finally, once foreign students are seen as a rich recruitment ground for skilled immigrants, there is an additional reason beyond revenue generation and knowledge production for expanding the size of the foreign student pool.

Concluding Comments

I opened the chapter by noting that the topic of foreign student recruitment is often discussed in over-hyped language concerning the need to "compete for talent." In considering policy design in this area, there needs to be a careful debate about what Canada hopes to accomplish by the recruitment of foreign students, with particular emphasis on its effects on Canadian students and the broader economy. My review of the various sources of costs and benefits suggests that well-designed systems of foreign student recruitment can provide net benefits. But for these net benefits to result—in particular for foreign student recruitment to increase the available quantity and quality of educational opportunities for younger

Table 9.5 Structural Incentives to Improve the Benefit-Cost Balance

Channel of Influence	Potential Benefit	Potential Cost	Structural Incentive
Revenue Generation	Increased places/ quality for domestic students	Crowding out of domestic students	Floor on number of domestic places
Competition	Competition-induced improvements in performance	Competition-induced lowering of selection standards	Quality control in foreign student body
Diversity	Enriched learning environment	Impediments created by communication difficulties	Strict language competency requirements
Research Output	Lower costs and higher research output	Fewer domestic graduate students	Two-tier system of stipends
Immigrant Selection	Greater Canada-specific human capital	Greater share of education costs falls on Canada	Differentially recognize Canadian education in points allocation

Canadians—it is important that an appropriate incentive structure is put in place. I close the chapter, then, by recapping elements of an incentive structure that should increase the odds that such recruitment will prove an overall plus (see also table 9.5).

- *Revenue generation.* Universities should be allowed to enhance their revenues without crowding out domestic students. This could be accomplished by placing floors on the number of domestic students, leaving institutions free to expand their student bodies by recruiting foreign students. The institutions should be allowed to keep the resulting revenues, and the government should not reduce future appropriations based on success in raising these revenues. Institutions need to pay close attention to ensuring that strong financial incentives do not lead to reduced standards and diminished reputations.
- *Diversity.* An internationally diverse student body can enhance the learning experience relevant to a more global society, provided that all students meet rigorous standards, including standards for language competence.

- *Competition.* The government should avoid placing a cap on foreign student intake so that institutions have an incentive of better margins to attract foreign students by improving quality. However, to ensure that domestic students benefit from the improved quality, it is essential to avoid a two-tiered system.
- *Knowledge production.* Foreign graduate students can significantly boost the research capabilities of Canadian universities and also increase the return to government support for research and development. But it is important to minimize the extent to which foreign graduate students drive domestic students out of research careers due to their willingness to work for lower stipends. It is thus important to keep stipends for domestic students at a competitive level with other opportunities in the economy. A two-tiered stipend system—with more generous stipends for domestic students—could help balance the goals of increasing research output, reducing research cost, and ensuring that Canadian students are attracted to research.
- *Links to the immigration system.* The immigration points system should recognize that a Canadian education tends to be more valuable than a foreign education in the Canadian economy. Foreign students should not be impeded from gaining valuable work experience during their time as students, and the process of obtaining temporary work permits after graduation should be streamlined.

NOTES

1. I thank Industry Canada and Human Resources and Skills Development Canada for financial support. I am also grateful to Daniel Boothby for his support and encouragement and to Devesh Kapur, Thitima Songsukul, Keith Rogers, and two anonymous referees for valuable feedback.
2. A recent *New York Times* editorial raised alarm about the competition for students:

   The fact is that the competition for students has become far more intense. While American campuses are still by far the favorite destination, they have been steadily losing share for years, especially to Canada, Australia and Europe. Now the European Union is considering offering citizenship to foreign students who complete their doctorates at European universities.... Indeed, the competition for brains and ideas is where the battle for global influence should be waged.... After so many years of near-hegemony in this field, it is good for the United States to be reminded that those people banging at the door have ever more other addresses to try if they are rebuffed. ("Imported Brains," *New York Times*, December 3, 2005.)

3. Devesh Kapur and I discuss the broader effects of skill recruitment on developing countries in a recent monograph published by the Center for Global Development (Kapur and McHale, 2005).

4. Of course, Canada has the additional competitive advantage that it is also attractive to students seeking instruction in French.

5. This comparison is not entirely fair, since the 19 percent studying in the United Kingdom includes some Canadians.

6. Quebec students typically pay between C$2,000 and C$3,000 (inclusive of ancillary fees) at Quebec universities.

7. The median foreign graduate student share for the universities listed with significant graduate programs is 20.9 percent.

8. A similar crowding out argument is often heard in relation to the recruitment of foreign workers. The fear is that foreign workers will take jobs from domestic workers. Many economists are dismissive of this argument, however, as they see this as an example of the "lump of labour fallacy," whereby the total number of jobs is mistakenly view as fixed. Expansions in the labor force are typically associated with broadly matching expansions in the number of jobs available. In effect, supply creates its own demand. But fear of crowding may have greater warrant in the case of foreign student recruitment; for example, if administrators place a cap on the total number of places available.

9. In regard to the latter concern, it is clear the schools have can have a very strong financial incentive to recruit additional foreign students, which can create strong pressures to admit marginally qualified students. This danger is even greater if the price is set in advance, so that the financial gain from admitting an additional student is equal to the potentially substantial gap between marginal cost and price, which can put pressure on recruiters to hit ambitious recruitment targets. This concern—that quality standards are stretched too far for financial gain—is often heard in relation to deregulated MBA programs.

10. New government regulations allow the fee for U.K. students to give to £3,000 for the academic year 2005/2006.

11. However, see Rothstein (2004) for a critical analysis of Hoxby's construction and use of instrumental variables for competition based on geographic features of the locality.

12. I consider the issue of retaining foreign graduates from Canadian institutions in the domestic skilled workforce in the next section.

13. The current pass mark is 67. In addition to educational attainment and adaptability, 24 points are available for language skills (English and French), 21 points for experience, ten for age, and ten for arranged employment.

14. In recent work, Ferrer and Riddell (2004) allow separately for the effects of years of completed education and the actual attainment of credentials—what they term the "sheepskin effect." They find that this effect is quite important for Canadian immigrants, and that not allowing for it can lead to downward biased inferences about how foreign education is rewarded in the Canadian labor market. Interestingly, they find the "sheepskin effect" is especially pronounced for immigrants from outside the United Kingdom and the United States.

BIBLIOGRAPHY

Agrawal, Ajay, Devesh Kapur, and John McHale. 2004. *Defying Distance: The Role of the Diaspora*. Working Paper, University of Toronto, Harvard University, and Queen's University.

Alborim, Naomi, Ross Finnie, and Ronald Meng. 2005. "The Discounting of Immigrants' Skills in Canada: Evidence and Policy Recommendations." *IRPP Choices* 11 (2): 1–28.

Baker, Michael, and Dwayne Benjamin. 1994. "The Performance of Immigrants in the Canadian Labor Market." *Journal of Labor Economics* 12 (3): 369–405.

Baker, Michael, and Daniel Trefler. 2002. *The Impact of Education on Urbanization and Productivity*. Toronto: Institute for Competitiveness & Prosperity. Available online at: http://www.competeprosper.ca.

Bhandari, Rajika, and Patricia Chow. 2009. *Open Doors 2009: Report on International Educational Exchange*. New York: Institute of International Education.

Borjas, George. 2005. "The Labor Market Impact of High-Skill Immigration." Paper presented at the American Economic Association Meetings, Philadelphia, January 2005.

Burt, Ronald. 1992. *Structural Holes: The Social Structure of Competition*. Cambridge: Harvard University Press.

Citizenship and Immigration Canada. 2004. *Facts and Figures 2003: Immigration Overview Permanent and Temporary Residents*. Ottawa: Citizenship and Immigration Canada.

Citizenship and Immigration Canada. 2005. *Foreign Students in Canada 1980–2001*. Ottawa: Citizenship and Immigration Canada. Available online at: http://www.cic.gc.ca.

Citizenship and Immigration Canada. 2005. *The Monitor*. Ottawa: Citizenship and Immigration Canada.

Ferrer, Ana, and Craig Riddell. 2004. *Education, Credentials, and Immigrant Earnings*. TARGET Working Paper No. 020, TARGET. Vancouver: University of British Columbia.

Ferrer, Ana, David Green, and Craig Riddell. 2005. *The Effect of Literacy on Immigrant Earnings*. TARGET Working Paper No. 011, TARGET. Vancouver: University of British Columbia.

Friedberg, Rachel. 2000. "You Can't Take It with You? Immigrant Assimilation and the Portability of Human Capital." *Journal of Labor Economics* 18 (2): 221–251.

Green, David, and Christopher Worswick. 2004. *Immigrant Earnings Profiles in the Presence of Human Capital Investment: Measuring Cohort and Marco Effects*. Working Paper, University of British Columbia and Carleton University. Vancouver and Ottawa: University of British Columbia and Carleton University.

Hoxby, Caroline. 2000. "Does Competition among Public Schools Benefit Students and Taxpayers?" *American Economic Review* 90 (5): 1209–1238.

Kapur, Devesh, and John McHale. 2005. *Give Us Your Best and Brightest: The Global Hunt for Talent and Its Impact on the Developing World*. Washington, DC: Center for Global Development, The Brookings Institution Press.

McHale, John, and Keith Rogers. 2005. *Design of an Optimal Immigration Points System*. Working Paper Queen's University. Kingston: Queens University.

National Science Board. 2004a. *Science and Engineering Indicators–2004*. Arlington, VA: National Science Board.

National Science Board. 2004b. "An Emerging and Critical Problem in the Science and Engineering Workforce (Companion to *Science and Engineering Indicators–2004*)." Arlington, VA: National Science Board.

Organisation for Economic Co-operation and Development (OECD). 2004. *Internationalisation and Trade in Higher Education: Opportunities and Challenges*. Paris: OECD.

Ottaviano, Gianmarco, and Giovanni Peri. 2004. *The Economic Value of Cultural Diversity: Evidence from Cities*. National Bureau of Economic Research (NBER) Working Paper 10904. Cambridge, MA: NBER.

Reitz, Jeffrey. 2005. "Tapping Immigrants' Skills: New Directions for Canadian Immigration Policy in the Knowledge Economy." *IRPP Choices* 11 (1): 2–18.

Romer, Paul. 2000. Should the Government Subsidize Supply or Demand in the Market for Scientists and Engineers? NBER Working Paper 7723. Cambridge, MA: NBER. Romer.

Rothstein, Jesse. 2004. *Does Competition among Public Schools Benefit Students or Taxpayers? A Comment on Hoxby (2000)*. Working Paper No. 10. Princeton, NJ: Princeton University Education Research Section.

Schaafsma, Joseph, and Arthur Sweetman. 2001. "Immigrant Earnings: Age at Immigration Matters." *Canadian Journal of Economics* 34 (4): 1066–1099.

Sweetman, Arthur. 2004. *Immigrant Source Country Educational Quality and Canadian Labour Market Outcomes*. Analytical Studies Branch Research Paper Series, Statistics Canada. Ottawa: Statistics Canada.

Terenzini, Patrick, Alberto Cabrera, Carol Colbeck, Stephani Bjorklund, and John Parente. 2001. "Racial and Ethnic Diversity in the Classroom: Does It Promote Learning?" *Journal of Higher Education* 72 (5): 509–531.

Chapter 10

Can Speak, Will Travel: The Influence of Language on Global Student Mobility

Veronica Lasanowski

International student mobility is booming, with the demands of a globalizing economy influencing patterns of student movement across borders. Importantly, however, the rapidity with which mobility is growing is part of a larger context in which tertiary education is expanding more generally.

Fueled by a shift to postindustrial society and the rise of services-oriented knowledge economies, the world's middle class is growing, resulting in an increase in worldwide tertiary participation. Between 1999 and 2004, reduction in the number of people suffering extreme poverty was almost entirely due to rapid economic progress in Asia's two economic powerhouses—China and India (Elliot 2007). And, indeed, globally, the number of people classified as middle class is projected to swell from 440 million to 1.2 billion in the coming decades, with most of the new entrants coming from these two countries (National Intelligence Council 2008).

To a large extent, tertiary education growth mirrors in-country economic growth. Global tertiary education demand is forecast to exceed 262 million places by 2025, contributing to the massification of the tertiary education subsector (Meares 2003). It is, moreover, influencing patterns of growth in the overseas tertiary education subsector.

As an increasing number of students access tertiary education, more and more are likely to access it overseas. Global tertiary enrollments grew from 100.8 to 152.5 million between 2000 and 2007 alone, a growth of nearly 53 percent (UNESCO 2009). Over the same period, the number of internationally mobile students increased from roughly 1.9 to 2.8 million, a comparable rise of 49 percent, much of which is attributable to Asian student mobility (Ibid.).

Rapidly developing economies affect the magnitude and direction of mobility flow because they require a great amount of skilled labor to support them (de Wit 2008). Students from families that are recent entrants to the middle class, many of whom believe that by going overseas they benefit in terms of both educational quality and improved return on investment via enhanced career opportunities, are consequently going abroad in greater numbers to "get skilled" (Banks et al. 2008). For example, over the past 25 years, average economic growth in China was close to 9.5 percent per year, an economic performance that, by alleviating poverty and improving levels of per capita wealth, is fueling the development of an emerging middle class (Gallagher et al. 2009). Whereas roughly 19 percent of China's population was considered to be middle class in 2003 it is expected to grow to 40 percent by 2020 (Graddol 2006).

Mirroring China's economic growth is Chinese tertiary enrollment and, consequently, Chinese tertiary enrollment overseas. China reportedly educates 25 percent of the world's students, with enrollments having increased roughly fivefold over the past decade (Gallagher et al. 2009). Total tertiary enrollments currently number around 26 million (Ibid.). At the same time, the total number of Chinese students studying abroad between 1978 and the end of 2008 exceeded 1.3 million, with United Nations Educational, Scientific and Cultural Organization (UNESCO) estimating that in 2007 alone the number of Chinese students studying abroad was as many as 421,000 (People's Daily Online 2009; UNESCO 2009).

This chapter first provides an overview of overseas student flows into key English-speaking destinations such as the United States, the United Kingdom, and Australia, while analyzing the role of the English language in current patterns of international student mobility. By emphasizing the interconnectedness of today's global workplace, it furthermore addresses the comparative value of English in future employment opportunities in a shifting economy. Lastly, it considers the strategic policy implications of a multilingual educational provision as it pertains to overseas student recruitment and migration.

Overseas Student Mobility Flows and the "Pull" of Language

In *Vision 2020: Forecasting International Student Mobility—A U.K. Perspective* (2004), Böhm and colleagues forecast that total global demand for international student places is likely to increase to 5.8 million by 2020 (Böhm et al. 2003). Of these projected 5.8 million places, 2.6 million, roughly 45 percent, are expected to go to the five main English-speaking destinations—the United States, the United Kingdom, Australia, Canada, and New Zealand (Ibid.).

In 2008, the United States attracted 624,000 overseas students, 40,800 more than the year before, representing a 7 percent increase in total foreign enrollments in the past academic year, and more than a 10 percent rise within the last two (IIE 2008). Like the United States, the United Kingdom is now attracting more international students than it has at any point in the past, with the Higher Education Statistics Agency (HESA) suggesting that by counting overseas students by nationality, rather than domicile, the United Kingdom hosts close to 514,000 students and actually rivals the United States in terms of total numbers (Lipsett 2009). Indeed, three in every ten overseas students currently choose to study either in the United States or the United Kingdom, making them the two most popular overseas student destinations in the world.

As in the United States and the United Kingdom, surging overseas student enrollments have also benefited Australia, Canada, and New Zealand over the past decade, largely as a result of the advent of English as a "global" language (Tremblay 2008). More than 20 percent of the world's population is English-speaking to some degree, with countries such as highly populous India, where it is spoken as a second language, especially contributing to the language's ubiquity (Graddol 2006). Graddol (2006) states that while only 50 percent of India's middle class (in itself, less than 10 percent of the population) was reportedly English-speaking in the mid-1980s, as much as 30 percent of the *entire* population now claims to "use" English—according to some estimates, roughly 333 million people (Ibid.).

With at least 75 countries having English as an official or affiliated language, as many as 750 million people worldwide speak English as their first or second language, and millions more are learning, or already speaking it, as an additional one (Ibid.). More people are learning English in China than in any other country, with an estimated 176.7 million Chinese students reportedly studying English within the country's formal education sector in 2005 alone (Ibid.).

Given that student mobility patterns tend to exist more strongly between countries sharing a common language (or several languages), the fact that English is so widely spoken partially explains why the United States, the United Kingdom, Australia, Canada, and New Zealand are five of the world's most popular overseas student destinations. Collectively, they currently share approximately 50 percent of the international student market. Yet a second— and arguably more significant—reason why these destinations have until now attracted large numbers of overseas students is because English is the current lingua franca of today's global workforce (Tremblay 2008).

Foreign No More: English as a Global Economy Language

The dominance of English is staggering. According to the British Council, more than 66 percent of the world's scientists read in it, 75 percent of the world's mail is written in it, and 80 percent of the world's electronic information stored in it (British Council 2000; Power 2005). It is, as the current language of international diplomacy, sport, technology, business, and academia, accelerating economic globalization as economic globalization encourages the ubiquity of its use (Graddol 2006). And, indeed, in a world where so many people—and more—speak English as a "foreign" language as a first or second one, its "otherness" disappears, making it a foreign language no more (Ibid.). Rather, "English" is today synonymous with "global" and students see it as a passport to travel and study abroad in the shorter term (Tremblay 2008).

In the longer term they see English as a means to employment. According to Davis (2003), English is responsible for 30 percent of world gross domestic product (GDP) (in 2007, an estimated US$54.6 trillion), a percentage calculated on the basis of approximate GDP apportionment by language— roughly, GDP per country and the number of English speakers in each one. The fact that the English-speaking United States is the world's largest economy with US$13.8 billion GDP (2007 est.) gives English a significant share of world GDP (Ibid.). With the United Kingdom and Canada also being English-speaking, three of the G7 economies are English-speaking, and this goes a long way toward explaining the economic predominance of the English language.

GDP by language is methodologically problematic (Ibid.). Language is often misrepresented by economic activity, with French, for example, playing an important business role in Maghreb countries, despite available data (the number of French speakers) underestimating the language's economic performance in the region (Ibid.). Yet despite such caveats, Davis argues that trends are accurate enough to chart an overall picture of relative levels of economic activity—and by implication, strategic value—of different languages.

The interconnectedness of today's global economy suggests that in terms of future employment opportunities an international skill set is invaluably advantageous to the higher education student. In response, the education sector is more actively embracing the international dimension by integrating it into curricular development in an attempt to mirror developments in the economic sector (Tremblay 2008). Globally oriented firms seek global-minded graduates, internationally competent workers articulate both in foreign languages and in intercultural skills (Ibid.). The students most likely to be global-minded are likely to be those capable of communicating within an international environment—in other words, students with the ability to speak English (Ibid.). This argument, that the ability to speak English is highly conducive to future employment opportunity, goes even further toward explaining the attractiveness of the English-speaking destinations.

Language: A Key Mobility Driver

The fact that the United States, the United Kingdom, Australia, Canada, and New Zealand are English-speaking thus influences their incoming mobility. In a Council for International Education (2006) survey of international student drivers for studying in U.K. further education colleges, respondents cited the opportunity to learn or improve English as one of the best aspects about living and studying in the United Kingdom (UKCOSA 2006). Similarly, the fact that Australia is an English-speaking country was an influential factor for respondents participating in Yang's (2007) study profiling what attracts mainland Chinese students to Australian higher education. The most important factor influencing international students' choice of New Zealand as a study destination in the Ministry of Education's international student experience survey (2007), meanwhile, was New Zealand's status as an English-speaking country. Notably, this factor was more important than any other factor in the choice of study destination (safety, the quality and recognition of New Zealand qualifications, the student's individual preference, etc.).

Certainly, there are other factors as well that influence overseas student mobility to these main English-speaking destinations, not least the quality of education—and educational experience—they offer. In the first instance, the quality of education in these five countries is often higher than that available in overseas students' own home countries. Importantly, unmet demand for domestic tertiary provision—or quality tertiary domestic provision—is contributing to the growth of international tertiary education. Between 1970 and 2007, worldwide tertiary enrollment grew by an average annual rate of 4.6 percent, with the number of tertiary students doubling every 15 years (UNESCO 2009). Demand is outstripping supply, despite rapid growth in the number of tertiary education providers.

Private tertiary education provision, which now accounts for 30 percent of global enrollment, is partially addressing surging demand in Africa, Latin America, and Southeast Asia. And indeed, the remarkable growth of private higher education worldwide is one of the most striking developments in global higher education in recent years, and not only within developing economies. While enrollment in private higher education accounts for 50 percent of total student enrollments in Chile, Indonesia, and the Philippines, it accounts for 70 percent of all higher education enrollment in Japan and South Korea (Altbach et al. 2009).

Yet although the private sector is absorbing some of the demand for tertiary education, demand is still unmet in many places, especially in highly populated countries with rapidly developing economies. Forecasts previously made in regards to China, for instance, substantially underestimated the current tertiary education supply needed to meet the demands of the country's burgeoning economy. Blight (1995) predicted that demand for higher education in China would grow to 21 million university places by 2020, and 27 million by 2025 (Olsen 2002). Böhm and King (1999) estimated a demand of 50 million by 2020, signaling China's inability to meet this demand even in the most conservative scenario (Ibid.). Given that China's student-age (18–22) cohort—now approximately 120 million—is projected to decrease after 2015, more recent forecasts suggest that higher education demand will eventually decline (British Council 2008). Yet despite considerable progress since the early 1990s, at which time China's tertiary education participation rate was less than 10 percent, it is still only 22 percent (Gallagher et al. 2009). As a result, soaring demand guarantees China's incapacity to supply in the foreseeable future.

Estimates suggest that as in China, tertiary education demand in India will eventually exceed supply. Böhm and Chaudhri (2000) forecast demand to reach 20 million in 2015, making India unable to supply at least 9 million university places needed to meet the demands of its rapidly developing economy. India's gross enrollment ratio is only 11–12 percent, and although there were around 12 million enrollments in 2006/2007—more than double the number in 1990/2001—tertiary demand is overwhelmingly unmet by available domestic provision (U.K. HE International Unit 2008).

In 2006, approximately 3,500 out of 178,000 students who undertook examination for entry to the Indian Institutes of Technology (IITs), India's "elite" group of institutions for chemical, electrical, and computer engineering, successfully qualified for application (note: acceptance *only* to seek application, not acceptance itself). In a country whose population exceeds 1.1 billion, less than 2 percent of applicants qualify for prospective entry to the IITs. In contrast, the published admission rate for the 2012 undergraduate class at Harvard University is 7.9 percent (CBS News 2008).

Unmet domestic provision is, therefore, one of the key factors driving the growing demand for overseas tertiary education. Given that students often believe overseas qualifications to be more valuable than "local" ones, the fact that the United States, the United Kingdom, Australia, Canada, and New Zealand provide quality, internationally recognized qualifications is a prime motivational factor "pulling" international students toward them.

In a second instance, overseas students are drawn to the quality of educational experience provided by key English-speaking destinations. With respect to lifestyle and climate, these countries are as different as they are similar, providing widely varying accommodation, student support, as well as financial and welfare services for incoming overseas students. Increasingly "consumer conscious" foreign students, many of whom now consider tertiary education in economic terms, consequently see education in these countries as a sound investment, and this is why overseas students believe that they provide better comprehensive value—the "total student package." As a result, they more successfully attract and recruit a higher number of overseas students.

New Global Languages: Challengers to English Language Dominance

Significantly, however, these leading host countries are less likely to attract as successfully in the longer term, with several key reasons explaining why. Predominant among them is the changing strategic value of the English language. Simply put, other languages are beginning to challenge the position of English as the definitive global language. Demographically, Arabic is growing more quickly than any other language in the world (Graddol

2006). Spanish now has roughly as many native speakers as does English. Mandarin is the world's most widely spoken language in terms of first language speakers (Ibid.).

In contrast, not only is English likely to be spoken as a first language by a declining proportion of the global population, but also it is no longer the only language in global business (Ibid.). By analyzing projections of economic growth for the so-called BRIC economies (Brazil, Russia, India, and China), Davis extrapolates that demand for other languages—and GDP apportionment—is growing (Davis 2003; Graddol 2006). Chinese, Russian, Indic, and Portuguese are set to account for a higher proportion of global GDP, most significantly after 2010 (Ibid.).

English meanwhile, is likely to account for the same amount—or less—of global GDP (Davis 2003). From 1975 to 2002 whereas English contributed to 29.2 percent, Chinese accounted for only 12.5 percent. Between 2002 and 2008, however, while English's contribution actually fell by 1.1 percent to 28.2 percent, Chinese share grew to 22.8 percent (Graddol 2006). Importantly, Chinese is now second only to English in market share, suggesting not only that it is, like Spanish and Arabic, contributing to the economic depreciation of English, but also that it is more economically valuable than it once was (Davis 2003).

What the growing economic value of Chinese translates to is the growing popularity of Chinese as a foreign language. The Office of Chinese Language Council International reports that 40 million people are now learning Chinese, with 3,000 higher education institutions in 109 countries having launched Chinese courses for their students (The University of Hong Kong 2009). Educational instruction in it, moreover, is likely to only grow as Mandarin continues to grow more economically relevant and the language thus appears more attractive to employment-seeking students (Graddol 2006, 61). Chinese-taught courses already exist in the Netherlands, for instance (Tremblay 2008).

At the same time, the growth of English-taught curricula worldwide is depreciating a premium strategic advantage once enjoyed only by the main English-speaking destinations, namely, English-language provision. Now a rapidly growing number of tertiary education institutions in Europe are offering English-language provision, with English-taught courses available in a widening range of countries. More than 50 percent of all degree programs in the Netherlands are currently offered in English, making the country Europe's leader in the provision of English-taught education, followed by Finland and Cyprus (Wächter and Maiworm 2008). Yet English-taught programs are also becoming a regular feature in Sweden, Switzerland, Denmark, Norway, and Germany, especially at the postgraduate level. More than 500 master's programs are English-taught in Swedish universities, while as much as 80 percent of the postgraduate-level provision available in some institutions in Switzerland are taught in English (Becker et al. 2009). The highest providers of English-medium education are countries in Northern Europe, with German universities currently offering a further 415 master's programs at least partly in other languages—the majority in English (Tremblay 2008).

The first reason why such countries are expanding their English-taught provision is to prove more attractive to overseas students. Denmark, Finland, and Greece, among others, find it more challenging to attract international students than the key English-speaking destinations because their national languages are not widely spoken outside their borders. Lacking adequate proficiency to follow an educational program in these languages, foreign students—not wanting or, as in many cases, actually unable to learn such languages—consequently choose to study elsewhere (Ibid.). They choose to study in countries with widely spoken language(s) of instruction because they are more likely to be proficient in such languages (Ibid.). And indeed, as discussed, the competitive advantage of the main English-speaking destinations is at least partially attributable to their use of English, a widely spoken language, as a language of instruction (Wächter and Maiworm 2008).

Yet the second reason why these countries are expanding English-taught provision is that it would benefit their own students. Significantly, the development of language abilities among domestic student populations is a tool to enhance their outward mobility; the higher students rate their foreign language proficiency the more likely they are to go overseas (Tremblay 2008). In many cases, European and Asian students are seeking English-medium provision because by studying in English, the global economy's current lingua franca, they are likely to widen the study and employment opportunities later available to them (Ibid.). The growing emphasis on tertiary provision in foreign languages—at this point, mainly English—derives from the acknowledgment that lacking foreign language proficiency and, more generally, international experience creates somewhat of a glass ceiling in today's employment market (Ibid.). Just as importantly, overseas students arguably gain added advantage by studying *in* English, for international experience—and the intercultural skills gained through it—is a highly valuable commodity within a global economy. If monolingualism is preventive of mobility, multilingualism is thus encouraging it—a fact increasingly acknowledged by today's global economy students.

For this reason, "domestic" student demand is arguably driving the introduction of English-medium provision in non-English-speaking countries as much as overseas student recruitment. Yet regardless of which is the greater driver, the institutions—and more widely, countries—now offering English provision stand to benefit. Co-opting one of the key factors incentivizing English-speaking destinations, namely, the fact that they are English-speaking, is likely to prove advantageous to, for instance, South Korea, to successfully promote itself as an overseas higher education destination and subsequently recruit overseas students.

South Korea's government sees English as a determined consequence of the country's future socioeconomic reality, for the country can more effectively compete in a world market once it knows it—and its language—well. From this perspective, English-medium instruction is obligatory, not least as a means to strengthen its position in a global market. And indeed, it is in an effort to do both that several of the country's universities have in recent years "gone English" (Becker 2007). As well as "English only" zones, where, as the name suggests, only English is spoken, some of the country's best internationally known institutions are rapidly introducing English-taught provision. At Korea University, one of South Korea's best known universities internationally, as many as 35 percent of its courses are now English-taught, with plans to increase provision to more than 60 percent by 2010. All lectures are given in English at the Korea Advanced Institute for Science and Technology (KAIST), where a bilingual (English/Korean) language policy is officially in place as part of the institution's ambition to become a global campus.

English-Language Provision: Advantageous Necessity?

Clearly, English-language provision is not disadvantageous to recruitment. By complementing the amount and variety of provision available in native languages, English is contributing to the internationalization of higher education within these countries. The level (or lack thereof) of English-language provision on offer in Spain, for example, is arguably an obstacle challenging the internationalization of Spanish higher education. Together with France, Italy, and Portugal, Spain is currently one of Europe's lowest providers of higher education in the English language. Reasons for the absence of English language within Spanish universities presumably include lack of faculty members with adequate language skills or insufficient financial resources for the development of English-medium courses, but perhaps more saliently, historical mobility patterns into the country suggest that until quite recently there was a less intrinsic need for it.

The large majority of Spain's overseas students have traditionally come from countries such as Colombia, Argentina, Mexico, Peru, and Ecuador, countries that, as well as sharing significant sociohistorical connections, are Spanish-speaking. As a result, Spain was (and, arguably, still is) not dependent on English-medium provision to attract international students, at least not to the same extent as other countries. As much as 50 percent of Spain's total higher education population has come from Central and South America in the past years, including thousands of students from Venezuela and Chile. By virtue of being Spanish-speaking, therefore, Spain is already an attractive study destination for a significant number of overseas students.

The same is true of France. The fact that France is French-speaking is part of the reason why it is an attractive destination for students from a host of African countries. Francophone Africa annually sends the largest number of students to the country, with Morocco, Algeria, Tunisia, and Senegal historically responsible for the bulk of France's international enrollments. Since 1999, these four countries have consistently accounted for 27 percent (on average) of France's total overseas student population, with a record total of 80,700 combined enrollments in 2006 alone.

Other African "source" countries include Djibouti, Benin, Mauritania, Cameroon, and the Ivory Coast. Eight out of every ten mobile African students is currently studying in North America or Europe; of the eight, between three and four are going to France. Many of these students undoubtedly find it easier to pursue higher education studies in France than in a non-French-speaking country. French higher education is arguably more accessible for them, much like it is for the many Lebanese and, to a lesser extent, Syrian students who annually pursue higher education in France. Total enrollment from Lebanon is continuing to grow, it nearly doubled from 2,500 to 5,900 between 1999 and 2007. Interestingly, nearly quintupling over the same period is the number of Vietnamese students, making Vietnam—a former French colony—one of France's "top ten" overseas student "sources" (CampusFrance 2008). Thus at present the French language is advantageous to France's recruitment of overseas students. Moreover, because the education systems in countries such as Morocco, Algeria, and Lebanon are often modeled on that in France, France can rather enviably offer significant numbers of overseas students an international experience from within a common language setting. Therefore, in marked contrast to the United States, the United Kingdom, Australia, Canada, and New Zealand (each of which primarily attracts students from Asia), France has Africa and the Middle East as its most important "source" regions for recruitment.

Conclusions: Recruitment, Migration, and Changing Linguistic Hegemony

Ironically, in the longer term the fact that English is a global language is potentially marginalizing in the continued competition among the main English-speaking destinations. First, rapid growth in the amount of English-language provision in non-English countries is depreciating its once-premium value, with countries across Europe and Asia offering a higher number of English-taught courses. By doing so, they are attracting an increasing number of "eager-for-English" students from beyond their traditional recruitment "pools" or "source" countries. The use of English as a language of instruction in Germany, for example, is removing a "mobility barrier" that may have previously prevented overseas students from enrolling in tertiary education there. Germany's growing English-language curricula is consequently one of the factors explaining why it is gradually becoming a more popular destination among students from Brazil and Vietnam. At the same time, English *only* provision is likely to be less advantageous to overseas student recruitment than it is now. With more and more English educational provision, the language is arguably set to devalue as a competitive recruitment advantage, especially as other languages (Mandarin, Spanish, Arabic, etc.) become increasingly valuable toward future employment.

Opportunity for employment is the predominant reason why if given the chance, a large number of overseas students want to stay, at least temporarily, in a country following their studies. In Yang's (2007) study of what attracts mainland Chinese students to Australian higher education, future migration opportunity was cited as the key reason by 97 percent of the respondents. It is why roughly 80 percent of Indian students studying in Canada apply for permanent residency following completion of studies (Bird 2008). And it is why 66 percent of foreign citizens who received science or engineering doctorates from U.S. universities in 2003 were reportedly still living there two years later (Wadhwa et al. 2009).

Given that the aim of staying in a country of study to work and make a career is one of the strongest factors "pushing" students to prioritize some destinations over others, a shifting global economy is set to gradually influence "traditional" patterns of student movement across borders (Altbach 2004). In respect to speed and directional flow, the transfer of economic power currently underway—roughly "West" to "East"—is remarkable, with growth projections for the BRIC nations indicating that they are on target to collectively match the original G7's share of global GDP by

2050 (National Intelligence Council 2008). China in particular is rapidly transforming itself into an economic superpower, one that by 2025 will trail only the United States in terms of GDP output (Ibid.). The country's economy, now the world's third largest, is growing at an unparalleled pace, having reportedly grown tenfold over the past 30 years.

The primary reason why the newly emerging destinations such as China are likely to attract more overseas students is, therefore, their potential to provide comparable value in terms of educational investment in the longer term. In the latter part of the twentieth century, mobility flow was largely unidirectional, with students from developing economies migrating toward developed ones, buoyed by the appeal of quality education and promising employment prospects. With the center of economic gravity gradually shifting toward Asia, however, directional flow is partly reversing, with students once "brain drained" from their own countries now more frequently returning. Students (and job seekers) from developed countries are, moreover, "brain gaining" rapidly developing economies. A shift in the destinations where employment is available is contributing, therefore, to a directional shift in the flow of overseas students toward them.

A second reason why newly emerging destinations are becoming more competitive is language, however. At present, the ubiquity of English as a spoken language benefits the main English-speaking destination countries because overseas students understand the language to be a key educational investment toward future employment. As the current lingua franca of the global economy, English is a must if students want to successfully participate in the global workforce. Yet with the rise of other global languages and more and more English-taught curricula, in terms of recruitment, English provision is a depreciating advantage. Future employers will increasingly seek more global (read multilingual) graduates in the longer term, making the opportunity to learn in more than one language or study in English in a non-English context grow comparably more popular. The appeal of "English-only" degrees is consequently set to weaken among international students, and most advantageously positioned to benefit within this context are non-English-speaking countries offering foreign language provision, including, but not limited to, English (Becker et al. 2009). Therefore, what is now a strategic recruitment advantage for English-speaking countries—namely, the English language—may eventually become a liability. Why is this significant?

Importantly, within one generation the populations of select OECD nations may be 30 percent smaller than they are now, with fertility rates in countries such as Australia (1.8 percent) and Canada (1.5 percent)—where significant proportions of the population are already foreign-born—falling below replacement population levels (Hawthorne 2010). With negative population growth restricting future economic development, such nations of aging local populations need to deal with a serious skills shortage that, combined with the international financial turmoil, is intensifying the global "talent" race.

Within this context exists the overseas student whose attributes include, among others, youth, relevant professional training, international experience, and, critically, host country language ability (Hawthorne 2009, 2010). Culturally aware, diverse, and, in many cases, multilingual, the international student contributes a series of sociocultural benefits to the host country, benefits that, because they provide no readily measurable economic value, are difficult to quantify (Vickers and Bekhradnia 2007).

More easily quantifiable is their economic benefit, certainly in terms of actual expenditure, but more acutely, human capital. In New Zealand, whereas 2.3 million arrivals from 1955 to 2004 netted a population gain of only 208,000 people, 88 percent of skilled migrants by 2006 first arrived as students or temporary workers (Hawthorne 2009). Simply put, incoming mobility to the country is tantamount to the country's "demographic survival" (Hawthorne 2009).

Cognizant of what is inherently a highly desirable source of skilled workforce, migration countries are consequently implementing innovative recruitment strategies in an effort to put their "best foot forward" toward them. One of the factors that can help them do so is language. Language proficiency is advantageous in international student recruitment—and later migration—because it facilitates, first, the arrival of overseas students and, second, their integration into society. With technology changing the nature of today's workplace, "softer" skills (teamwork, presentation, reportage, etc.) are becoming more important to global employers, placing an even higher premium on the ability to "speak the local lingo" (Keeley 2009). Within this context, the extent of host country language(s) knowledge is quite plausibly the most important human capital component with respect to integration (Ibid.).

Sharing a common language (or languages) with a destination country makes the overseas experience potentially that much more attractive to the incoming "foreign" student because it ultimately is an "easier" one. With prominent ethnic Chinese, Indian, and Malay communities, Singapore, for instance, is able to provide a "home away from home" for students from a variety of countries. Its multicultural atmosphere renders it an attractive destination for a large majority of Asian students, especially those sharing (Chinese, Tamil, and Malay) linguistic and cultural ties.

At the same time, Singapore's multiculturalism is rendering it more attractive to students beyond Asia because it is English-speaking. One of the strengths of the city state's education system is the fact that it is multilingual, which, when coupled with a high-quality life and a safe living environment, goes a long way toward explaining why more and more "Western" (and English-speaking) students are now preferring to study there. By capitalizing on its colonial history, Singapore is thus exploiting one of its most competitive advantages: language (Graddol 2006).

Importantly, because mobility is made "easy" by language, language policy is almost certainly going to more heavily influence tertiary education reform in the coming years. Governments, seeking to reap the sociocultural and economic benefits afforded by incoming overseas students—a highly desirable source of skilled migration—are increasingly likely to allow the delivery of tertiary education programs in a foreign language. In the longer term, such delivery is going to be in emerging global languages now challenging the dominance of English, including Mandarin, Arabic, and Spanish. Advantageously positioned within this context are countries such as Singapore and Malaysia, as well as aspiring regional education "hubs" in the Middle East, namely the United Arab Emirates, Qatar, Kuwait, and Bahrain. In the future, it is through provision of both English and a foreign language that countries might potentially regain the competitive edge now provided by English-language provision.

BIBLIOGRAPHY

Altbach, Philip G. 2004. "Higher Education Crosses Borders." *Change* 35 (2): 18–24.

Altbach, Philip G., Liz Reisberg, and Laura E. Rumbley. 2009. *Trends in Global Higher Education: Tracking an Academic Revolution.* Paris: UNESCO.

Banks, Melissa, Alan Olsen, and Daniel Pearce. 2008. *Global Student Mobility: An Australian Perspective Five Years On.* Canberra: IDP Education.

Becker, Rosa. 2007. The Growth of English-Medium Instruction in East Asia: The Key to Competitiveness? London: The Observatory on Borderless Higher Education.

Becker, Rosa, Veronica Lasanowski, Helen Goreham, Don Olcott Jr., Steve Woodfield, Robin Middlehurst, and Joan-Anton Carbonell. 2009. *U.K. Universities and Europe: Competition and Internationalisation.* London: U.K. Higher Education Europe/International Unit.

Bird, Jessica. 2008. Four Fifths of Indian Students in Canada Apply for Permanent Residency. London: Canadian Visa Bureau. Available online at: http://www.visabureau.com/canada.

Böhm, Anthony, Marcelo Follari, Andrew Hewett, Sarah Jones, Neil Kemp, Denis Meares, David Pearce, and Kevin Van Cauter. 2003. *Vision 2020: Forecasting International Student Mobility—A U.K. Perspective.* London: British Council.

British Council. 2008. What Does the Future Hold? China Country Report: The Outlook for International Student Mobility. London: British Council.

CampusFrance. 2008. Les *étudiants internationaux: chiffres clés*. Paris: CampusFrance.

Council for International Education (UKCOSA). 2006. New Horizons: The Experiences of International Students in U.K. Further Education Colleges—Report of the UKCOSA Survey. London: UKCOSA.

Davis, Mark. 2003. *GDP by Language*. Technical Note No. 13. Mountain View, CA: UNICODE. Available online at: http://unicode.org.

de Wit, Hans. 2008. Changing Dynamics in International Student Circulation: Meanings, Push and Pull Factors Trends and Data. In *The Dynamics of International Student Circulation in a Global Context*, ed. H. de Wit, Pawan Agarwal, Mohsen Elmahdy Said, Molatlhegi T. Sehoole, and Muhammad Sirozi. Rotterdam/Taipei: Sense Publishers.

Elliot, Larry. 2007. "World Poverty Reduced by Growth in India and China." *The Guardian*, April 16. Available online at: http://www.guardian.co.uk.

Gallagher, Michael, Abrar Hasan, Mary Canning, Howard Newby, Lichia Saner-Yiu, and Ian Whitman. 2009. *OECD Review of Tertiary Education: China*. Paris: OECD.

Graddol, David. 2006. *English Next?* London: British Council.

Hawthorne, Lesleyanne. 2010. "Demography, Migration and Demand for International Students." In *Globalisation and Tertiary Education in the Asia-Pacific: The Changing Nature of a Dynamic Market*, ed. Christopher Finlay, and William G. Tierney. Singapore: World Scientific.

Hawthorne, Lesleyanne. 2009. "Two-Step Migration": The Growing Competition for International Students as Skilled Migration in the Asia-Pacific Market." Paper presented at the Asia Pacific Rim University Senior Staff Forum, Melbourne, March 18–19, 2009.

Institute of International Education (IIE). 2008. *Open Doors 2008: Report on International Educational Exchange*. New York: IIE.

Keeley, Brian. 2009. International Migration: The Human Face of Globalisation. Paris: OECD.

Lasanowski, Veronica. 2009a. *International Student Mobility: Status Report 2009*. London: The Observatory on Borderless Higher Education.

Lasanowski, Veronica. 2009b. Entering into the Ring? The Spanish Government Announces the Creation of an Overseas Promotion Agency as Part of Higher Education Internationalisation. London: The Observatory on Borderless Higher Education.

Leung, Rebecca. 2003. "Imported from India." *CBS News*, June 22.

Lipsett, Anthea. 2009. "See More Overseas Students than Thought." *The Guardian*, May 21. Available online at: http://www.guardian.co.uk.

Meares, Denis. 2003. Global Student Mobility 2025: The Supply Challenge. Sydney: IDP Education.

National Intelligence Council. 2008. *Global Trends 2025: A Transformed World*. Washington, DC: National Intelligence Council.

New Zealand Ministry of Education. 2008. The Experiences of International Students in New Zealand: Report on the Results of the National Survey 2007. Wellington: Ministry of Education.

Olsen, Alan. 2002. *E-Learning in Asia: Supply & Demand*. London: The Observatory on Borderless Higher Education.

Organisation for Economic Co-operation and Development (OECD). 2009. *Education at a Glance 2009*. Paris: OECD.

People's Daily Online. 2009. "Chinese Students Studying Abroad Exceed 1.39 Million." 2009. *People's Daily Online*, March 26, Available online at: http://english.peopledaily.com.cn.

Power, Carla. 2005. "Not the Queen's English." *Newsweek*, March 7. Available online at: http://www.newsweek.com.

Tremblay, Karine. 2008. Internationalisation: Shaping Strategies in the National Context. In *Tertiary Education for the Knowledge Society: Volume 2*, ed. P. Santiago, K. Tremblay, E. Basri, and E. Arnal. Paris: OECD.

U.K. Higher Education International Unit. 2008. *Country Briefing: India*. London: Universities U.K.

UNESCO. 2009. Global Education Digest 2009: Comparing Education Statistics across the World. Paris: UNESCO.

University of Hong Kong. 2009. *China Education News Issue 6*. Hong Kong: Wah Ching Centre for Research on Education in China.

Vickers, Phil, and Bahram Bekhradnia. 2007. *The Economic Costs and Benefits of International Students*. Oxford: Higher Education Policy Institute.

Wächter, Bernd, and Friedhelm Maiworm. 2008. *English-Taught Programmes in European Higher Education: The Picture in 2007*. Bonn: Lemmens.

Wadhwa, Vivek, AnnaLee Saxenian,Richard B. Freeman, and Alex Salkever. 2009. *Losing the* World's Best and Brightest: America's News Immigrant Entrepreneurs, Part V. Kansas City, Missouri: Ewing Marion Kauffman Foundation.

Yang, Molly. 2007. "What Attracts Mainland Chinese Students to Australian Higher Education." *Studies in Learning Evaluation, Innovation and Development* 4 (2): 1–12.

Chapter 11

Regional Education Hubs: Mobility for the Knowledge Economy

Jane Knight

Introduction

The emergence of the knowledge society and economy, a direct manifestation of globalization, has had a profound impact on the higher education subsector—the international dimension in particular. Cross-border education is booming in response to three important developments: (1) the escalating demand for a skilled workforce by nations wanting to engage in the knowledge economy, (2) a pronounced orientation to a market economy and commodification of education, and (3) the escalating numbers of students wanting higher education opportunities and in many cases a foreign credential (Knight 2008). Who could have imagined two decades ago the massive investments in global international student recruitment campaigns now clearly linked to more relaxed immigration policies and national innovation strategies? No one predicted the substantial increase in the number of branch campus centers being established by traditional universities and new higher education providers. Finally, the growth in franchising, twinning, double/joint degree partnerships, and, of course, the new virtual worlds of education has been unexpected and unprecedented. Linked to these cross-border initiatives is the latest trend, the positioning of countries as regional hubs for higher education.

It is revealing to read newspaper headlines in Hong Kong, Dubai, Bahrain, Singapore, Botswana, and Seoul all announcing major new investments in establishing regional education hubs or education cities. Higher education is a key economic and political actor critical to countries wanting a leadership position in the new knowledge economy and a geopolitical footprint in the marked trend toward regionalization. It is a new era when one sees higher education as an anchor for positioning a country's economic, technological, and innovation competitiveness in their region and beyond. The diversity of rationales, partnerships, strategies, financing, and regulatory frameworks for establishing regional education hubs demonstrates that each country adopts an approach consistent with its national/regional context and policy.

This chapter will focus on three countries in the Middle East (the United Arab Emirates, Qatar, and Bahrain) and three in Asia (Singapore, Hong Kong, and Malaysia) and explore the potential and challenges for regional hubs in each place. Of interest is that these countries are all relatively small in size and are committed to the hub model not only for education but also for other sectors. In fact, it may be justified to say that hubs (transportation, innovation, education, health, trade, fashion, etc.) are definitely the current rage making the question of long-term sustainability very relevant.

The purpose of the chapter is to examine the different models of education hubs being developed in these six countries with a specific focus on the driving rationales and the key actors. While these initiatives include familiar strategies such as branch campuses and franchises, they are of another magnitude as they try to co-locate foreign universities with private companies, research and development enterprises, as well as science and technology parks in order to support and develop new knowledge industries.

New Actors and New Terminology

The development of "international education cities" and "regional hubs" is new territory for the higher education subsector. That being said, it is important to recognize that it is not necessarily the higher education subsector that is sponsoring or guiding these new education initiatives. Economic development boards, tourism authorities, multinational investment companies, as well as science and technology enterprises are capitalizing on the important role of higher education as a key actor in the preparation of future knowledge workers and the production of new knowledge through partnerships with the private sector.

There is no lack of new terms to describe an education hub. Each country (in fact, each sponsor) chooses different concepts to brand its initiative. Current terms being used include education hot spot, gateway, hub, cluster, free economic zone, global schoolhouse, world city, knowledge village, international academic city, university town, and the list goes on. An analysis of the terms reveals that except for "higher education free economic zone," the terms are more oriented to carving out a marketing niche than indicating a particular business or academic approach. In fact, the diversity and use of terms can lead to major confusion. For instance, Education City is a preferred term but is used in starkly different ways. Bahrain Education City refers to a complex of buildings, recreation and commercial facilities, as well as laboratories and residential areas, while Hong Kong Education City is an Internet-based portal for teachers, students, parents, and the community. A term that has not been used for obvious reasons is "education/knowledge marketplace" but in reality it might be the most accurate description for many of the hubs.

New Developments in the Middle East

United Arab Emirates: Dubai International Academic City and Knowledge Village

This country of 2.4 million inhabitants, of which 30 percent are under 18 years of age, is in the process of moving from an oil-based economy to a knowledge- and services-oriented economy. This requires major investments to develop the necessary infrastructure and to attract businesses from the region and beyond. A key priority is having skilled and professional workers to support the growing knowledge economy. Of the seven emirates making up the United Arab Emirates (U.A.E.), three—Dubai, Abu Dhabi, and Ras al Khaimah—are currently active in recruiting international universities, faculty, and students. This chapter focuses on one specific emirate—Dubai.

A key element of Dubai's Strategic Plan 2015 is the development of the region's "talent pool" thereby giving high priority to attracting education organizations, institutions, and companies. The Dubai International Academic City (DIAC) is being developed by a leading investment and holding company in Dubai and is one of several theme-oriented cities that this private company is promoting. DIAC was formally launched in 2007 and builds on the successful creation of the Dubai Knowledge Village (KV), established in 2003. The Knowledge Village, home to over 400 business partners, is shifting its emphasis to short-term training and professional development by private firms. It is expected that foreign universities that offer undergraduate- and graduate-level programs will move to DIAC as it appears to be the current priority for developing Dubai as a regional base for international higher education institutions and students (Dubai Holdings 2008).

The owner/sponsor of both DIAC and the Knowledge Village is TECOM Investments, a subsidiary of Dubai Holdings. The mission of TECOM Investments is to create and manage business clusters that contribute to the development of knowledge-based industries. Their five business clusters (also known as theme cities) include (1) education; (2) information, communication, and technology (ICT); (3) media; (4) life sciences; and (5) clean technology. CNN and Reuters are part of the Media City, while Microsoft and IBM are part of the ICT cluster. DIAC and KV and their "tenant" universities are part of the education business cluster. TECOM has described DIAC as a regional base for premier international higher education institutions located in an area of 25 million square feet with modern educational, housing, recreational, sport, and commercial facilities available for students and faculty. This 3.27 billion dollar business venture is concrete proof of the U.A.E.'s commitment to develop education as a profitable commercial industry, an approach that might not please those academics who question whether higher education should be treated as a commodity.

Dubai sees higher education as a sector critical to developing brain power for their new knowledge-based economy. Fundamental to their strategy is the recruitment of reputable international higher education institutions that can (1) lend their brand equity, (2) offer their already established academic programs, and (3) provide experienced faculty to teach national and international students. It is somewhat surprising that higher education institutions are being recruited more as business partners to educate and train future knowledge workers and less as research and innovation experts. This may change over the years given that the production and application of new research is fundamental to the knowledge enterprise. The involvement of Johns Hopkins University in Dubai's Medical City is concrete evidence of the recruitment of universities for their research expertise (Bardsley 2008).

There are currently over 25 international universities of higher learning in Dubai Knowledge Village and Dubai International Academic City. They come from different parts of the world including the United States, Australia, India, Pakistan, Iran, Russia, Belgium, and the United Kingdom. Examples of higher education institutions include the University of Wollongong, Michigan State University, St. Petersburg State University of Engineering and Economics, the International Institute of Coffee and Barista Training, Harvard University's Medical School Branch, Boston University, London Business School, Université Lyon 2, Rochester Institute of Technology, and Murdoch University. Total enrollment in 2008 was estimated at 11,000 students representing 102 nationalities, indicating small enrollment rates for most DIAC tenant universities. Academic program durations range from one to four years and include engineering, computer science, finance, media, fashion and design, biotechnology, environmental studies, quality management, and business management programs. The plans for the future include an expansion to 40 universities catering to students from the Middle East, North Africa, and Asia.

Partners in DIAC and KV, in fact, any business in the Free Economic Zones (FEZ), are not subject to federal U.A.E. or Emirates Law. In terms of financial arrangements they are assured of 100 percent foreign ownership, 100 percent freedom from taxes, 100 percent repatriation of profits and assets, and smooth visa-issuance procedures for students, faculty, and staff. There is no question that these are attractive features for tenants of DIAC and KV in terms of minimizing some of the significant financial risks involved in establishing a branch campus or teaching center in foreign countries.

The fact that Free Zones are not under the direct authority of federal U.A.E. or Dubai Emirate law means that the power for selecting institutions and controlling the quality of academic programs rests with the Free Zone authority. The establishment of the University Quality Assurance International Board (UQAIB) in 2008 by the Knowledge and Human Development Authority Dubai (KHDA) does not change this but it puts a mechanism in place to provide advice to the Free Zone authority.

The primary task of the UQAIB is "to ensure that branches of universities and colleges accredited by foreign associations comply with the same standards of academic quality found at the 'home' campus programs" (OBHE 2008, 1). This assumes, of course, that the home institution has been accredited by a bona fide accreditation agency (Knight 2006). The mandate of the board includes, first, reviewing applications of all institutions applying to the Dubai Free Zones and making recommendations to the licensing board of the Free Zone authority, and, second, approving the academic programs of licensed institutions. (KHDA 2008). The UQAIB is an ambitious undertaking and a necessary and welcome one. It will be important to monitor the developments and decisions of the UQAIB as it is breaking new ground in terms of assessing education institutions and organizations that work under an independent authority that manages and promotes the business ventures of an Economic Free Zone.

Qatar Education City

Qatar was the first country in the Middle East to act on the concept of developing an Education City. More than a decade ago it developed its strategy for Qatar Education City (QEC). The idea originated with the emir and the Qatar Foundation was mandated to implement the ambitious plan. As of 2008, QEC is a 2,500 acre well-equipped complex fully functioning with eight foreign universities offering a variety of undergraduate and graduate programs (Qatar Foundation 2010a). Currently the vast majority of students are local residents of Qatar but future plans include recruiting students from the entire region.

The Qatar Foundation (QF) for Education, Science and Community Development is a private, nonprofit organization established in 1995 by the emir of Qatar. The QF is committed to human resource development through a network of innovative centers and partnerships, all dedicated to making the knowledge society in Qatar a reality. The QF believes that a highly educated population is a key prerequisite for success in the knowledge economy. Their commitment is to provide quality education at all levels to prepare today's generation for their leadership role in a global society.

In terms of their higher education mandate, the QF has been strategic and highly selective in inviting foreign universities to become partners in their endeavor. To date, only American universities have actually established their operations in QEC, but as of late 2008, two U.K. universities have been asked to participate. The Imperial College of London has plans to set up a branch campus in QEC (OBHE 2008). The critical factors for selection are an internationally recognized curriculum and high-level expertise in disciplines that are central to broadening Qatar's range of higher education programs. Given that each university has a niche area of curriculum, there is no overlap of or competition between academic programs being offered by the international higher education institutions (HEIs) operating in Qatar Education City. It operates on a differentiated academic model that is responsive to the clearly articulated Qatar priority to develop human resource requirements for the twenty-first-century knowledge economy. The American universities currently operating in Education City include Virginia Commonwealth University, Weill Cornell Medical College, Texas A&M University, Carnegie Mellon University, Georgetown University School of Foreign Service, and Northwestern University.

As research is a priority for the QF, each university has a research element to its work. In addition to these American institutions, the Qatar Faculty of Islamic Studies offers a postgraduate program in Islamic Studies and a master's degree in contemporary *Fiqh*, the study of Islamic law, and is part of an international center that promotes Islamic thinking, dialogue, and research (Qatar Foundation 2010b).

Qatar has invested over a billion dollars to attract American universities. For example, Cornell University reportedly received US$750 million over 11 years, for offering its programs and qualifications at QEC (OBHE 2005). Similar arrangements are in place with the other institutions. Modern education facilities are provided at no cost for all resident HEIs in Education City and university salaries and administrative expenses are covered as well.

Qatar Education City shares a similar rationale of educating its population for the knowledge economy with other education hubs or cities in the Middle East but its approach is dramatically different. The master plan for QEC goes beyond the current institutions that were invited because of their specialized program area. This model avoids overlapping of curriculum and prevents unnecessary competition in student recruitment. It leads to stable undergraduate- and graduate-level programming. To date, the majority of enrollments are local Qatari students but future plans include recruitment of other regional students. The Qatari approach is one of direct funding of expenses of foreign institutions offering their programs instead of tax incentives or repatriation of profit arrangements. QEC is deliberately not part of the Qatar Free Trade Zone. It is a very expensive proposition to buy the education services and brand of selected universities from the United States and the United Kingdom. Whether this model is replicable in other countries or even sustainable in Qatar is still an unanswered but critical question.

Bahrain—Higher Education City

In late 2006, Bahrain announced its intention to establish a world-class higher education city at a total cost of US$1 billion. The Executive Development Board of the Kingdom of Bahrain made the announcement after agreeing to jointly undertake this major initiative with the Kuwait Finance and Investment Company. It is expected to be completed in 2010 and by 2015 have a projected enrollment of 25,000 students. These are ambitious plans and high expectations for a small state such as Bahrain and for a Kuwaiti multinational company. An announcement in late 2008 that the Sorbonne University of Paris would be the first tenant of Higher Education City indicates that it is en route to attracting respected institutions.

The drivers and anticipated benefits of the Higher Education City include the following: (1) to provide a technologically skilled workforce for the current and future labor market in Bahrain and the region; (2) to encourage innovation; (3) to leverage increased direct investments into the kingdom; and (4) to reposition the kingdom as a regional specialist center in higher education. Plans include the establishment of laboratories, an international center for research, a branch of a U.S.-based university, and a specialist academy. The courses offered will focus on three areas of study: engineering, business, and science. The ancillary facilities such as housing, sports, and recreation complexes will also be built to service the university students and faculty (Gulf News 2006).

Bahrain has also launched a Science and Technology Park to attract regional and international businesses working on new technologies such as renewable energy, environment, information and communication, and clean technology. It is intended that the Higher Education City will complement and contribute to the work of the Science and Technology Park by training the necessary skilled and professional knowledge workers as well as providing ongoing professional development opportunities (Science and Development Network 2008).

It is far too early to report on the progress, success, and challenges of Bahrain's Higher Education City. Of note is the fact that it is a Kuwait-based investment firm (not a Bahrain-based one) that is leading this initiative. There are more questions than answers related to quality assurance, recognition of degrees, diversity of programs offered, and selection criteria, but it will be informative to see what lessons they learn from the developments in the U.A.E. and other countries in the region.

Approaches to Regional Education Hubs in Asia

Singapore: The Global Schoolhouse

The Global Schoolhouse is the official name of the Singapore initiative to develop a regional educational hub of students, scholars, and researchers. Such a name evokes global scope but local impact. Plans to attract foreign institutions to Singapore started in 1997 with Singapore's goal of attracting ten world-class universities by 2007. In fact, they surpassed their expectations. In 2003 Singapore Education was launched as the umbrella brand to lead developments toward establishing Singapore as a premier education hub. In the following year, 2004, the Global Schoolhouse project was announced by the Singapore Economic Development Board and promoted by the Singapore Tourism Board (Ministry of Trade and Industry 2002). Edu-tourism and edu-nomics appear to be high priorities for this small nation state void of both natural resources and a vibrant manufacturing sector. It is thus committed to become a world player in the knowledge economy, and the Global Schoolhouse project is a part of the overall strategy. As of 2008, the education sector (all levels) contributed about 2 percent of Singapore's GDP and is forecast to reach 5 percent by 2015.

The major objectives and expected benefits driving this project include, first and foremost, economic development through foreign investment, second, recruitment of "foreign talent," and, third, attracting research and development firms as well as multinational companies specializing in the knowledge economy and service industries (Gribble and McBurnie 2007).

The Global Schoolhouse is a multifaceted and ambitious project. It includes providing secondary and university-level education, corporate training, e-learning opportunities, and education services such as the preparation of standardized tests for the region. The focus on tertiary education is clear as it aims to improve the quality and capacity of Singapore's higher education subsector by (1) inviting and providing financial support for "world-class universities" to establish programs, research partnerships, and a branch campus in Singapore; (2) recruiting 150,000 international students from Asia and beyond by 2015; and (3) modernizing domestic higher education institutions through international partnerships with elite universities from around the world.

It is worth noting that the Global Schoolhouse initiative is focused on supporting both teaching and research at higher education institutions. This distinguishes it from other regional hubs that are mainly oriented to the recruitment of international students and foreign universities for training and profit purposes. In fact, the 2006–2010 national research and development agenda for Singapore is supported by a US$8 billion fund. The establishment of a US$600 million Campus for Research Excellence and Technological Enterprise (CREATE) is part of Singapore's long-term approach to create sustainable research expertise rather than relying on short-term commercially driven research and development projects (Sidhu 2007).

To achieve the objectives and targets for the Global Schoolhouse, reputable universities have been invited from China, the United States, Australia, France, India, Germany, and the Netherlands to offer niche programs according to their individual strengths. To date, the higher education institutions include Stanford, Institut Européen d'Administration des Affaires (INSEAD), Massachusetts Institute of Technology (MIT), University of Chicago Graduate School of Business, Wharton Business School, S. P. Jain Centre of Management (India), New York University School of Arts, and the DigiPen Institute of Technology. Two well-known institutions have withdrawn from the Global Schoolhouse project in the last two years: the Bio-Medical Research facility of Johns Hopkins University from the United States and New South Wales University from Australia. The reasons are varied but the latter institution cites low enrollments, high startup costs, and lack of faculty commitment as major issues.

A salient feature of the Singapore approach has been selectivity, differentiation, and attention to the quality of the educational institutions and businesses involved in professional development and training. Although it has invited world-class universities to Singapore, it has also attracted private education institutions that can be commercial or nonprofit organizations dedicated to the business of education and training. These entities may or may not be registered with the Ministry of Education, indicating that there is no regulatory overview. In response to the growth in the private education sector Singapore has also developed its own quality assurance system—the Singapore Quality Class. It recognizes private education organizations that have attained a commendable level of performance in business excellence and is based on the Singapore Quality Award Business Excellence Framework. The benefits for both the business and the student are reduced visa-processing time and a brand that signifies some kind of quality control of business practices, but not the quality of the actual academic offer. This is an important difference. According to a recent study, "the government has not yet imposed any form of regulatory framework to ensure that academic standards are upheld. Rather, private schools are relying heavily on their own initiatives to safeguard teaching quality" (Lim 2009, 79).

To date, there has been no evaluation of the results and impact of the Global Schoolhouse project, at least no public assessment. However, there appear to be valuable lessons learned from this five-year-old initiative. The withdrawal of two foreign institutions that were invited to develop a branch campus signals a gap between expectations and realities. It demonstrates the need for both the foreign institution and the Singapore Economic Development Board to develop solid business plans and a pragmatic approach to the costs and expected return on the investments for foreign public and private universities and to be aware of the social, cultural, and political issues at play.

A key element of the Global Schoolhouse strategy is capacity building of local higher education institutions in terms of research expertise, governance, curriculum innovation, and recruitment of international students. How much collaboration has taken place for this capacity building to happen? Is collaboration likely if, in fact, there is competition between local and foreign institutions for the best and brightest of students, faculty, and research partnerships? Are there some potential areas of conflict here? Singapore has a long history of franchise, twinning, and articulation models of cross-border education but, like other countries in the world, it has limited experience in integrating these initiatives with new ones into a coherent and strategic regional hub model. The complexities of doing so should not be underestimated (Sidhu et al. 2007; Sidhu 2008).

Hong Kong: Regional Education Hub

Hong Kong has also joined the club of countries wanting to establish regional education hubs. The Chief Executive's 2004 Policy Address announced a plan "to promote Hong Kong as Asia's world city" (Lam 2004). A critical element of being Asia's world city was building Hong Kong's capacity to serve as a regional higher education hub. The University Grants Commission (UGC) supported the vision of Hong Kong as "the education hub of the region because of its strong links with Mainland China, its geographical location, its internationalized and vibrant higher education subsector, and its very cosmopolitan outlook" (UGC 2004, 5). A key theme in the UGC policy paper, which has relevance for their hub model, is the development of an interlocking system where the whole higher education subsector is viewed as one force, with each institution fulfilling a unique role based on its individual mission and particular strengths. Differentiation of role and international competitiveness of each institution's teaching and research strength are identified as the backbone for domestic reform and an important feature for the hub (UGC 2004).

Attracting international students for study and work in Hong Kong is the main engine driving the development of the hub. There is no plan to invite foreign institutions to establish branch campuses, instead foreign students will be accommodated by increasing the admission quotas assigned to domestic institutions. The impact on domestic enrollments is unknown. Since the announcements in 2004 and 2007, more scholarships have been provided for international students and the immigration policies have been liberalized. Changes have focused on relaxing employment restrictions for non-local[1] students both during and after their study programs. For example, foreign students are now able to undertake internships, part-time campus employment, and a summer job during their study period. New graduates are able to stay on for 12 months as locally engaged employees. A particularly interesting aspect of the immigration reform has been a change in regulations for international graduates who left Hong Kong after their studies but wish to return for employment purposes. This has major implications for the multitudes of Mainland Chinese graduates. The aim of these changes is to strengthen Hong Kong's human capital and competitiveness, enhance the quality of the workforce, and, of course, make Hong Kong more attractive to international students (Education Bureau 2007).

In the 2007–2008 Policy Address, the importance of Hong Kong as a regional education hub was addressed again and this time included more specifics about expanding the international school subsector and attracting outstanding students. It stated that

> [Hong Kong] will make available a number of greenfield sites at nominal premium for the development of new international schools or the expansion of existing schools with interest-free capital works assistance loans. In terms of international student recruitment, it was announced that "the government will introduce a package of measures which includes increasing the admission quotas for non-local students to local tertiary institutions, relaxing employment restrictions on non-local students as well as providing scholarships to strengthen support for local and non-local students." (Hong Kong Government 2007)

Have these policy announcements and reforms made a difference? A recent study (HKIEd 2008) focused on the perceptions of foreign students and the number of non-local students currently in Hong Kong. The findings indicate that the vast majority of non-local students come from the mainland. For example, 92.6 percent of the UGC funding for international students went to Mainland Chinese students. With less than 8 percent coming from other countries in the region one can question whether Hong Kong is serving as a regional hub or perhaps as a gateway for students from the mainland. In 2007, over 1,370 students living in Mumbai, New Delhi, Jakarta, and Kuala Lumpur were interviewed regarding their knowledge and interest in the Hong Kong postsecondary system. A very small minority had any understanding of Hong Kong's education programs or were aware of any promotion to study there. Lack of brand visibility is a major issue and appears to be a significant challenge for Hong Kong, especially when one considers the aggressive recruitment campaigns by its regional neighbors such as Malaysia and Singapore.

Although work may continue on shaping Hong Kong as an education hub for international students, very little information has been forthcoming with respect to further regulatory changes or financial incentives. Is the absence of information indicative of a lack of any substantial progress? Even the goals for establishing the hub seem to be unclear as articulated by the following comment: "The hub plans may be at risk of getting lost without a clear roadmap. In Hong Kong, we are not even clear about the goals of the education hub from the government's perspective. Is it for benchmarking against top universities internationally? Capacity building in neighboring countries? Workforce planning? Developing institutions' reputations? Providing a global perspective for our own Hong Kong students?" (SCMP 2008). In spite of major policy announcements, the establishment of a steering committee, changes to the immigration policies, and a new quota system, there still seems to be a lack of momentum and direction to develop and promote Hong Kong as a regional education hub.

Hong Kong is still in the early stages of taking the necessary steps and making investments to position itself as a regional education hub. Furthermore, Hong Kong is operating within a region where there is strong competition from neighboring countries to be seen as a regional education hub for research excellence, recruitment of bright international students and faculty, and development of successful partnerships with foreign universities, all strongly geared toward an overall profile as a center of education activity (Hackett 2006).

Malaysia: Kuala Lumpur Education City

In 2007, as part of the Ninth National Plan, Malaysia announced the creation of the Kuala Lumpur Education City (KLEC). Planners for KLEC have a vision that it will be "a Global Education Hub that fosters international unity and learning through Education, Culture and Lifestyle as the core of a modern 21st century city." Its mission is to create "an environment of learning, living and leisure as a haven for individual education institutions and organizations who converge for Knowledge, Peace and Progress" (KLEC 2008, 1). The intention is to "translate a global view into local living." These are lofty and ambitious plans and a different approach than that of other countries.

In the past ten years, Malaysia has been well known and respected for its education reforms such as encouraging domestic private colleges to establish two-plus-two programs with institutions that grant foreign degrees, establishing branch campuses of foreign universities, and developing a comprehensive qualifications framework. These measures have already increased domestic student access to higher education and attracted sizable numbers of international students. Thus it is interesting to examine its new efforts to establish education cities and include universities in their economic free zones.

Both social and economic motives are driving the new KLEC enterprise. On one hand, there is a pressing need to invest more into developing the human capital necessary for Malaysia's knowledge economy and, on the other hand, KLEC provides the opportunity to showcase Malaysia as an environment-friendly, energy efficient, and connected knowledge-based regional center. The plan is to gain greater access to the global education market especially from the three nearby population giants, India, China, and Indonesia. Second, the strategy includes the development of the necessary research infrastructure to position Malaysia as a regional center of excellence in education and the central node for an international network of academic institutions, companies, and services (*Financial Express* 2007).

KLEC Ventures, a private investment firm managing this initiative, intends to open the first phase of the 1,000 acre commercial and residential site in 2012. The strategy is to co-locate world-class academic institutions with Malaysian colleges and universities in a single complex. Royal Holloway University of London from the United Kingdom is one of the first universities to indicate their plan to establish a branch campus there. Research will have a central place in KLEC as plans include a research park involving independent or university-affiliated international research institutes in the areas of life sciences, biomedical engineering, educational, and media technologies.

The Malaysian government sees KLEC and other smaller education cities as a way to bring important benefits such as an increase in the higher education participation rate to 40 percent, a larger pool of international and local graduates in the domestic workforce, a wider selection of program offers, and an enhanced world-class education platform for both teaching and research.

KLEC is an example of an ambitious multi-use commercial, academic, residential complex. It is a sign of the times that education institutions are becoming the anchors of these profit-making ventures that seek to position a country regionally and globally in the twenty-first-century knowledge economy. But can these ambitious plans be realized? For instance, KLEC envisions that within four years of its startup, that is, by 2011, there will be 110,000 students and faculty plus a residential population of 30,000 living in Malaysia's newest education city. This is an ambitious plan, especially in light of the fact that nearby neighbors such as Singapore and Hong Kong, plus other Asian countries such as Japan, Korea, and India, are all working toward increasing the numbers of international students in their country. There are some critical issues to be addressed: Is this plan realistic? Will quality be maintained? Is it sustainable?

Diversity of Motivations and Expectations

The first questions to ask when analyzing the driving rationales and intended outcomes of these new cross-border developments are what the benefits are and for whom. Because it is often multinational investment firms or government economic boards, not the higher education subsector, that are spearheading these initiatives, the obvious benefit for students is not necessarily a top priority. It depends on the national agenda and the expectations of the sponsoring entity. For instance, an international holding company in Bahrain will have different intentions than a social/cultural/educational not-for-profit organization such as the Qatar Foundation. A government-funded and -guided initiative such as in Hong Kong uses a different policy framework than an entity such as the Free Economic Zone Authority in Dubai.

A common element to all initiatives is a clear acknowledgment of the need to prepare a skilled job-ready workforce for the knowledge economy. This is particularly true for nations with limited natural resources or a weak manufacturing sector such as Singapore or for states moving from an oil-dependent economy to service industries such as Dubai. In these scenarios, education is a means to an end—usually an economic outcome. But for others, rationales rest on the belief that foreign credentials are a hot commodity for students and employers alike. Thus promoting and centrally locating branch campuses of foreign providers can (1) offer increased access for local students, (2) attract international students who may be eventually interested in a foreign credential plus short- or long-term employment opportunities, (3) bring economic benefits to the education providers, (4) provide a source of potential employees and immigrants for the country, and (5) serve to increase competitiveness in the knowledge economy.

In terms of education benefits, broader course offering as well as access to foreign expertise in pedagogy and research are often cited but usually less so than economic and human capital motives. The traditional internationalization benefits such as increased international knowledge and intercultural skills for faculty and students as well as enhanced quality are seldom identified. Overall, economic, immigration, and employment reasons are cited more often than social, cultural, and education rationales.

The "push and pull" of attracting world-class institutions to a regional hub is a goal (and struggle) that many countries are facing. Brand recognition and world rankings of foreign institutions are current factors (sometimes called obsessions) motivating and influencing the development of new hubs. In fact, having one or two prestigious institutions from the United States or the United Kingdom as an anchor, or so-called big names, is becoming a prerequisite. The university as a "prize collectable" is a new and more prevalent phenomenon than one could have imagined just two decades ago.

Table 11.1 provides a comparative analysis of the six different approaches that countries take to education hub or cities in terms of date of establishment, the sponsor or implementing body, the approach used, and the driving rationales. It is clear that, with the exception of Qatar, which is significantly different from the others, these hubs are very recent

Table 11.1 Comparison of Country Approaches to Education Hubs and Cities

	Bahrain	Qatar	U.A.E.	Hong Kong	Singapore	Malaysia
Name	Higher Education City	Education City	Knowledge Village	Regional EducationHub	Global School house	Kuala Lumpur Education City
Date of Establishment	2007	1998	2003	2004	2004	2007
Sponsor/ Organizer	Bahrain Economic Development Board	Qatar Foundation	Dubai Holdings/ TECOM Investments	Hong Kong Trade Development Council	Singapore Economic Development Board	KLEC Ventures
Approach	Economic Free Zone Regional Hub Model	Invited Academic City Model	Economic Free Zone Regional Hub Model	Academic Gateway Model	Selective Academic City Model	Selective Academic City Model
Rationales						
Skilled workforce	xx	xxx	xxx	xxx	xxx	xx
Grow Knowledge Economy	xxx	x	xxx		xx	xx
Foreign Direct Investment	xxx		xxx	x	xx	xx
Improve Domestic HE System and Access		xxx		xx	x	xx
Status/ Competitiveness	xxx	xx	xxx	xxx	xxx	xxx

xxx – very important, xx – medium importance, x – low importance
Source: Knight (2010).

developments that are being used to build a cluster of knowledge-based industries where foreign education and training institutions and companies play an important role.

Table 11.1 shows that the two top rationales across the board are the preparation of a skilled workforce and improvement of their status and competitiveness as a center of higher education excellence contributing to the knowledge economy. It is clear that the approaches used by the three Asian countries, more than those employed in the U.A.E. or Bahrain, are closely linked to enhancing their domestic higher education subsector and increasing access for local as well as foreign students. Qatar stands out in its orientation to providing higher education opportunities first to its local students through invitations and generous financial arrangements with foreign universities who aim to provide the same curriculum and education experience in Qatar as at their home base.

Lack of clear information on governance structures, quality assurance and accreditation policies, selection and licensing criteria, enrollment data, faculty employment contracts, and tuition fees makes it difficult to undertake any kind of detailed comparative analysis on the academic frameworks and business models used to establish nationally based but region-wide education cities or hubs. As these initiatives take root and grow, more substantive information should become available.

Of key importance is the sustainability of the hubs and cities. Whether these new developments will be able to survive unpredictable economic and political ups and downs is yet to be seen. But the responsibility of education providers to offer education programs until the granting of the qualification is paramount. A sound business plan and academic framework are mandatory. This may seem obvious but the importance of it bears repeating when one sees closure of campuses such as some of those in Singapore and the U.A.E. due to unfulfilled expectations. The prospect of financial benefits and increase in reputation is great. Universities have to be clear, pragmatic, and realistic about (1) the size of the market, (2) the ability to deliver quality education programs and related faculty, (3) compliance with foreign regulatory requirements, (4) the hidden expenses and burden on home administrative and program departments, and (5) competition with local and other foreign institutions. These are but a few of the issues that have to be rigorously thought through to ensure a sustainable business plan and a rigorous academic framework.

The explosion of the knowledge economy is escalating competition between nations and regions and increasing the importance of higher education as a political and economic actor. As a result the international dimension of higher education is experiencing a fundamental shift in its approach, values, and strategies. No matter how distasteful many academics will find the treatment of education as a commercial commodity, the development of these education hubs and cities is positive proof of the importance education has in developing the required human capital to gain a competitive advantage in the knowledge economy. That being said, there are also unforeseen risks at play. A major challenge facing education, trade, immigration, and industry policymakers is to ensure that the quality, sustainability, and ultimate integrity of cross-border education/research is preserved so that it can serve the social, cultural, economic, and technological development of their country and region.

NOTE

1. The term non-local student is used in Hong Kong to refer to international or foreign students.

BIBLIOGRAPHY

Bahrain Economic Development Board. 2008. *Education and Training*. Manama: Bahrain Economic Development Board. Available online at: http://www.bharainedb.com.

Bardsley, Daniel. 2008. "Dubai Plans Education Hub of 40 Universities." *The National Newspaper*, August 14, 7. Available online at: http://www.thenational.ae.

Dubai Holding. 2008a. *Dubai International Academic City and Knowledge Village*. Personal Correspondence, Dubai Holding.

Dubai Holding. 2008b. "DIAC Showcases Higher Education Model at THE-QS World University Rankings Workshop in Korea." *Dubai Holding Media Centre*, July 9. Available online at: http://dubaiholding.com/media-centre/news/2008/july/diac-world-university-rankings-workshop-in-korea/

Education Bureau. 2007. *Legislative Brief: Developing Hong Kong as a Regional Education Hub*. Hong Kong: Education Bureau of the Government of Hong Kong Special Administrative Region of the People's Republic of China. Available online at: http://www.edb.gov.hk.

Financial Express. 2007. *Strategies towards a Global Education Hub*. Dhaka: Financial Express. Available online at: http://www.thefinancialexpress-bd.com/

Gribble, Cate, and Grant McBurnie. 2007. "Problems within Singapore's Global Schoolhouse." *International Higher Education* 48 (Summer): 5–6.

Gulf News. 2006. "Bahrain Plans Hub for Education with KFIC." *Gulf News* (online), December 26. Available online at: http://gulfnews.com.

Hackett, J. 2006. "Hong Kong—The Regional Education Hub: New Kid on the Block." Paper presented at the 4th Asia-Pacific Conference on Continuing Education and Lifelong Learning, Hong Kong, December 6–8. Available online at: http://www.hkuspace.hku.hk.

Hong Kong Government. 2007. *The 2007–08 Policy Address: A New Direction for Hong Kong.* Hong Kong: Legislative Committee of the Hong Kong Government. Available online at: http://www.policyaddress.gov.hk.

Hong Kong Institute for Education (HKIEd). 2008. Press Release: Academics Call for Designated Agency to Boost Hong Kong's Position as Regional Education Hub. Hong Kong: HKIEd.

Hong Kong University Grants Council. 2004. *Hong Kong Higher Education to Make a Difference to Move with the Times.* Hong Kong University Grants Council. Available online at: http://www.ugc.edu.hk.

Knowledge and Human Development Authority. 2008. *Stakeholders Consulted on Quality Assurance Manual.* Dubai Internet City: Government of Dubai. Available online at: http://www.khda.gov.ae.

Knight, Jane. 2010. "Quality Dilemmas with Regional Education Hubs and Cities." In *Quality Assurance and University Rankings in Higher Education in the Asia Pacific: Challenges for Universities and Nations,* eds. Sarjit Kaur, Morshidi Sirat, and William G. Tierney, 33–47. Penang, Malaysia: Universiti Sains Malaysia Publishers.

Knight, Jane. 2008. Higher Education in Turmoil: The Changing World of Internationalization. Rotterdam. The Netherlands: Sense Publishers.

Knight, Jane. 2006a. Higher Education in the World: Cross-Border Higher Education: Issues and Implications for Quality Assurance and Accreditation. Global University Network for Innovation. Available online at: http://upcommons.upc.edu.

Knight, Jane. 2006b. Internationalization of Higher Education: New Directions, New Challenges. 2005 IAU Global Survey Report. Paris: International Association of Universities.

Krieger, Zvika. 2007. "Dubai, Aiming to Be an Academic Hub, Strikes a Deal With Michigan State." *The Chronicle of Higher Education* 54 (8): A33.

Kuala Lumpur Education City. 2008. *Academic Masterplan.* Kuala Lumpur: KLEC. Available online at: http://www.kualalumpureducationcity.com.

Lam, Alice. 2004. "Welcome Speech." Twenty-first Digby Memorial Lecture, University of Hong Kong, July 10, 2004. Available online at: http://www.ugc.edu.hk.

Lim, Fion Choon Boey. 2009. "Education Hub at a Crossroads: The Development of Quality Assurance as a Competitive Tool for Singapore's Private Tertiary Education." *Quality Assurance in Education* 17 (1): 79–94.

Ministry of Trade and Industry. 2002. Panel Recommends Global Schoolhouse Concept for Singapore to Capture Bigger Slice of US$2.2 Trillion World Education Market. Singapore: Singapore Government. Available online at: http://app.mti.gov.sg.

Ministry of Trade and Industry. 2003. *Growing Our Economy.* Singapore: Singapore Government. Available online at: http://app.mti.gov.sg.

Mok, Ka Ho. 2008. "Singapore's Global Education Hub Ambitions: University Governance Change and Transnational Higher Education." *International Journal of Educational Management* 22 (6): 527–546.

OBHE. 2005. Trouble at Knowledge Village? Unexpected 29% Rent Increase Gives Foreign University Tenants Pause for Thought. London: OBHE.

Observatory for Borderless Higher Education (OBHE). 2008. Onto Something Good? Dubai's Knowledge and Human Development Authority Launches an International Quality-Monitoring Board. London: OBHE.

Qatar Foundation. 2008. Why Education City? Doha: Qatar Foundation. Available online at http://www.qf.edu.qa.

Qatar Foundation. 2010a. *Education City*. Doha: Qatar Foundation. Available online at: http://www.qf.org.qa.

Qatar Foundation. 2010b. *Qatar Faculty of Islamic Studies*. Doha: Qatar Foundation. Available online at: http://www.qf.org.qa.

Royal Holloway University of London. 2008. *MOU signed with Kuala Lumpur Education City*. Egham, England: Royal Holloway University of London. Available online at: http://www.rhul.ac.uk/Resources/Helper_apps/Message.asp?ref_no=1647.

Science and Development Network. 2008. "'Higher Education City' to Boost Middle East Science." London: Science and Development Network. Available online at: http://www.scidev.net.

Sidhu, Ravinder. 2008. "Knowledge Economies: The Singapore Example." *International Higher Education* 52 (Summer): 4.

Sidhu, Ravinder, K-C. Ho, and Brenda Yeoh. 2007. "The Global Schoolhouse: Governing Singapore's Knowledge Economy Aspirations." Paper presented at the Workshop for the Transnational Education and Migration in Globalizing Cities, Singapore, July 2007.

South China Morning Post (SCMP). 2008. "Hub Plans at Risk of Getting Lost Without a Clear Road Map." *South China Morning Post*. February 2.

University Grants Commission. 2004. Hong Kong Higher Education—To Make a Difference—To Move with the Times Report. Hong Kong: University Grants Commission.

Contributors

Tony Adams is Director and Principal Consultant of Tony Adams and Associates, an international education consultant firm that has been working in Australia, the United States, Mexico, the United Kingdom, Botswana, Italy, Canada, and the Netherlands. He comes from a computer science teaching background. In 1991 Adams was appointed to the position of Dean of International Programs at RMIT University in Melbourne, a position he held until 1998. In 1998 he took up the position of Director of International Programs and later of PVC International at Macquarie University in Sydney until January 2007. At Macquarie he led the internationalization effort, taking Macquarie's rank among Australian destinations for international students from twenty-third in 1998 to fourth in 2006 and built the strongest outward-bound mobility program in Australia with over 19 percent of its UG graduating cohort having an international experience. Adams was the Foundation President of the International Education Association of Australia (IEAA). He is Vice Chairman of the International Student Exchange Program (ISEP) and co-editor of the *Journal of Studies of International Education* (JSIE). In 1997 he was awarded the inaugural IDP award for excellence in International Education and in 2006 he received the Charles Klasek award from the AIEA jointly with John Hudzik.

Pawan Agarwal is an Indian civil servant and the current principal secretary to the Government of West Bengal in India. He earlier served as Director in the Indian government's Ministry of Human Resource Development, and as Financial Advisor and Coordinator of New Initiatives for India's University Grants Commission—a position in which he developed substantial expertise in higher education policy and practice and gained a broad understanding of the issues and challenges faced by the Indian higher education. He is a member of the consultative committee set up by the planning commission to review higher education in the eleventh five-year plan (2007–2012). During the year 2005–2006, Agarwal was a Fulbright New Century Scholar on higher education from India, and in 2009 he was a visiting scholar at the Centre for the Study of Higher Education in the

University of Melbourne on an Endeavour Executive Award granted by the Australian government. He has been affiliated to the Indian Council for Research on International Economic Relations (ICRIER), Science and Engineering Workforce Program at Harvard University, and the India-China-America Institute at Emory University. His recent book *Indian Higher Education: Envisioning the Future* is the most comprehensive and up to date review of Indian higher education so far and has received very good response from India and abroad. Argarwal's other important studies and publications focus on private higher education for the Observatory on Borderless Higher Education, higher education and labor markets for the World Bank, Indian higher education from a Latin American perspective for the Inter-American Development Bank, privatization and internationalization trends in South Asian countries for the South Asia Network of Economic Research Institutions, and liberal arts education in India for the Institute of Higher Education Policy, Washington.

Melissa Banks is a consultant in international education. With around 20 years of experience encompassing a variety of roles across multiple education sectors and service providers, she has gained comprehensive firsthand experience and skills across many aspects of international education in Australia. She has held senior positions in two Australian universities heading up their international student recruitment operations and was the Head of Research at IDP Education Pty. Ltd. Her research interests encompass outcomes and impacts of international education, global student mobility, skilled migration of former overseas students, data capture methodologies and analysis of international student data, retention and transition policies, processes and systems in Australian tertiary education, customer service and the international customer experience, and Australian transnational tertiary education. Banks has contributed many chapters, papers, and presentations to industry forums and publications throughout her professional career.

Rajika Bhandari is Deputy Vice President of Research and Evaluation at the Institute of International Education (IIE) in New York where she leads two major research projects—*Open Doors* and *Project Atlas*—that measure international higher education mobility at the domestic (U.S.) and international levels. She is a frequent speaker and author on the topic of mobility and serves on the Global Advisory Council of the Observatory on Borderless Higher Education, and also on the editorial board of the *Journal of Studies in International Education*. Bhandari is also the author of two other recent books on higher education mobility and exchanges, *International India: A Turning Point in Educational Exchange with the U.S.* and *Higher Education on the Move: New Developments in Global*

Mobility, which won the Best Book Award given by the Comparative and International Education Society's Higher Education Special Interest Group. Bhandari also conducts program evaluations of IIE's international scholarship and fellowship programs. Before joining IIE, she was a Senior Researcher at MPR Associates, an educational research and evaluation firm in Berkeley, California. She also served as the Assistant Director for Evaluation at the Mathematics and Science Education Network at the University of North Carolina, Chapel Hill. She holds a doctoral degree in Psychology from North Carolina State University and a BA (Honors) in Psychology from the University of Delhi, India.

Peggy Blumenthal is Executive Vice President and Chief Operating Officer of the Institute of International Education (IIE). Responsible for the overall programmatic and administrative operations of the IIE, she also directly supervises its research activities, corporate and foundation-funded scholarships, and specialized programs such as the Global Engineering Educational Exchange Consortium. Before joining IIE in 1984, Blumenthal served as Assistant Director of Stanford University's Overseas Studies and then as Coordinator of Graduate Services/Fellowships for the University of Hawaii's Center for Asian and Pacific Studies. Her earlier work focused on the development of U.S.-China exchanges, as a staff member of the National Committee on U.S.-China Relations and the Asia Society's China Council. Selected publications include the co-edited volume *Academic Mobility in a Changing World: Regional and Global Trends;* "Virtual and Physical Mobility: A View from the U.S.," an article in the ACA publication *The Virtual Challenge to International Cooperation in Higher Education;* and a co-authored chapter in *The Europa World of Learning,* "Global Student Mobility: Moving towards Brain Exchange." Her recent co-authored article "Expanding Study Abroad in the STEM Fields: A Case Study of U.S. and German Programs" was published in *The Online Journal for Global Engineering.* Blumenthal holds a BA from Harvard University in Modern Chinese History and an MA in American Studies from the University of Hawaii at Manoa.

Christian Bode is Secretary General of the German Academic Exchange Service (DAAD). Before joining DAAD, he was head of the planning group at the Federal Ministry of Education and Research and then, from 1982 through 1990, Secretary General of the Western German Rectors' Conference. Bode graduated in law from the University of Bonn, where he also obtained his PhD in 1971. He is a member of several national and international professional associations and administrative boards, including Academic Cooperation Association (ACA), and has been awarded several honorary degrees from universities around the world.

Martin Davidson CMG is Chief Executive of the British Council, a position he has held since April 2007. Prior to this appointment, he served as Deputy Director General since September 2005. When he left the Hong Kong government to join the British Council as Assistant Representative in Beijing in 1984, British Council China employed six people. Davidson played a pivotal part in building it up to its present strength of more than 230 people in four offices. He himself was responsible for opening the South China office in Guangzhou and returned to Beijing in 1995 as Director. He speaks fluent Mandarin and Cantonese. Davidson has held various posts in the British Council's Geographical Directorate with responsibilities that have included South East Europe, in a particularly troubled time in the region's history, the Middle East, East Asia, and the Americas.

Allan E. Goodman is President and CEO of the Institute of International Education (IIE) which is the leading not-for-profit organization in the field of international educational exchange and development training. IIE administers the Fulbright program, sponsored by the U.S. Department of State, and 200 other corporate, government, and privately sponsored programs. Previously, he was Executive Dean of the School of Foreign Service and Professor at Georgetown University. He has authored books on international affairs (published by Harvard, Princeton, and Yale University presses) and *Diversity in Governance,* published by the American Council on Education. Goodman also served as Presidential Briefing Coordinator for the Director of Central Intelligence and as Special Assistant to the Director of the National Foreign Assessment Center in the Carter Administration. He was the first American professor to lecture at the Foreign Affairs College of Beijing. He also helped create the first U.S. academic exchange program with the Moscow Diplomatic Academy for the Association of Professional Schools of International Affairs and developed the diplomatic training program of the Foreign Ministry of Vietnam. He has also served as a consultant to Ford Foundation, the Woodrow Wilson National Fellowship Foundation, the United States Information Agency, and IBM. He is a member of the Council on Foreign Relations. Goodman has a PhD in Government from Harvard, an MPA from the John F. Kennedy School of Government and a BS from Northwestern University. He also holds honorary degrees from Toyota and Chatham Universities, Mount Ida, Ramapo, and Middlebury colleges, and the State University of New York. He has received awards from Georgetown, Johns Hopkins, and Tufts universities, and the French Légion d'honneur.

Robert Gutierrez is Director of Research Support, Office of the Provost, at the New School in New York City. Prior to taking his current position, Gutierrez served as Senior Manager of Research and Evaluation at the Institute of International Education (IIE), where he managed IIE's research and evaluation projects, including Project Atlas, the Meeting America's Global Education Challenge policy research series on expanding study abroad capacity, and program evaluations for various government, foundation, and NGO sponsors. Gutierrez also managed IIE's new research project for developing a classification system for higher education institutions in the Middle East and North Africa. He holds an MSc in Public Policy and Management from Carnegie Mellon University and a BA in English and Spanish from the University of Notre Dame.

Isabel Cristina Jaramillo specializes in the international relations of higher education through the observation, analyses, and international comparisons of institutional development, related to the objectives, strategies, policies, and management in universities in Latin America and other regions in the world. She has participated in and coordinated several studies related to the international dimension of higher education for several multilateral organizations, one of which, for the Secretaría General Iberoamericana, SEGIB, surveyed the flows of academic mobility (students and professors) in Iberoamerica in 2007. Simultaneously, she coordinated a comparative analysis, financed by the European Commission–Alfa Program named "Practices and Tendencies of the Internationalization and the Cooperation among Universities in Latin America and the European Union," published in 2007. With the support of the World Bank and the Institutional Management of Higher Education (IMHE) of the OECD, she co-edited a comparative study ("Higher Education in Latin America: The International Dimension," published in 2005) that examined the challenges Latin American universities face in their international process. In 2003, Jaramillo published the first survey that analyzed the development of the international dimension of higher education in Colombia. She worked as Director of International Relations at the Colombian Association of Universities (ASCUN) where she coordinated the international dimension of the universities in the country and was in charge of several programs of academic cooperation, for example, ALFA and ALBAN, between Colombia and other regions such as the European Union, Canada, Cuba, and México, among others. She has also participated as a lecturer in national and international seminars and conferences. Jaramillo is currently working as a professor, an assessor, and a consultant for different universities in Colombia and for international organizations.

Roshen Kishun is Executive Director of BA ISAGO University College in Gaborone, Botswana. He has a PhD from the University of Southern California, Los Angeles. He is a founding member of the International Education Association of South Africa (IEASA), established in 1997, and was President of IEASA until 2006. He is a member of the Atlas International Advisory Group that was constituted by the International Institute of Education (IIE) in New York to look at the data on the global mobility of international students. Currently he is the Chair of *African Network for International Education* (ANIE). ANIE's primary focus is to facilitate the internationalization of education, in particular the higher education in Africa, and to meet the professional needs of individuals active in international education. The goal is to locate African higher education as an integral part of the global community. Kishun has presented papers at national and international conferences on internationalization and is responsible for various publications promoting African higher education internationally.

Jane Knight is a Visiting Professor at the Ontario Institute for Studies in Education, University of Toronto. Her research focuses on the international dimension of higher education at the institutional, systemic, national, and international levels. Her work in over 60 countries with UN agencies, universities, foundations, and professional organizations helps to bring a comparative, developmental, and international perspective to her research, teaching, and policy work. She is the author of numerous articles, chapters, and reports on internationalization concepts and strategies, quality assurance, institutional management, mobility, cross-border education, trade, and capacity building. Her latest books include *Higher Education in Turmoil: The Changing World of Internationalization* (author), *Financing Access and Equity in Higher Education* (editor), and *Higher Education in Africa: The International Dimension* (co-editor). Knight is an adjunct professor at the Ontario Institute for Studies in Education, was a Fulbright New Century Scholar in 2007–2008, and sits on the advisory boards of several international organizations and journals. Currently, she is a visiting professor at the National Higher Education Research and Policy Institute at the Universiti Sains Malaysia.

Veronica Lasanowski is Senior Research and Marketing Officer at the Observatory on Borderless Higher Education (OBHE), a global strategic information service based in London. Responsible for tracking recent developments in cross-border higher education worldwide, she analyses policy trends likely to become strategically important to higher education decision-makers. Her previous work experience includes posts at the European Commission's Directorate-General for Education and Culture (Belgium), the former Canadian Education Centre (Australia), and the Fairtrade Foundation (the United Kingdom). Since joining the Observatory, she has contributed to publications focused on international student mobility, international branch campuses, and regulatory frameworks. Her principal interests include cultural politics, regionalism, language, and mobility. Lasanowski received an undergraduate degree in English and Hispanic Studies from McGill University, Canada, and an MSc in International Relations and History from the London School of Economics and Political Science.

John McHale is Established Professor and Head of Economics at the National University of Ireland, Galway. Before joining NUIG he held positions as Assistant Professor of Economics and Associate Professor of Economics at Harvard University, and as Associate Professor of Managerial Economics and Toller Family Research Fellow at the Queen's University, Ontario. McHale received his PhD and AM degrees from Harvard in 1996 and also holds first-class BComm (1988) and MEconSc (1990) degrees from the National University of Ireland. He has published numerous articles in refereed journals and edited volumes, in addition to co-authoring (with Devesh Kapur) *Give Us Your Best and Brightest: The Global Hunt for Talent and Its Impact on the Developing World* (Brookings Institution Press). His shorter articles have appeared in publications such as the *Financial Times*, the *Irish Times*, and the *Wall Street Journal*. McHale has been a consultant to the World Bank on various migration and development projects.

Alan Olsen is Director of Strategy Policy and Research in Education Limited. Olsen, an Australian living and working in Hong Kong, is a consultant in international education, carrying out research in strategy and policy advice for client institutions and organizations on international education, transnational education, and international student programs. He has worked in international education in Australia, Singapore, and Hong Kong and has published extensively, with 40 items on Australia's Database of Research on International Education. In October 2009 Olsen was recognized by his colleagues with an International Education Excellence Award from the International Education Association of Australia for his distinguished contribution to the field of international education.

Hans de Wit has been Professor (Lector) of Internationalization of Higher Education at the School of Economics and Management of the Hogeschool van Amsterdam, University of Applied Sciences, since August 2009. He is also a private consultant at De Wit International Higher Education Consultancy. He is the co-editor of the *Journal of Studies in International*

Education. In 2005–2006, he was a New Century Scholar of the Fulbright Program Higher Education in the 21st Century, and in 1995 and 2006 a visiting scholar at the Center for International Higher Education of Boston College and in 2002 and 2009 in Australia. De Wit has written and co-written several books and articles on international education and is actively involved in assessment and consultancy in international education, for organizations such as the European Commission, UNESCO, and the World Bank. He has been Director of the Office of Foreign Relations, Vice-President for International Affairs, and Senior Advisor International at the Universiteit van Amsterdam between 1986 and 2005, and Director of International Relations at Tilburg University in 1981–1985. He was assistant professor in Latin American Studies at Utrecht University, 1979–1981. He has a PhD from the University of Amsterdam. Hans de Wit is founding member and past president of the European Association for International Education (EAIE). Currently he is Member of the Board of Trustees of World Education Services. On September 11, 2008, he received the Constance Meldrum Award for Vision and Leadership from the EAIE in Antwerp. Previous awards he received from the University of Amsterdam (2006), AIEA (2006), CIEE (2004 and 2006), NAFSA (2002), and EAIE (1999).

Yang Xinyu joined the Ministry of Education in 1986 after graduating from Heilongjiang University with a BA in English Language and Literature. She studied at Nottingham University from 1988 to 1989 under a British Council Scholarship and received her Master of Education in 1989. She worked in the ministry as Senior Program Officer until 1995 when she was appointed Second Secretary for Education in the Chinese Embassy in Canada. She joined the China Scholarship Council (CSC) in 1998 as Deputy Director and later became Director of the Division of Studying Abroad Programs. She took the position as the Deputy Secretary General of CSC in 2003.

Index

Note: Page numbers in **bold** refer to references in figures or tables. If references are located in both a figure or table and the body of the text on the same page then pager numbers are left without bold demarcation.

Printed and bound by CPI Group (UK) Ltd, Croydon, CR0 4YY